The Soviet Union under Brezhnev

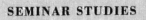

SEMINAR STUDIES IN HISTORY

The Soviet Union under Brezhnev

WILLIAM TOMPSON

PEARSON
Longman

PEARSON EDUCATION LIMITED

Head Office:
Edinburgh Gate
Harlow CM20 2JE
Tel: +44 (0)1279 623623
Fax: +44 (0)1279 431059

London Office:
128 Long Acre
London WC2E 9AN
Tel: +44 (0)20 7447 2000
Fax: +44 (0)20 7447 2170
Website: www.history-minds.com

First published in Great Britain in 2003

© Pearson Education Limited 2003

The right of William Tompson to be identified as Author
of this Work has been asserted by him in accordance
with the Copyright, Designs and Patents Act 1988.

ISBN 0 582 32719 9

British Library Cataloguing in Publication Data
A CIP catalogue record for this book can be obtained from the British Library

Library of Congress Cataloging in Publication Data
A CIP catalog record for this book can be obtained from the Library of Congress

Transferred to digital print on demand, 2006

Typeset by 7 in 10/12 Sabon Roman
Produced by Pearson Education Asia Pte Ltd.,

Printed and bound by CPI Antony Rowe, Eastbourne

CONTENTS

INTRODUCTION TO THE SERIES

Such is the pace of historical enquiry in the modern world that there is an ever-widening gap between the specialist article or monograph, incorporating the results of current research, and general surveys, which inevitably become out of date. *Seminar Studies in History* is designed to bridge this gap. The series was founded by Patrick Richardson in 1966 and his aim was to cover major themes in British, European and world history. Between 1980 and 1996 Roger Lockyer continued his work, before handing the editorship over to Clive Emsley and Gordon Martel. Clive Emsley is Professor of History at the Open University, while Gordon Martel is Professor of International History at the University of Northern British Columbia, Canada, and Senior Research Fellow at De Montfort University.

All the books are written by experts in their field who are not only familiar with the latest research but have often contributed to it. They are frequently revised, in order to take account of new information and interpretations. They provide a selection of documents to illustrate major themes and provoke discussion, and also a guide to further reading. The aim of *Seminar Studies in History* is to clarify complex issues without over-simplifying them, and to stimulate readers into deepening their knowledge and understanding of major themes and topics.

ACKNOWLEDGEMENTS

I am indebted to the staffs of the Institute of Scientific Information in the Social Sciences in Moscow, the library of the School of Slavonic & East European Studies in London, and the Bodleian Library in Oxford, where the bulk of the research for this book was done. The assistance of the superb Carole Menzies, who has ruled over the Bodleian's Slavonics Reading Room for many years, was – as I have always found it – especially valuable. I am grateful, too, to Casey Mein and Magda Robson of Pearson Education, who handled the manuscript with professionalism and with all the speed and efficiency that I had lacked in writing it, as well as to the series editor, Professor Gordon Martel, whose patience I sorely taxed in taking so long to produce the final text. Finally, my wife Julia Tompson, a veteran of the publishing world herself, proof-read both the manuscript and the page proofs with a better eye for detail – both stylistic and substantive – than I could ever have managed. Her labours have undoubtedly reduced the number of mistakes and inconsistencies in the text. Sole responsibility for those errors of fact and judgement that remain is, of course, entirely my own.

The publishers are grateful to the copyright owners whose material appears in this book.

Table 7.1 from Economic Growth and Slowdown in *Brezhnev Reconsidered* edited by E. Bacon and M. Sandle, published by Palgrave and reproduced with permission of Palgrave Macmillan (Harrison, M. 2002).

In some instances we have been unable to trace the owners of copyright material, and we would appreciate any information that would enable us to do so.

1964

14–15 October   Nikita Khrushchev removed from power, replaced by Leonid Brezhnev as party leader and by Aleksei Kosygin as head of government.

November   Soviet Union declares its support for North Vietnam in the event of an American attack.

6 November   Brezhnev speech declaring that the Soviet Union seeks improved relations with the West.

1965

January   *Novyi mir* anniversary issue arouses hopes for further cultural liberalisation.

Willy Brandt publishes proposals that become the basis for West Germany's *Ostpolitik*.

February   Kosygin's effort to mediate the US-North Vietnamese conflict fails; US action against North Vietnam escalates.

Spring   Demotion of a series of high officials linked to Brezhnev rival Nikolai Podgornyi.

24 April   Demonstration in Yerevan marking the 50th anniversary of the Turkish genocide of the Armenians.

August–
September   Indo-Pakistani war deepens Sino-Soviet rift as the two Communist giants back opposite sides.

24 August   Crackdown on nationalist dissent in Ukraine begins with dozens of searches and arrests.

September   Arrest of writers Andrei Sinyavskii and Yulii Daniel on charges of anti-Soviet agitation and propaganda.

September   Khrushchev's *sovnarkhoz* reform scrapped; ministerial system of economic management restored in conjunction with the launch of the Kosygin reforms.

December   Abolition of Party–State Control Commission signals demotion of Brezhnev critic A. N. Shelepin, who also loses his post of Deputy Prime Minister.

1966

3–10 January   Kosygin mediates successful peace negotiations between India and Pakistan in Tashkent.

10–14 February	Trial of Sinyavskii and Daniel.
18 April	Chinese press attack on Beijing party chief Peng Zhen signals the start of the Great Proletarian Cultural Revolution in China.
4 May	Soviet government reaches agreement with Fiat on the construction of automobile factory in Togliatti, near Kuibyshev.
10–13 May	Brezhnev visits Romania, apparently in response to Romanian leader Nicolae Ceaucescu's 7 May declaration that Romania seeks improved ties to West European countries.
1 December	Grand Coalition formed in West Germany; Brandt becomes Foreign Minister and begins to pursue his *Ostpolitik*.

1967

18 May	Central Committee Secretary Yuri Andropov appointed Chairman of the KGB.
5 June	Six-Day War in the Middle East begins.
10 June	USSR severs diplomatic ties with Israel.
23 June	Kosygin meets President Lyndon Johnson in Glassboro, New Jersey.
24 August	US and USSR submit identical drafts of a nuclear non-proliferation treaty to the UN Disarmament Committee in Geneva.
October	Soviet intervention in Yemeni Civil War prevents royalist victory.

1968

3–5 January	Alexander Dubček replaces hardliner Antonin Novotny as First Secretary of the Czechoslovak Communist Party.
12 January	Aleksandr Ginzburg and three other Soviet writers convicted of 'anti-Soviet activities'.
30 April	Launch of *samizdat* journal *Chronicle of Current Events*.
9 May	Joint Soviet-Polish military manoeuvres conducted near the Czechoslovak-Polish border in an effort to intimidate reformist Czechoslovak leaders.
20 June	Start of Warsaw Pact manoeuvres in Czechoslovakia.
1 July	Treaty on the Non-Proliferation of Nuclear Weapons (also known as the 'Non-Proliferation Treaty', or the 'NPT') opened for signature in London, Moscow and Washington, with the USSR among the sixty-two initial signatories.
14 July	USSR halts the withdrawal of Soviet troops from Czechoslovakia following manoeuvres there.
15 July	Joint letter to Czechoslovak leaders from the leaders of the USSR, Poland, East Germany, Hungary and Bulgaria calls for end to Prague Spring.

29 July–3 August	Czechoslovak, Soviet and other East European leaders meet in Cierna nad Tisou and Bratislava but fail to resolve the Czechoslovak crisis.
20–21 August	Warsaw Pact forces invade and occupy Czechoslovakia.
16 October	Five Soviet citizens sentenced to exile or hard labour for protesting in Red Square against the invasion of Czechoslovakia.
12 November	Brezhnev, in Warsaw, enunciates the 'Brezhnev doctrine' of limited sovereignty of socialist states.

1969

January	Richard Nixon becomes President of the United States and signals that the US no longer requires strategic superiority over the USSR.
2 March	Border conflict with China escalates after skirmish over Damanskii Island, triggering a series of clashes along the frontier over the next half-year.
6 October	Brezhnev, in speech marking 20th anniversary of the founding of the GDR, expresses a willingness to cooperate with West Germany.
15 October	Mohammed Siad Barre seizes power in Somalia, which then becomes the Soviet Union's first non-Arab client in Africa.
21 October	Social Democrats win West German election; Brandt becomes Chancellor.
12 November	Aleksandr Solzhenitsyn expelled from the Union of Soviet writers.
November	US and Soviet negotiators begin first round of Strategic Arms Limitation Talks in Helsinki.

1970

March	Non-Proliferation Treaty enters into force.
12 August	Soviet-West German Renunciation of Force Treaty (the 'Treaty of Moscow').
8 October	Aleksandr Solzhenitsyn awarded the Nobel Prize for Literature.
7 December	Signing of the Warsaw Treaty.

1971

22 March	Kosygin, unveiling broad outlines of the Ninth Five-Year Plan, calls for closer economic ties with Western Europe and promises an emphasis on higher living standards.
July	Announcement that Richard Nixon is to visit China in 1972.
3 September	Signing of Four-Power Agreement on the status of Berlin.

1972

February	Nixon–Mao summit in Beijing.
22–30 May	Brezhnev–Nixon summit in Moscow; signing of SALT I and other agreements.
8 July	President Nixon announces $750m, three-year agreement on sale of US grain to the USSR.
18 July	Egyptian President Anwar Sadat expels 17,000 Soviet advisers from his country in response to Soviet reluctance to sell arms to Egypt.
3 October	Signing of the Anti-Ballistic Missile (ABM) Treaty.
20 December	Signing of Basic Treaty between the two Germanys leads to the exchange of permanent missions between the two and the accession of both to the UN.

1973

2 April	Announcement of major reorganisation of industrial management, bringing related plants together in large 'production associations'.
April	Ukrainian party leader Petr Shelest sacked for his advocacy of Ukrainian language and culture and protection of nationally inclined intellectuals.
18–25 June	Nixon–Brezhnev summit in Washington; signing of agreements on the peaceful development of nuclear energy and the prevention of nuclear war.
3 July	Publication in Sweden of article by physicist Andrei Sakharov describing the Soviet system as 'anti-democratic in its essence'.
August–September	Sakharov and Solzhenitsyn convene press conferences in Moscow.
6–25 October	Yom Kippur War in the Middle East; crisis in US-Soviet relations; first 'oil shock'.

1974

13 February	Expulsion of Solzhenitsyn from the USSR.
March	Construction of the Baikal–Amur Mainline (BAM) begins.
April	Fall of the Caetano regime in Portugal; new leaders set 11 November 1975 as the date for granting independence to Angola.
27 June–3 July	Nixon–Brezhnev summit in Moscow; signing of further arms control and cooperation agreements.
July	Nixon Administration approves CIA support for UNITA and the FNLA in Angola.

9 August	Nixon resigns to avoid impeachment over the Watergate scandal and is succeeded by Gerald Ford.
12 September	Ethiopian Emperor Haile Selassie overthrown and replaced by a Marxist junta.
23–24 November	Brezhnev–Ford summit in Vladivostok produces accords that are to form the basis for a SALT II agreement; Brezhnev suffers major stroke just after the summit; formation of the 'Little Five' group of officials to coordinate arms control policy.

1975

January	Moscow abrogates US-Soviet trade agreement in protest at December 1974 US trade bill linking Jewish emigration from the USSR to trade arrangements.
March	USSR accedes to aid request from the Popular Movement for the Liberation of Angola (MPLA).
April–May	Final defeat of US client regimes in Indochina.
17–19 July	Joint US-Soviet space mission (Apollo–Soyuz).
1 August	Signing of the Helsinki Accords of the Conference on Security and Cooperation in Europe.
Autumn	Soviet/Cuban support for the MPLA escalates in response to South African intervention and cut-off of US aid to UNITA and the FNLA; the MPLA holds power in most of Angola after independence.
9 October	Andrei Sakharov wins the Nobel Peace Prize for his human rights activities.

1976

July	Sadat terminates the Soviet-Egyptian Treaty of Friendship and Cooperation, thereby completing Egypt's exit from the Soviet orbit.
15 September	Mao Zedong dies and is succeeded by Hua Guofeng.
2 November	Jimmy Carter defeats Ford for the US presidency.
December	Ethiopian leader Mengistu Haile Mariam visits Moscow.

1977

18 January	Brezhnev delivers his 'Tula speech', rejecting pursuit of military superiority and declaring that victory in a nuclear war is impossible.
20 January	Carter takes office as US President.
14 February	Carter repudiates the Vladivostok Accords agreed by Ford and Brezhnev in November 1974.
February	Carter writes to dissident Soviet physicist Andrei Sakharov.

15 March	Dissident Anatolii Shcharanskii is refused permission to emigrate to Israel and arrested on charges of treason and espionage.
May	Mengistu visits Moscow again.
16 June	Brezhnev replaces Podgornyi as Chairman of the Presidium of the Supreme Soviet (head of state).
July	Somali forces invade Ethiopian territory in the Ogaden; the USSR agrees to an Ethiopian request for assistance.
1 October	Joint US-Soviet communiqué commits the superpowers to work together towards a comprehensive settlement of the Arab-Israeli conflict.
7 October	Adoption of a new USSR Constitution.
November–December	Soviet airlift helps Ethiopia expel Somali forces from the Ogaden; Siad Barre expels Soviet advisers from Somalia and deprives Soviet forces of the use of naval facilities at the port of Berbera.
19 November	Sadat arrives in Israel.

1978

April	Overthrow of Afghan leader Mohammad Daoud by the People's Democratic Party of Afghanistan (PDPA).
13 July	Aleksandr Ginzburg convicted of 'anti-Soviet agitation and propaganda'.
17 September	Camp David Accords between Israel and Egypt agreed as the basis for an eventual peace treaty.

1979

17 February	Chinese invasion of Vietnam.
March	Rising in Herat triggers first consideration of possible Soviet intervention in support of the PDPA regime in Afghanistan.
26 March	Conclusion of Israeli-Egyptian peace treaty.
15–18 June	Carter–Brezhnev summit in Vienna; signing of SALT II, which is never ratified.
16 September	Hafizullah Amin overthrows rival Mohammad Taraki in Afghanistan, triggering further destabilisation of the PDPA regime.
December	Brezhnev awarded the Lenin Prize for Literature for ghost-written war memoirs.
12 December	NATO decision to deploy Pershing-2 and cruise missiles in Europe in response to Soviet SS-20 deployments.
24–27 December	Introduction of Soviet forces into Afghanistan; installation of Babrak Karmal as president in place of Amin, who is removed and killed.

1980

3–4 January	Responding to the intervention in Afghanistan, US President Carter suspends ratification of SALT II and imposes sanctions against the USSR, including an embargo on the sale of grain or advanced technology to the USSR.
22 January	Dissident physicist Sakharov exiled to Gorky.
19 July	Opening of XXII Summer Olympic Games in Moscow.
July–August	Labour unrest in Poland in response to officially mandated food price rises leads to formation of Solidarity Trade Union.
October	Ailing Kosygin is replaced as premier by Brezhnev crony Nikolai Tikhonov.
2 December	Soviet troop manoeuvres near Polish border prompt US warning against intervention in Poland.

1981

20 January	Reagan inaugurated as US president.
19–26 March	Warsaw Pact manoeuvres in a number of countries are extended to 7 April in response to unrest in Poland.
6 August	Reagan announces the stockpiling of neutron bombs by the United States.
4 October	Polish government announces new food price hikes, which trigger a wave of strikes and other disturbances through November.
19 October	Defence Minister General Wojciech Jaruzelski replaces Stanislaw Kania as leader of the Polish United Workers Party.
November	Reagan unveils his 'zero option' proposal for controlling the deployment of theatre nuclear weapons, which Moscow promptly rejects.
12–13 December	Jaruzelski imposes martial law in Poland; Solidarity is banned.

1982

May	Yuri Andropov leaves the KGB to return to work in the CPSU Secretariat.
May	CPSU Secretary Andrei Kirilenko suffers major heart attack, effectively eliminating him as a contender to succeed Brezhnev.
10 November	Brezhnev dies.
12 November	Andropov becomes party leader.
30 December	Jaruzelski suspends martial law in Poland.

1983

23 March	Reagan announces his Strategic Defence Initiative.

16 June	Andropov becomes Chairman of the Presidium of the Supreme Soviet (head of state).
August	Andropov last seen in public.
1 September	Shooting down of Korean Air Lines flight 007 in Soviet air space.

1984

9 February	Andropov dies.
13 February	Konstantin Chernenko becomes party leader.
11 April	Chernenko becomes Chairman of the Presidium of the Supreme Soviet (head of state).
5 July	Chernenko readmits Stalin's long-serving lieutenant, 94-year-old V. M. Molotov, to the CPSU, from which Khrushchev had expelled him in 1957.

1985

10 March	Chernenko dies.
11 March	Mikhail Gorbachev succeeds Chernenko as party leader.

PART ONE   INTRODUCTION

CHAPTER ONE

THE SOVIET UNION AT THE END OF THE KHRUSHCHEV ERA

Late on 15 October 1964, Soviet news agencies issued a terse statement informing Soviet citizens and the world that Nikita Sergeevich Khrushchev, First Secretary of the Central Committee of the Communist Party of the Soviet Union (CPSU) since 1953 and Chairman of the USSR Council of Ministers since 1958, had been released from his duties in connection with his advancing age and deteriorating health. After almost a dozen years in power, Khrushchev was pensioned off to live out the remainder of his life in obscurity. His name disappeared from the official media overnight: even the denunciations of his mistakes and defects of character that followed his removal did not mention him by name [*Doc. 1*]. The new party leader was Khrushchev's long-time protégé and colleague in the CPSU Secretariat, Leonid Brezhnev, while the post of head of government passed to the head of the USSR State Planning Committee (Gosplan), Aleksei Kosygin. Seen by many at the time as transitional figures, these two men would in fact lead the USSR for more than a decade and a half.

THE FALL OF NIKITA KHRUSHCHEV

It was Khrushchev's distinction, and to some extent his achievement, to be the first – and until Gorbachev's resignation from the presidency of a collapsing state the only – Soviet leader to be removed from office before his death. That his removal was both bloodless and orderly, if not exactly democratic, was in no small measure a reflection of the changes he had wrought while in power. One reason for the smooth transfer of power was that Khrushchev's removal enjoyed the overwhelming support of the country's political elite (Tompson, 1991 and 1995). While some observers at the time saw him as the victim of an anti-Stalinist backlash, he was in fact overthrown by a broad coalition bringing together the Stalinist and (relatively) liberal wings of the political elite. Leading representatives of all the key institutions of the regime, including the party, the state bureaucracy and the secret police took part in the plot; only the military remained on the sidelines, choosing to back neither Khrushchev nor his opponents.

By 1964, virtually every major elite constituency had significant grievances against Khrushchev. Senior party and state bureaucrats ('cadres', in Soviet parlance) were fed up with his endless and often ill-considered administrative reorganisations, his public bullying of subordinates and his frequent changes of course with respect to policy. Party officials, who constituted the largest share of the anti-Khrushchev coalition, were angered by his attempts to impose term limits on party officials and mandatory turn-over requirements on leading party bodies. His 1962 decision to split the Communist Party's territorial apparatus into 'agricultural' and 'industrial' segments was an administrative disaster and a major blow to incumbent officials, who found half their authority transferred to newly appointed rivals. Conservatives, especially in the military and the security organs, were antagonised by his determination to control military expenditure, his pursuit of détente with the West and his increasingly aggressive pursuit of de-Stalinisation. More reform-minded members of the elite had come to see him as an unreliable patron for the causes of both de-Stalinisation and economic reform. A series of foreign setbacks, most notably over Berlin and Cuba, had damaged Khrushchev's authority, while his economic policies were failing to deliver the promised rates of growth. This last concern was made more acute by his incautious rhetoric about the pace of Soviet development, which risked arousing popular expectations that could not be met and thus endangering social stability.

Thus, while policy failures clearly undermined the First Secretary, it appears to have been Khrushchev's leadership style that really triggered his removal. He fell because the Soviet elite had come to regard him as un-manageable. His impulsive decision-making, arbitrary behaviour and high-handed treatment of senior officials alienated both his colleagues in the party Presidium and the wider elite. The other members of the Presidium believed that his personal dominance was undermining the oligarchic arrangements around which they had tried to fashion a stable political order since Stalin's death, while lower-level officials saw his endless re-shuffles – the so-called 'leapfrogging of cadres' – as a permanent threat to their job security. In denouncing Stalin's crimes against the elite in his 'secret speech' to the Twentieth Party Congress in 1956, Khrushchev had offered the country's political-administrative elite a promise of physical security: never again would a campaign of terror be directed against them. By 1964, how-ever, they wanted more: they wanted the professional security that Khrushchev's perpetual reorganisations and personnel shake-ups denied them. The October Plenum was, above all else, an attempt by the political elite to replace an increasingly erratic and autocratic leader with a stable, predictable collective leadership. It was therefore natural that the oligarchs should turn to Brezhnev and Kosygin as Khrushchev's successors.

THE NEW LEADERS

In both the USSR and the West, it was long believed that Brezhnev had succeeded to the party leadership almost accidentally, either as a compromise candidate or as the figure chosen by the real king-makers (Suslov and/or Shelepin, depending on which account one accepts – see Tatu, 1969; Medvedev, 1982; Burlatsky, 1988 and 1990). In fact, Brezhnev's selection to succeed Khrushchev to the party leadership reflected both his own leading role in the plot – he was the prime mover behind Khrushchev's removal – and the extent to which he offered the elite exactly what it wanted in a new First Secretary: stability and predictability.

Born in 1906 to a working-class family in the Ukrainian city of Kamenskoe (later Dneprodzerzhinsk), Leonid Brezhnev worked in agriculture and industry in his youth and qualified as a surveyor in 1927. He worked as a fitter for a time, while studying part-time at the metallurgical institute in Dneprodzerzhinsk. After graduating from the institute in 1935, he became a shift leader in a factory, but he was soon called up for military service, which he completed as the political instructor of a tank company before returning to Dneprodzerzhinsk in 1936. Soon Brezhnev's career began to take off, launched (as were the careers of so many of his contemporaries) by the opportunities for rapid promotion that arose during the Great Terror of 1936–38. By February 1939, he had risen to the post of propaganda secretary for the Dnepropetrovsk Provincial Party Committee (*Obkom*). Brezhnev spent the war as a political officer, rising to the rank of major-general. Despite later attempts to establish his reputation as a war hero, his military record was not particularly distinguished. He did, however, make a good impression on Ukraine's Communist Party boss, Nikita Khrushchev, who was to act as Brezhnev's patron for almost two decades.

After the war, thanks to Khrushchev's favour, Brezhnev rose rapidly, heading the Zaporozhe *Obkom* and then that of the much larger Dnepropetrovsk. In 1950, shortly after Khrushchev's return to Moscow as a Central Committee Secretary, Brezhnev was summoned to the capital for a short stint in the Central Committee apparatus. Later that year, he was dispatched to Kishinev (Chisinau) as first secretary of the Central Committee of the Moldavian Communist Party. Like a number of younger officials, Brezhnev suffered demotion in the immediate aftermath of Stalin's death in 1953, but Khrushchev's patronage did not fail him, and he soon began his political recovery. Over the ensuing six years, he faithfully supported Khrushchev and was rewarded with appointments as second secretary (1954) and then first secretary (1955) of the Kazakh party organisation, before joining the Central Committee Secretariat in 1956. Brezhnev became a candidate member of the CPSU Presidium at the same time, attaining full membership in 1957 as a result of his support for Khrushchev against the so-called 'anti-party group'. In 1960, Brezhnev was 'kicked upstairs' from the Secretariat to the largely ceremonial post of Chairman of the Presidium of the Supreme Soviet – formally the country's head of state. However, the April 1963 stroke which ended the political career of Frol Kozlov, who had been widely seen as Khrushchev's most likely successor, triggered Brezhnev's return to the Secretariat, although he remained head of state.

By this time, Khrushchev's own political stock was falling. The First Secretary's frantic efforts to realise his aims were alienating almost every important elite constituency. From early 1964, therefore, his closest colleagues, led by Brezhnev and Nikolai Podgornyi, began to plot his removal. Brezhnev's role in this conspiracy has often been played down, at least partly as a reflection of his posthumous political reputation as a dim-witted, unimaginative and colourless *apparatchik*. In fact, the evidence strongly suggests that he was the chief conspirator, although some witnesses claim that he panicked in the autumn, when he learned that Khrushchev knew of the plot (Tompson, 1991). Panic or no, the coup succeeded, and the October 1964 Central Committee plenum relieved Khrushchev of all his duties, choosing Brezhnev and the long-serving technocrat Kosygin to take over the leadership of the party and government, respectively.

In his address to the October plenum, Brezhnev affirmed his commitment to collective leadership and emphasised his determination to strengthen the role of party organs in all spheres of social and economic life. In light of the regime's subsequent development, it is noteworthy that Brezhnev stressed not the leading role of the *party* but the leading role of *party organs*. He promised more than once to 'stick up for cadres', beginning to develop the themes of 'trust in cadres' and 'stability of cadres' that would be the hallmarks of his rule. In any case, Brezhnev had no real rivals for the party leadership. He was already the *de facto* second secretary, he had long experience in senior party posts and he was a man whose work style was generally recognised as 'collegial'. He was expected to show greater respect for the norms of collective leadership than had the increasingly arbitrary and autocratic Khrushchev. He was perceived as a safe pair of hands, who could provide stability at the top, and he was generally regarded as a 'decent' character (Tompson, 1991: 1115). To be sure, Brezhnev was also a compromise figure. He was not strongly identified with any particular ideological tendency and was thus more or less acceptable to both right and left – the anti-Khrushchev conspiracy had brought together representatives of all strands of opinion within the elite. He was also acceptable both to older members of the elite, like Suslov, and rising younger men, like Shelepin, Semichastnyi and Voronov (Burlatsky, 1988: 214). In short, Brezhnev stood at the intersection of a number of cleavages involving both policy issues and generational splits.

Aleksei Kosygin's succession to the chairmanship of the Council of

Ministers was the culmination of a career that had in many ways been even more remarkable than Brezhnev's. Born in 1904, Kosygin joined the Red Army during the Civil War. After being demobilised, he completed his secondary education in a *tekhnikum* (a specialised secondary school) in the field of trade and thereafter occupied a number of managerial posts in the consumers' cooperatives of Siberia. In 1931, he entered the Leningrad Textile Institute, graduating in 1935 and going to work first as a foreman and then as a shop head in a Leningrad textile factory. It was from there that his political career was launched. During the Great Terror, the young Kosygin received a dizzying succession of promotions to fill vacancies created by the arrests of numerous senior officials and the transfer of many more to fill their posts. By late 1938, he was chairman of the Executive Committee of the Leningrad City Soviet. Kosygin was transferred to Moscow in 1939 as USSR People's Commissar for Light Industry – at the age of 35 and just four years after completing his course at the textile institute. In 1940, he was named Deputy Chairman of the USSR Council of People's Commissars (effectively deputy prime minister), a post he retained throughout the rest of the Stalin period. Kosygin joined the Politburo as a candidate member in 1946 and was promoted to full member in 1948. Like Brezhnev, however, Kosygin was dropped from the Presidium after Stalin's death, returning as a candidate member only in 1957. Kosygin was neither a client nor a particularly close supporter of Khrushchev, but he was one of the most able Soviet administrators and also a man who knew how to avoid being drawn into factional intrigues. Khrushchev thus came to appreciate both his ability and his reliability, and in 1959 Kosygin returned to the front rank of Soviet politicians as chairman of the State Planning Committee (Gosplan), regaining his full membership of the Presidium the following year. His elevation to the premiership, too, reflected above all the widespread recognition of his administrative talents. It was certainly no reward for his role in Khrushchev's removal. While Kosygin clearly knew of the plot and supported it, there is no evidence to suggest that he played a key role in the conspiracy.

Brezhnev and Kosygin were, in many ways, an odd couple, and that may be why the elite chose them. In Brezhnev, the party apparatus had a safe, reliable leader who could be counted on to advance its interests and to eschew the abrupt and often arbitrary changes in policy that had characterised Khrushchev, as well as his often high-handed treatment of senior officials. In Kosygin, they chose an able administrator whose technocratic bent and failure to manifest any real leadership ambitions of his own minimised the risk of rivalry with Brezhnev. Moreover, Kosygin's more reformist inclinations would counterbalance Brezhnev's cautious conservatism and reassure those who hoped that Khrushchev's removal would not bring an end to reforms but would rather allow them to continue without the zigzags associated with Khrushchev. The first of these calculations with respect to Kosygin turned out to be largely justified. While his relations with Brezhnev were never close and cooled markedly in the 1970s, he remained in post until shortly before his death in 1980 without ever challenging Brezhnev's position. The second calculation, however, proved unwarranted. Kosygin's modest reformism marked him out from Brezhnev throughout the ensuing decade and a half, but his major economic reform drive came to nothing by 1970, and further attempts at reform went nowhere.

SOVIET SOCIETY A DECADE AFTER STALIN'S DEATH

The country that Khrushchev's successors inherited was a very different one from that which Stalin had bequeathed to Khrushchev and his heirs. It was, to begin with, a predominantly urban society: during the dozen years since Stalin's death, the rural population had declined slightly, while the urban population had risen by just under 22%. This raised the urban population from 43% to 53% of the total Soviet population, a development that made Soviet society easier to mobilise but arguably more difficult to manage, not least because its social structure and occupational profile were far more complex. It was also a better educated and very much wealthier society. Even relatively conservative Western estimates – which were far lower than the official data – pointed to growth rates for the economy as a whole averaging around 5.8% per year during the Khrushchev era. Industry grew even faster, at rates of perhaps 6.2% on Western estimates (Gros & Steinherr, 1995: 66). This performance, coupled with such obvious and high-profile technical successes as Soviet achievements in space exploration, suggested to most observers within the country and without that the Soviet system was fundamentally sound and that its performance posed a major challenge to the capitalist West.

This growth performance was reflected in popular living standards to an extent unknown in the Stalin era. According to official Soviet data, *per capita* consumption of meat had risen by more than 57%, and that of fish, vegetables and fruit by 80, 41 and 155% respectively. At the same time, consumption of grain products and potatoes, which had long formed the basis for most Soviet citizens' diets, actually declined, by about 9.3% in the case of grain and a staggering 41.9% in the case of potatoes. Khrushchev's housing construction drive had dramatically reduced the proportion of the population living in communal apartments and dormitories, and many con- sumer durables were becoming ever more widely available. The Khrushchev era saw dramatic increases in production of radios, refrigerators, washing machines and vacuum cleaners. Many of these goods remained relatively hard to come by – the huge percentage increases were often from very low bases – but a large and rapidly growing minority did indeed possess them.

In 1953, television sets had been virtually unknown in the Soviet Union; by 1965, around one-quarter of Soviet households owned them (TsSU, 1966: 595–9).

Politically, too, the country was much changed, although the institutional architecture of the system was, on the whole, that inherited from Stalin. The CPSU retained the monopoly on political and economic power it had claimed in the years following the Civil War, and its organs monitored and directed every social, economic or political institution of any significance, from the government of the USSR down to the shop floor of the smallest factory in the most remote provincial town. The party tolerated no opposition and maintained a tight grip on the media and the arts. While Khrushchev had tinkered extensively with the organisation of economic management, the basic principles and priorities of the command economy created by Stalin – state ownership of the means of production, central planning of virtually all economic activity of any significance and the priority development of heavy industry – remained intact. Yet this institutional continuity did not prevent dramatic changes in the political atmosphere in the decade or so to 1964.

The most important change was the abandonment of the use of terror against members of the elite. Khrushchev's 1956 denunciation of Stalin's crimes against the leading party and state officials, along with his treatment of defeated rivals, who were removed from office rather than arrested and shot, signalled to the wider Soviet elite that the days of arbitrary terror against them were over. Ironically, this very fact reduced the risks faced by would-be plotters and doubtless contributed to the political upheavals of the Khrushchev era – including his removal. The wider society, too, felt the lessening of police controls. While de-Stalinisation proceeded in fits and starts, with partial retreats following each new advance, the trend was towards greater freedom, not least in the arts. Even the crackdown on abstract artists and heterodox writers launched in late 1962 was relatively mild by comparison with what had gone before. In short, Khrushchev bequeathed his successors a society that was both wealthier than it had ever been before and freer than it had been for a generation or more. However, as his successors would learn, these developments, though clearly positive, did not necessarily make it easier to govern successfully.

THE SOVIET UNION AND THE WORLD IN 1964

The new leaders were aware that Khrushchev's legacy in foreign affairs was, at best, mixed. On the positive side, he had done much to break down the Soviet Union's isolation after 1953. The sense that the USSR and its European allies constituted a besieged camp gave way to a new sense of confidence and activism world-wide. The USSR was to challenge American imperialism throughout the world. This transformation owed much to Khrushchev's doctrinal innovations. Khrushchev had rejected as outmoded Leninist theses concerning the inevitability of war between capitalism and socialism and the role of war as the 'midwife of the revolution'. Instead, he affirmed the possibility of long-term peaceful coexistence between states with different social systems.

These innovations opened up new opportunities for Soviet diplomacy, particularly in the post-colonial world, where Khrushchev had demonstrated the potential benefits for the USSR of close links to national liberation movements, even where these were not communist in orientation. Unlike Stalin, Khrushchev took a keen interest in the newly independent states of Africa and Asia, and spent much time and energy building closer ties to them. Recognising that most of the new states of the developing world would not move rapidly to Soviet-style socialism, Khrushchev accepted the need for a relatively non-ideological approach, extending aid to non-communist governments that adopted a suitably 'anti-imperialist' stance and largely side-lining Third World communist parties. His successors thus inherited close ties to such states as India and Indonesia. Khrushchev's post-colonial involvements were not by any means risk-free, and he did suffer reverses as Soviet-backed leaders fell from power in a number of black African and Arab countries. These setbacks highlighted the need for caution but did not deter Khrushchev's successors from pursuing their own ambitions in the developing world, which increasingly became a major battleground in the contest between the superpowers.

Other aspects of Khrushchev's record were more problematic. The most serious was the apparent failure of his policies towards the West. Khrushchev found himself stymied in his attempts to revise the post-war status of Berlin, which greatly aggravated East–West tensions and which culminated in the construction of the Berlin Wall in 1961, one of the great Soviet propaganda defeats of the Cold War. His elaborate efforts to deceive the West into believing in Soviet strategic superiority were exposed, but not before fear of this mythical 'missile gap' had helped fuel a genuine arms build-up in the United States. When his missile deception was exposed, Khrushchev responded by trying to achieve strategic parity with the United States quickly and cheaply: the result was the Cuban missile crisis and the humiliating Soviet climbdown that resolved it. For his successors, the lesson was obvious: the Soviet Union had to achieve military equality with America so as to preclude the possibility of any such humiliation in the future. Indeed, Soviet leaders concluded in the wake of the Cuban crisis that they must pursue strategic nuclear *superiority* in order to counterbalance the arsenals of America's allies and the presence of American nuclear forces in Europe which were capable of hitting Soviet territory (Savel'ev & Detinov, 1995: 3).

Nevertheless, although Khrushchev's ambitions in East–West relations were never realised, much progress was made. This was particularly true after Cuba, not least because both sides had been so shaken by the missile crisis. A Soviet-American hotline was installed to facilitate direct contact between the two leaders in a crisis, a partial nuclear test ban was agreed, and Khrushchev's relationship with the US President, John Kennedy, developed. Had Kennedy lived and Khrushchev remained in office, more might have been achieved. Even as things stood, Khrushchev's successors inherited a much more relaxed climate of East–West relations than he had. They also inherited a more stable European order. While the status of Germany, and in particular of Berlin, had yet to be settled formally, the two sides had come to accept as normal the spheres of influence that had emerged after 1945. Moreover, as subsequent events demonstrated, the heirs of both Kennedy and Khrushchev had learned at least one key lesson from the missile crisis: henceforth the two superpowers carefully avoided direct confrontations. Their conflict was waged by proxy and confined for the most part to the developing world. The two sides showed greater respect than ever for each other's 'core' spheres of influence; even during the period of high tensions after 1979 that became known as the Second Cold War, the superpowers behaved with restraint in areas of the world where their vital interests intersected (e.g. the Middle East). Mutual provocation was generally reserved for areas of secondary importance to one side or the other (Angola, Nicaragua).

Khrushchev's pursuit of détente with the West aggravated relations with China, which broke with Moscow at the end of the 1950s, thereby dividing the Communist bloc and leaving Soviet leaders with a second Cold War to manage. Relations with China had begun to sour even under Stalin, but things had gone from bad to worse under Khrushchev. The two giants of the Communist world quarrelled over a range of issues, including ideology, leadership of the 'Socialist camp', policies towards the West and the developing countries, Soviet aid for China's nuclear programme and a number of other regional and bilateral issues. The Chinese challenge to Soviet leadership both within the Socialist Commonwealth and in the developing world was by 1964 regarded as an extremely serious threat.

Khrushchev's removal did little to change the major priorities of Soviet diplomacy, which were to remain remarkably constant until the late 1980s. However, the October plenum did bring about a significant shift in the means by which those goals were pursued. Khrushchev had frequently operated by bluff, bluster and deception, and the results had all too often been less than satisfactory. His successors, by contrast, emphasised patience and prudence, showing little inclination for either risk-taking or bluff. The installation of the Brezhnev–Kosygin leadership thus ushered in a more stable, predictable period in Soviet diplomacy.

PART TWO   ANALYSIS

CHAPTER TWO

LEADERSHIP POLITICS

HIGH POLITICS AND BREZHNEV'S CONSOLIDATION OF POWER

Brezhnev's consolidation of power was slow but relatively smooth. While he took longer to establish his dominance than had Stalin or Khrushchev, he managed to do so without the upheavals and eruptions of open conflict that had characterised their struggles for supremacy. The caution with which Brezhnev moved to consolidate his position was no doubt a reflection of the balance of forces in the party's highest policy-making body, the Presidium of the CPSU Central Committee (renamed the Politburo in 1966, when Brezhnev's own title reverted to 'General Secretary', as had been the case under Stalin). While both Stalin and Khrushchev had shown that the position of party leader was a promising one from which to bid for dominance, it was not yet clear that the party leadership was in fact the pre-eminent position in Soviet politics. Brezhnev's caution may also have reflected his awareness that Khrushchev had been removed largely because his fellow oligarchs found him unmanageable. A period of 'collective leadership' was clearly in order.

There was, however, more to it than this. Members of the Soviet leadership who later described Brezhnev's accession were more or less unanimous in asserting that his position was somewhat shaky at the start (Tompson, 1991: 1116). While he was more than a figurehead installed by Suslov or Shelepin, Brezhnev was viewed by some of his colleagues as a transitional figure. Ukrainian party boss Petr Shelest (1989) claims that, from the beginning, Brezhnev feared a challenge from the younger members of the leadership, led by former KGB chief Shelepin, a claim supported by other observers (see Burlatsky, 1988; Rodionov, 1989), though denied by Shelepin (1991) himself. Another potential rival was Brezhnev's chief partner in organising Khrushchev's removal, Nikolai Podgornyi. Shelest (1989, 1991) claims that Podgornyi backed Brezhnev from the start and that the new party leader would not have survived his first year in power without Podgornyi's support. This may be so, but Brezhnev's subseqent sidelining of Podgornyi suggests that he saw Podgornyi himself as a threat. This does not necessarily contradict Shelest's account: it may well have been an early reliance on Podgornyi's support that prompted Brezhnev to marginalise him so quickly.

In any case, Shelepin and Podgornyi were the first victims of Brezhnev's consolidation of power. In April 1965, Podgornyi's protégé V. N. Titov was removed from his position as the junior Central Committee Secretary for Organisational Party Work, a post that would have involved him in personnel selection at the highest levels. Just three months later, a Central Committee report sharply criticised the Khar'kov *Obkom*, which Podgornyi had headed in the early 1950s and which remained very much his political base. Other Podgornyi protégés (many of them from Khar'kov) were demoted throughout 1965, and Podgornyi himself was transferred in December from the powerful Central Committee Secretariat, effectively the administrative 'nerve centre' of the party, to the largely ceremonial post of Chairman of the Presidium of the Supreme Soviet – the USSR's titular head of state (Hough & Fainsod, 1979: 256–7).

Shelepin, for his part, found himself increasingly engaged in foreign affairs, which appears to have been part of a deliberate effort to keep the ex-KGB chief out of domestic politics. In December 1965, the Party–State Control Commission, which Shelepin had headed since 1962, was abolished, a move which also cost Shelepin his position as a deputy prime minister. He remained in the Secretariat until 1967, but with the much less important portfolio of trade and light industry, before finally being transferred to the post of Chairman of the All Union Central Trade Union Council, a post with even less to recommend it than Podgornyi's. Throughout 1966–68 a number of high-ranking officials linked to Shelepin were demoted, including the heads of the KGB, the *militsiya* (the ordinary police), Communist Youth League and the official news agency, TASS (Hough & Fainsod, 1979: 257–8; Shelest, 1991).

At the same time, Brezhnev slowly but surely promoted a growing number of former subordinates who had served under him in Moldavia and Ukraine to key positions at the centre. The rise of the so-called 'Dnepropetrovsk mafia' was particularly clear evidence of Brezhnev's ascendance. Brezhnev's former second secretary in Zaporopzh'e and his successor in Dnepropetrovsk, Andrei Kirilenko, entered the Secretariat and took over responsibility for cadres policy (personnel). N. A. Shchelokov, who had served under Brezhnev in Dnepropetrovsk and Moldavia, took up the post of USSR Minister for the Preservation of Public Order (later renamed Minister of Internal Affairs) in 1966, remaining in post until after Brezhnev's death. Konstantin Chernenko, Brezhnev's favourite and virtual 'shadow' since his Moldavian days, was appointed in early 1965 to head the Central Committee's 'General Department'. The General Department functioned as the party leader's *de facto* chancellery and largely controlled the flow of classified information within the upper echelons of the party apparatus. Many other former Brezhnev subordinates were installed in key posts in the KGB, the government bureaucracy and the diplomatic service (Hough & Fainsod, 1979: 259).

Increasingly, Brezhnev emerged as the 'public face' of the regime, both at home and abroad. While the Brezhnev cult did not really take off until about 1977, his public profile at home was markedly higher than that of any other member of the leadership. In foreign affairs, he increasingly took over the leading role, receiving foreign dignitaries and travelling abroad to meet foreign statesmen, even in situations in which protocol might ordinarily have called for either Kosygin, as head of government, or Podgornyi, as head of state, to take the lead.

BREZHNEV AS POLITICIAN: MANNEQUIN OR MACHIAVELLIAN?

Brezhnev's leadership style remains a matter of some controversy. In part, it has proved difficult to pin down because he stamped his own personality on the regime to a far lesser degree than either his predecessors or his successors – at least if one excepts the brief rule of the colourless Konstantin Chernenko, who was in many respects the 'poor man's Brezhnev'. As Colton (1986: 7) has observed, 'Admirers and detractors alike have found less to say about Brezhnev the leader than about the era over which he presided. His rule, by the lights of the Soviet past, was oddly impersonal'. Even in the late 1970s, when the Brezhnev cult began to flourish in the Soviet media, his image was marked by the very caution and blandness that had made him acceptable to such a wide range of elite opinion in 1964. It was, as Soviet wags (quietly) remarked, a personality cult without a personality. This is not entirely sur-prising. Given that Khrushchev was removed in large part on account of what colleagues saw as his autocratic and high-handed treatment of them, Brezhnev had good reason to adopt a more consensus-oriented, collegial style of decision-making, at least in the beginning. The fact that he was, by temperament, more of an 'organisation' man simply meant that his own inclinations pointed in the same direction as political necessity.

This lack of a clearly defined, robust public persona has made it par-ticularly easy for Brezhnev's harshest critics to present him as a complete mediocrity, untalented, unprincipled and uninterested in much beyond his own enjoyment of the perquisites of power. The dissident historian Roy Medvedev described him as a 'cynical…vain, stupid' man (Smith, 1990: 23) and argued that Brezhnev was nothing more than a place-man installed at the head of the party by others, a natural follower who never sought supreme power (Medvedev, 1991, vol. 1: 7). Medvedev's depiction may be the harshest yet published but it is by no means alone. Burlatsky (1988, 1990), too, presents Brezhnev as an essentially talentless apparatchik, a man chosen as a figurehead following a coup arranged and executed by others. Asked how Brezhnev became leader of the party, former Moscow party chief Nikolai Egorychev replied, 'Leonid Il'ich – the leader? He was never leader, before the October Plenum or after it' (Egorychev, 1989). These views are difficult to reconcile with the facts of Brezhnev's career. In a political system whose upper echelons have been likened by some observers to a Hobbesian 'war of all against all' (Linden, 1966: 1–10), Brezhnev reached the top and remained there longer than any Soviet leader except Stalin. If he was as limited a figure as his critics present, then this record requires a good deal of explanation.

To be sure, Brezhnev's limitations were evident even during his life and have occasioned much comment. He was certainly no intellectual – though, neither, it must be said, were his predecessor or most of his colleagues. His grasp of the Marxist classics was weak, as Brezhnev himself acknowledged (Suny, 1998: 423), and he so disliked reading that he preferred to have official papers read aloud to him by staff (Gromyko, 1991; Shelepin, 1991; Baibakov, 1991; Griko, 1997). It is also true that, as he grew older, Brezhnev's preference for promoting cronies and relatives to high positions grew more pronounced: by the end of the 1970s, he had promoted his son to first deputy foreign minister, his son-in-law to first deputy interior minister, and numerous protégés from his earlier career to posts for which they were manifestly ill qualified. In this, however, he may have been learning from the mistakes of his predecessor. Having shown great skill in promoting loyal subordinates during his rise to supremacy, Khrushchev had, after 1957 or so, become a rather more demanding boss – and a rather less loyal patron. Believing his position to be secure, Khrushchev had been all too ready to demote clients who failed to perform adequately in their posts, thereby generating a great deal of resentment among formerly loyal Khrushchevites, which ultimately contributed to his removal (Tompson, 1995). This was a mistake Brezhnev never repeated, although the price of his security was often the advancement to sensitive positions of mediocre toadies.

Brezhnev's love for the trappings of power also made him an easy target for ridicule. Indeed, as he grew older, he seemed more attached to the perquisites of power than to its exercise. His appetite for awards and honours was legendary, as was his love of expensive presents and hunting at his beloved Zavidovo retreat. Already a Hero of Soviet Labour when he came to power, Brezhnev after his accession was made a Hero of the Soviet Union no fewer than four times – the first in 1966, 21 years after his military career had ended. In 1978, he was awarded the Order of Victory, the Soviet Union's highest military award, having followed Stalin two years earlier in becoming a Marshal of the Soviet Union. In addition, Brezhnev collected numerous local orders, honours and other awards throughout the USSR and the world. By the end of his life, he had collected more state awards than all previous Soviet leaders combined (Kotkin, 2001: 50). In 1979, he was awarded the Lenin Prize for Literature for three slender booklets of ghost-written memoirs about the Second World War. Brezhnev was aware of the anecdotes to which his ever-expanding collection of medals gave rise. When told that people were joking about his having chest-expansion surgery, so as to make room for all his medals, Brezhnev replied, 'If they're telling jokes about me, it means they love me' (Shelest, 1991: 218).

Brezhnev's vanity also necessitated the re-writing of his rather undistinguished war record. In reality, he had begun the war as a political officer equivalent in rank to a colonel, and he recovered from a demotion in early 1943 to end it as a major general of no particular distinction. Official accounts of Brezhnev's record, however, inflated his achievements, in many cases simply falsifying the record to present Brezhnev as one of the major architects of victory – as in the claim that he had headed the Political Administration for an entire front at a time when he was in fact heading the Political Department of a single army (Kirsanov, 1991; Tabachnik, 1991). In this, it should be said, Brezhnev was arguably picking up where Khrushchev had left off. Nikita Sergeevich, too, had been made a Hero of the Soviet Union (albeit only once, in 1964) and the six-volume official history of the war published in the early 1960s presented him as a major military figure – until the final volume, that is: it appeared just months after his ouster and failed to mention him at all.

Where Brezhnev differed from Khrushchev was in his unconcealed love of luxury: he was as eager to accept expensive presents as new awards and showed a particular fondness for large, powerful – and preferably foreign – automobiles, of which he collected a substantial fleet. While his lifestyle was neither so opulent nor so open as that of post-Soviet Russia's elite, it was enough to give rise to a small genre of anecdotes all its own. In one such story, Brezhnev's mother, on seeing how her son lives, says how proud she is that he has done so well for himself but then asks, in a worried tone, what will become of him if the Bolsheviks return.

Nevertheless, it would be a mistake to overlook Brezhnev's real political skills. While Thatcher (2002: 32) goes too far in suggesting that Brezhnev should be 'praised as one of the most successful exponents of the art of Soviet politics', he rightly draws attention to Brezhnev's strengths as a political player in the Soviet system. As leader, Brezhnev succeeded in using his control over personnel decisions to secure his rule; he managed, on the whole, to hold together the broad coalition of elite interests that had backed the overthrow of Khrushchev; he brought a much needed period of stability and consolidation to politics and policy; and he projected to the outside world an image of the USSR as a stable, pragmatic and responsible super-power.

It is striking that, while authors like Burlatsky and Medvedev are dismissive of Brezhnev, those who worked most closely with him acknowledge his strengths as well as his faults. Their accounts suggest that, up to the early 1970s, at least, Brezhnev was a consummate backroom operator. Former Belorussian party boss K. T. Mazurov (1989) claims that Brezhnev 'in no way possessed the qualities of an outstanding figure' but nevertheless admits that he was a 'good student of the system'. Mazurov then describes how Brezhnev effectively sidelined the Politburo and increased the power of the Central Committee Secretariat, which Brezhnev dominated, at the Politburo's expense. Former Politburo member Gennadii Voronov (1991) presents Brezhnev as a man who knew very well how to undermine his opponents behind the scenes and prevail in disagreements over policy, on occasion overriding even the views of the Politburo majority. While he criticises Brezhnev for making ill-informed, arbitrary decisions, Voronov makes it clear that Brezhnev knew how to circumvent opposition to his plans. Former Foreign Minister Andrei Gromyko (1990: 522–30) gives Brezhnev modest praise for his effectiveness in representing the USSR abroad – an impression shared by many foreign statesmen who dealt with him – and for his consultative approach to decision-making. Shelepin (1991), who was certainly no Brezhnev partisan, suggests that Brezhnev's rise to the top job was entirely logical in terms of his wide experience of high office, as well as his 'composure, accessibility, democratic approach in conversation with comrades, his ability to form relationships with people and his benevolence'. Shelepin's claim that Brezhnev had the security organs place his highest-ranking colleagues under close surveillance suggests that the General Secretary may have been a dangerous boss but not a political incompetent.

'TWO BREZHNEVS'?

Many of those who observed Brezhnev at first hand during his years in power have tended to contrast the 'early' and 'late' Brezhnevs (see, e.g., Shelepin, 1991; Baibakov, 1991; Arbatov, 1993; Shelest, 1991; Egorychev, 1989; Bovin, 1991). These accounts emphasise that, in his first years in office, Brezhnev was inclined to listen to colleagues, to consult specialists and to work towards collective decisions. His mastery of policy issues was developing and – unlike his predecessor – he did not seem to have opinions on every conceivable subject which he insisted on imposing on those around him. The early Brezhnev, at least, knew what he did not know. By contrast, the 'late' Brezhnev was unwilling to brook opposition or accept criticism. He was ill informed about policy, highly susceptible to flattery and so insecure about himself that he blocked the careers of talented men while promoting toadies and mediocrities who would depend on him.

Some, including his physician Yevgenii Chazov (1992: 86–7; see also Griko, 1997: 16) are inclined to link this change to Brezhnev's deteriorating health. From about 1974, the General Secretary was in decline physically: he was, according to Chazov, dependent on tranquilisers, and he suffered a stroke following his summit with US President Gerald Ford in November 1974. A second stroke, in January 1976, reportedly left him clinically dead for a time. While his health fluctuated thereafter, the long-term trend was steadily downhill. According to Chazov (1992: 119–22, 132–3), Brezhnev's senior colleagues, including Andropov and Suslov, took great pains to ensure that information about Brezhnev's health remained restricted to a very small circle within the top leadership. Health, however, was not the only issue: many former colleagues follow Shelest in seeing the emergence of the 'late' or 'bad' Brezhnev as early as 1967–68, when he began to eclipse Kosygin and, in Shelest's words, 'to free himself' from his critics (Shelest, 1991: 217). On this view, it was not Brezhnev's health but his consolidation of power that allowed his faults to assert themselves fully. As long as he was constrained to some extent by the presence of alternative centres of power in the leadership, his weaknesses were less damaging.

How seriously should one take the 'two Brezhnevs' narratives? Clearly, there is much truth in them. Brezhnev was in power for 18 years, during the last nine of which he was suffering serious health problems. It would be astonishing if his physical deterioration did not affect his performance, and there is considerable evidence that during the last few years of his life his policy-making role was often quite marginal (see, for example, *chap.* 5 on the decision to invade Afghanistan). Nor is it difficult to imagine how, questions of health apart, Brezhnev's consolidation of power would have given him greater freedom to disregard colleagues' views, to promote favourites or to act arbitrarily. Former colleagues of Khrushchev, after all, often described him in similar terms, emphasising the increasingly arbitrary and autocratic nature of his behaviour after about 1958.

The simple periodisation of the two-Brezhnevs explanation is, however, problematic: Breslauer (1982) argues persuasively that Brezhnev was indeed ascendant during 1968–72, but that his authority was then challenged in the run-up to the Twenty-fifth Party Congress in 1976. Brezhnev, in Breslauer's account, successfully recouped his authority from about 1976. This period-isation is not wholly persuasive, but more recent first-hand accounts have confirmed that there was growing tension in the top leadership, most notably between Brezhnev and Kosygin, around the time of the Twenty-fifth Congress (Shelest, 1991; Baibakov, 1991). According to Shelest, Brezhnev was only narrowly deflected from sacking Kosygin and taking on the premiership; only after this ambition had been frustrated did he set his sights on Podgornyi's post as head of state, which Brezhnev assumed (for the second time) in June 1977 [*Doc. 2*].

Nor should one take claims about the faults of the 'late' Brezhnev at face value. Figures of more or less independent standing remained in the top leadership to the end of the Brezhnev era and beyond. Though hardly rivals or enemies of Brezhnev, men like Andropov, Gromyko, Suslov, Kosygin and Ustinov were scarcely his creatures. By the end of the Brezhnev era, Hodnett (1981: 94–5) could identify only three 'fully fledged clients' and one 'semi-client' of Brezhnev among the thirteen members of the Politburo (though Brezhnev was, to be sure, stronger in the Secretariat). Thatcher (2002) argues that the determination of Brezhnev's colleagues to protect him in his declining years was an indication that they still regarded him as having an important role to play. This does not mean that he remained effective: it could just as easily have reflected their desire to postpone the coming succession, which was fraught with uncertainty and which some of them had good reason to fear. For men like Ustinov, Andropov and Gromyko, moreover, an ailing and inactive Brezhnev left them with greater autonomy in their own domains (Brown, 1996: 54). Nevertheless, the few glimpses we have of Brezhnev in action during his latter years suggest that he was not wholly cut off from what was happening in the country; his speeches and other public pronouncements betray growing frustration with the performance of senior officials (see, e.g., Kelley, 1987: 15–16) and, after the Polish troubles began, a mounting sense of concern about the possible public reaction to the leadership's failure to deliver higher living standards (Breslauer, 1982: 239).

THE SOVIET ELITE IN THE BREZHNEV ERA

Brezhnev had become party leader largely because of the party elite's hostility towards Khrushchev's frequent reorganisations and even more frequent redeployment of subordinates. On replacing his former patron as party chief, Brezhnev promised that he would 'stick up for cadres'. He kept his word. 'Trust in cadres' and 'stability of cadres' became key themes of his leadership. Personnel turnover in top party and state bodies declined dramatically, with the result that the country's political elite aged steadily. This both reduced the scope for introducing new people – and hence new ideas – into the leadership and created greater opportunities for corruption than had previously existed, particularly in outlying republics with long-serving leaders.

The first indications that Brezhnev and his colleagues were serious about protecting the interests of senior party officials came almost immediately after the October Plenum. In November 1964, Khrushchev's hated bifurcation of the party's territorial apparatus was reversed, thereby restoring the authority of local party bosses over their fiefs and allaying fears that the Twenty-third Congress of the CPSU, due in 1966, would bring a major purge of the Central Committee. Also quickly scrapped were the rules imposing term limits on party officials and establishing mandatory minimum rates of turnover in party bodies. Opposition to the 'systematic renewal of cadres' appears to have loomed large in the reasons for Khrushchev's removal (Tompson, 1991: 1110–11) and the new leaders were quick to address this concern. Khrushchev had intended the term-limit and mandatory-turnover rules to help eradicate the formation within party organisations of 'family groups' involving 'elements of nepotism and of mutual concealment of shortcomings and mistakes' (*XXII S"ezd*, 1962, vol 1: 252–4). Khrushchev's aim was not to increase turnover but to preserve it. The danger he foresaw was that a gradual freezing of personnel policy would occur, blocking up the system and leading to stagnation. Khrushchev's fear was well founded: under Brezhnev, turnover levels fell far below the levels stipulated by Khrushchev, a development which contributed greatly to the sense of a stagnating political system (Tompson, 1991: 261–2).

In an exhaustive analysis of the CPSU elite from 1917 to 1991, White and Mawdsley (2000: 138, 170–2) show the consequences of this shift for the composition of the party elite. During the Khrushchev era, the composition of the Central Committee changed substantially each time a new Committee was elected by a party Congress: only 56% of the CC members elected at Stalin's last Congress in 1952 were re-elected just four years later, and only 50% of the 1956 committee was retained after the Twenty-second Congress in 1961. Death, of course, accounted for some of the turnover between Congresses, but close to half the surviving members of the CC lost their seats at each successive Congress. Under Brezhnev, by contrast, retention rates rose above 70%. Only 17% of the members of the 1961 Committee still living in 1966 were replaced – and most of those were close associates of Khrushchev. Retention rates in the Central Committees elected by the Twenty-fourth (1971), Twenty-fifth (1976) and Twenty-sixth (1981) Party Congresses were 73, 80 and 78% respectively. As the elite aged, moreover, death accounted for an increasing share of what turnover there was: the retention rates for *surviving* CC members reached 81% in 1971 and 89% in 1976. The CC was not the only institution to experience a remarkable degree of stability. The Politburo, too, was subject to extremely low rates of turnover: even men like Shelepin and Podgornyi remained long after Brezhnev had effectively sidelined them. Until the removal of Podgornyi in 1977, the four central figures in the leadership that emerged in October 1964 all remained in the Politburo: Brezhnev, Kosygin, Suslov and Podgornyi.

Stability of cadres had a number of effects. The first and most obvious was the ageing of the political elite. Brezhnev, Kosygin and many other members of the leadership had first risen to high office as relatively young men, winning rapid advancement as a result of the Great Terror of 1936–38.

By the early post-war period, they occupied party and government offices at the highest levels, and they showed no inclination to do anything but grow old in power. Thus, the so-called 'Class of '37' dominated Soviet politics until the early 1980s. Nor was this simply a case of incumbents growing older in office: from the early 1970s, it was quite common for *new* appointees in high positions to be as old as, or even older than, their predecessors; they were rarely much younger (Colton, 1986: 27; Brown, 1996: 332, n. 36). Perhaps the most striking example of this was the appointment of the 75-year-old Brezhnev crony Nikolai Tikhonov to replace the 76-year-old Kosygin in 1980. Even the expansion of the CC and of the party and state apparatuses did not do much to bring younger people into leadership positions. By the late 1970s, there was not a single Central Committee member under the age of 40 and the average age of new members was rising from Congress to Congress. According to White and Mawdsley, the average age of the CC elected at Brezhnev's last Congress in 1981 was 62. The Politburo was older still: the average age of the Politburo's full members after the Twenty-third Congress in 1966 was 58. This figure rose to 61 in 1971, to 66 in 1976 and to 70 in 1981 – despite the fact that the average for the 1981 Politburo was lowered by the inclusion for the first time of the 50-year-old Mikhail Gorbachev, then more than a decade younger than any other member of that body.

Similar patterns were observed for other elite groups. The average age of Central Committee secretaries and department heads and deputy prime ministers all rose by roughly a decade between 1966 and 1978, while the average ages of Politburo candidate members, government ministers and chairmen of state committees all increased by about 5–6 years over the same period (Hough & Fainsod, 1979: 272). This process took its toll on the effectiveness of leadership bodies: by the late Brezhnev era, Politburo meetings, which had run from three to six hours in the 1960s, were often as brief as 30–40 minutes (Gorbachev, 1995, vol. 1: 217; Afanas'ev, 1994: 38). Shortly after Brezhnev's death, the Politburo boldly, if belatedly, faced up to the age issue and resolved it – by setting limits on the hours and days its members should work (McCauley, 1998: 373). Nor did this ageing of the top leadership go unnoticed by ordinary Soviet citizens. When Konstantin Chernenko readmitted Stalin's old henchman, the 94-year-old Vyacheslav Molotov, to the party, more than a quarter-century after his expulsion by Khrushchev, sharp-tongued Muscovites suggested that Chernenko must be grooming a successor.

The ageing of the leadership could not but reduce the scope for introducing new blood – and new ideas. Over half of the 1981 Central Committee, for example, had reached adulthood by 1937. They were thus 'second-generation Stalinists' (Fitzpatrick, 1979). Their formative political experiences were the upheavals of the 1930s, which had forged the Soviet system and which had offered many of them stunning opportunities for upward social mobility, and the Second World War, which seemed to vindicate Stalin's policies of the previous decade and thus to demonstrate the essential soundness of the system. This in itself would have tended to introduce a conservative bias into their outlook. They were, moreover, men who had come out of the villages and factories of the 1920s and 1930s, rising to high office after crash courses in various technical subjects that were intended to prepare them to administer the emerging new order, an order in which they had a vested interest in believing. As a result, the country's leaders seemed at times to be stuck in a time warp. Presiding over an increasingly complex and rapidly changing society, much of the top elite was reluctant to acknowledge, and ill-equipped to comprehend, the emerging problems of the late twentieth century. The country's ruling elite was an anachronism, something a growing number of its subjects were coming to recognise.

'Stability of cadres' also created greater opportunities for corruption than had previously existed, particularly in outlying republics with long-serving leaders. The Transcaucasian republics saw mafia-like criminal structures take root, often with very close links to party bosses. In some areas, public office was bought and sold. But the most spectacular case of such localism was the Central Asian 'cotton affair' exposed in the late 1980s. During 1976–85, cotton production was overstated by around 385,000 tonnes per annum, facilitating the embezzlement of millions of roubles in state funds in a scheme that involved farm managers, republican leaders and leading officials of the USSR Ministry of Internal Affairs (Gleason, 1990: 107–9). The scale of the fraud, moreover, appears to have increased over time, suggesting that the participants grew bolder as it became clear that their activities would go unpunished. The cotton scam was unique only in its scale. Similar processes unfolded across the country as local elites entrenched themselves, quietly usurped the prerogatives of the all-union centre and administered their fiefs as they saw fit, enriching themselves and their families in the process.

CHAPTER THREE

POLICY-MAKING IN THE BREZHNEV ERA

Khrushchev's successors did not mention him by name after his removal, but the denunciations of 'voluntarism', 'subjectivism' and 'hare-brained' scheming clearly communicated the elite's rejection of his impulsive and often autocratic style of policy-making. The new leaders thus emphasised their 'scientific' and 'objective' approach to policy-making, as well as their commitment to the norms of collective leadership, which would prevent the inclinations and *idées fixes* of a single individual from distorting party policy. One important early signal of this shift was their speedy disavowal of the charlatan agronomist Trofim Lysenko, whose influence on Khrushchev had severely retarded the development of the biological sciences in the USSR. Lysenko's total rejection of Mendelian theory meant that genetics as a science was not only not acknowledged, it was explicitly rejected. Repairing the damage done by Lysenkoism took years; as late as 1966, approved Soviet textbooks still contained references to 'the so-called gene' (Medvedev, 1969; Joravsky, 1965 and 1970).

In rejecting Lysenkoism, the new leaders thereby indicated a greater willingness to give scientists scope to pursue their research free of political interference, as well as a readiness to consult with specialists, be they scholars, officials or managers, and to proceed with more careful, evidence-based policy-making. The breadth of the coalition that removed Khrushchev, which encompassed reformers, centrists and neo-Stalinists and included all the major institutional interests of the Soviet party–state, also necessitated a consensus-oriented, bargained approach to policy. Leonid Brezhnev was in many ways well suited to operate in just such an environment.

BREZHNEV AS POLICY-MAKER: FROM CONSENSUS TO STAGNATION?

Soon after coming to office, Brezhnev is said to have remarked that 'under Stalin people were afraid of repression, under Khrushchev of reorganisations and rearrangements... Soviet people should receive a peaceful life, so they can work normally' (Dokuchaev, 1995: 172, cited in Thatcher, 2002). This virtually amounts to a crystallisation of Brezhnev's approach to governing. He was chosen, above all, because it was believed that he would spare the elite and the country the sort of upheavals and abrupt changes of direction that had characterised not only the Khrushchev decade but the preceding half-century as well. By the late 1980s, it was relatively easy to attach the 'stagnation' label to this clear commitment to stability, but such an emphasis had much to recommend it in 1964. Over the preceding 60 years, the country had undergone three revolutions, two world wars, a civil war, the upheavals associated with collectivisation and forced industrialisation, the Great Terror, the post-war 'Lesser Terror' (Parrish, 1996), no fewer than four major famines, and the political roller-coaster ride that was the Khrushchev era. Arguably, the USSR needed a period of relative tranquility. Even the official formulation used to describe the Soviet Union in the Brezhnev era, 'developed socialism', avoided any hint of revolutionary transformation or utopianism [*Doc. 3*]. In Alex Pravda's (1982) words, the emphasis had shifted 'from getting there to being here'.

Brezhnev thus sought to provide a period of settled, orderly governance. The implicit bargain of the October plenum was, as Breslauer (1982) has argued, that the leadership would grant senior officials greater security of tenure and a stable working environment, in return for which they would respond by performing more effectively. For a time, at least, this formula appeared to work: the modestly improved economic performance of the late 1960s probably owed more to the end of Khrushchev's endless and disruptive reorganisations than to the limited economic reforms adopted in 1965. Over the years, however, the search for consensus, for incremental solutions and for stability at any price became a caricature of itself.

Nevertheless, there was more to Brezhnev's platform than stability for its own sake. As he tightened his grip on power, his distinctive approach to policy began to take shape. It would be a mistake to see him, as did some observers, as a mere 'broker' among competing elite interests. In the years before his health failed him, at least, Brezhnev proved to be both a shrewd political operator and a man with a clear, if cautious, understanding of the policies he wished to pursue (Breslauer, 1982; Thompson, 1989). In domestic politics, Brezhnev sought to preserve and strengthen the central party control over the economic and political systems. In Rigby's (1979: 206) view, his approach to domestic governance is best described as a reform of Stalinism rather than a return to it. While committed to the basic institutional architecture bequeathed by Stalin to his successors and proud of the system's achievements under Stalin, Brezhnev resisted pressure for a full-scale rehabilitation of Stalin or a return to the intense police controls applied to Soviet society in the latter years of Stalin's rule. Brezhnev brought Khrushchev's de-Stalinisation campaign to an abrupt halt, but the rehabilitation of Stalin's reputation was largely confined to his role in the Soviet victory over Nazi Germany. Otherwise, Brezhnev preferred simply to pass over the Stalin question in silence. In foreign affairs, Brezhnev's overriding aims were to ensure the primacy of the USSR in the world communist movement, to establish strategic parity with the United States and, on the basis of this, to secure western acceptance of the post-war order in Europe while extending Soviet power in the developing world.

Taken as a whole, this represented a middle-of-the-road formula in Soviet political terms, one which enabled Brezhnev to reconcile the competing ideological tendencies and institutional interests that had come together to overthrow Khrushchev. Over time, however, the differences between Brezhnev and Kosygin, in particular, became harder to conceal. Brezhnev's international ambitions meant that he was consistently less inclined than Kosygin or Podgornyi to resist the demands of the defence industrial complex in favour of Soviet consumers, while his commitment to party activism in the economic sphere brought him into conflict with Kosygin, particularly over the existence of Central Committee departments responsible for specific industrial sectors (Baibakov, 1991: 247). Kosygin and his supporters viewed these departments as a source of unnecessary and often disruptive interference by party officials in matters best left to the better qualified administrators in the ministries and the enterprise managers themselves. One former official of the State Planning Committee (Gosplan) has written that Kosygin valued Gosplan's skill at finding ways to deflect the latest unwelcome initiatives from the party officials in the CC departments (Zoteev, 1998b: 88). On the face of it, Kosygin and the state administrators seemed to have a good case against the CC over the issue of party interference, but subsequent events suggest that the situation was rather more complicated. The eventual abolition of the branch departments in 1988 proved enormously disruptive. The party organs involved in economic management did, for all their manifest faults, perform significant co-ordinating functions.

THE ROLE OF THE POLITBURO AND SECRETARIAT

As many western observers have noted, the post-Stalinist Soviet state encompassed both autocratic and oligarchic elements, which were permanently in tension with one another. Khrushchev's removal reflected the reassertion of the oligarchic elements (Hodnett, 1981). Over time, moreover, the oligarchic elements seemed to be growing stronger, as the regime's institutions stabilised and certain expectations and practices became sufficiently ingrained to impose constraints on the leader. As Brown (1980) observed, each successive CPSU General Secretary grew more powerful over time, as he consolidated his position, but each of Stalin's successors ended up less powerful than his predecessor.

Traditionally, the Politburo of the CPSU Central Committee was viewed as the supreme decision-making body in the post-Stalin Soviet Union, at least until the reforms of Mikhail Gorbachev marginalised it. However, recent accounts of decision-making under Brezhnev suggest that, while the most important decision-makers were in the Politburo, the full Politburo was rarely the forum for the making of key policy decisions; its meetings grew shorter over time, and fewer votes were taken. According to former Chernenko aide Vadim Pechenev, most key decisions were taken by an inner core of the Politburo, consisting of Brezhnev, Suslov, Gromyko, Ustinov, Andropov and, latterly, Chernenko, with Brezhnev by the late 1970s being the least active of the six (Pechenev, 1991, cited in Brown, 1996: 56). In general, serious issues were resolved before reaching the full Politburo, and *ad hoc* commissions headed by Politburo members handled different aspects of policy. Military policy was largely the preserve of the Defence Council, which Brezhnev chaired, and which appears to have enabled him to control to some degree the flow of sensitive military-security information to the rest of the Politburo (Hodnett, 1981: 93). Thus, a number of accounts claim that Brezhnev, Foreign Minister Andrei Gromyko, KGB chief Yuri Andropov and Defence Minister Dmitrii Ustinov took the final decision to invade Afghanistan, which their Politburo colleagues effectively rubber-stamped a few days later (Arbatov, 1993: 192; Shevardnadze, 1991: 26; Shubin, 1997). Politburo members based outside Moscow were least likely to have much input into policy-making at all-union level. Shevardnadze (1991: 26) even claims that, as a candidate member of the Politburo working in Tbilisi, he learned of the Soviet intervention in Afghanistan from the mass media. This marginalisation of members outside Moscow may explain why the complaints of Shelest (1991) and Mazurov (1989) about Brezhnev's sidelining of the Politburo are not echoed by men like Gromyko and Gorbachev, who were part of the central apparatus and thus more likely to be involved in pre-Politburo stages of decision-making.

From a very early stage, Brezhnev's position was stronger in the Secretariat of the CPSU Central Committee than in the Politburo. By the late 1960s he had installed reliable clients in critical positions in the CC apparatus and the Secretariat in particular – most notably those positions linked to cadres policy and the flow of information to members of the top leadership. Chernenko's position as head of the 'General Department' of the Central Committee was particularly important with respect to the latter. According to Mazurov (1989), a Politburo member for much of the Brezhnev era, the General Secretary increasingly used the Secretariat to prejudge decisions that were to come before the Politburo. Senior secretaries like Brezhnev, Suslov, Kirilenko, Kulakov and Ustinov were members of both bodies. If they could reach agreement among themselves ahead of a Politburo meeting – and the Secretariat generally discussed things before they reached the Politburo – then it could be relatively easy to present the rest of the Politburo with a *fait accompli*. This was all the more difficult to resist because so much of the information circulated to Politburo members originated in the CC apparatus, which was subordinate to the Secretariat.

TAKING ADVICE: INFORMATION, INSTITUTIONS AND EXPERTISE

Yet while much of the Politburo was thus excluded from the making of key decisions, it was not the case that the entire decision-making process rested in the hands of this small sub-group. On the contrary, the Brezhnev era witnessed a widening of the channels through which individuals, groups and institutions could influence the policy process. These remained, it must be said, quite narrowly circumscribed, and references to 'pluralism' grossly exaggerated the degree of openness of the policy process (Brown, 1983). Nevertheless, recent accounts by insiders confirm that policy-making was, as many western scholars argued at the time, characterised by competition and bargaining among various elite constituencies. Many of these conflicts took place between sectors that outsiders tended to see as allies, such as the persistent disagreements between the military and the defence industries over weapons procurement policies (Belanovsky, 1998). For all the references to the 'military-industrial complex', the military and the defence industrial complex were distinct institutions, whose interests often came into conflict.

There were several reasons for this change in the pattern of policy-making. The most important was the regime's repudiation of Khrushchev's 'subjectivism' and 'voluntarism', which implied a commitment to a more rational, pragmatic approach to policy-making. Khrushchev had sought constantly for panaceas that would enable him to solve a number of related problems quickly and cheaply, launching a succession of hasty and often ill-considered reorganisations and crash investment campaigns – usually with unrealistically ambitious targets. Impatient for results, he had tended to change direction rapidly when his pet schemes did not produce the desired results, amending or scrapping major initiatives and abruptly launching still newer ones. His successors turned their backs on this approach, preferring to break large problems up into smaller, more manageable ones, which they attempted to tackle via incremental measures devised and implemented in consultation with established experts in the relevant fields and with those institutions directly involved in policy implementation.

This problem-solving approach encouraged greater discussion and, on many issues, the scope for participation in policy-making by academic specialists and other experts broadened considerably. In general, the greater the technical complexity of the issues at stake, the greater was the role accorded to experts and established academic authorities in the relevant fields (Brown, 1974: 74ff). Much of this expertise was also brought 'in house', as a growing number of specialists were appointed to advise Central Committee departments and government bodies from within. The new leaders' dislike of grand theorising and the Khrushchevite search for cure-alls meant that individuals offering discrete solutions to specific problems stood a greater chance than ever of getting a hearing – provided, at any rate, that their proposals did not challenge the established order and that they were couched in the appropriate language. This latter requirement meant not only that they should be presented in an upbeat, optimistic tone, without too much comment on past mistakes, but also that novel concepts be cloaked in accepted Marxist-Leninist jargon, which often clouded meaning and made it difficult for outsiders to grasp the real import of what was being proposed. The Brezhnev years thus witnessed public debates over a wide range of policy issues, including reform of planning and economic management, the regime's investment strategy, energy policy, the promotion of technical innovation, legal development, federalism, private-plot agriculture, the role of trades unions, alcohol abuse and pollution. On some issues, the evidence strongly suggested that expert input from outside the leading echelons of the party–state did influence the direction of policy. Barry and Berman (1971) observed the influence of Soviet jurists over legal reforms, although the lawyers lost battles as well as won them, while Juviler (1967) traced the impact of family lawyers, in particular, on the revision of Soviet legislation concerning marriage and the family in 1968.

In a survey of a number of case studies of Soviet policy-making, Brown (1974: 85–9) observes that, even under Brezhnev, the role of the General Secretary was far more extensive than that of the chief executive in most other political systems. However, Brezhnev was far less inclined than his predecessor to meddle in the detail of policy, especially in matters of real technical complexity. Brown observes in addition that the greater emphasis on 'collective leadership' that followed Khrushchev also helped, as it reduced the likelihood that a single ambitious but wrong-headed scientist or adviser could gain the leader's confidence and secure the adoption of the kind of destructive policies pursued during Lysenko's ascendance. Even at the peak of his power, Brezhnev never became as autocratic as his predecessors had been. This meant that he was less inclined – and less able – to impose his own brand of irrationality on colleagues. It also meant that those seeking to influence policy need not gain his ear: access to Kosygin or other members of the leadership might be sufficient. However, the reduction in the leader's role in policy-making also reduced the scope for policy innovation on any scale at all. The conservative, incrementalist biases of the system were no longer countered by the ambitions of a strong leader. One reason Brezhnev enjoyed a relatively quiet political life on the domestic front was that, unlike his predecessors, he made little attempt to overcome the inertia of the party–state, choosing instead to accept it and to define his own policy agenda largely in terms of the interests of its major institutions and constituencies.

.   While there is little doubt that the policy process under Brezhnev and Kosygin was more rational and less exposed to the whims and *idées fixes* of the leader than it had been, there was still considerable scope for arbitrariness and irrationality. However, it was, more often than not, the forms of irrationality characteristic of the system itself, rather than the personal quirks of Brezhnev and Kosygin, that shaped policy. These included the emphasis on fulfilling output targets with little or no regard for cost or alternatives and the Soviet elite's boundless faith in economies of scale. Environmental externalities were downplayed or ignored, while technical problems were resolved with little or no regard for their broader socio-economic implications (Graham, 1993). Thus, even the 'rationalised' policy process of the Brezhnev era, with its higher levels of expert input, continued to generate the kind of massive industrial 'white elephants' that are perhaps the Soviet system's most lasting physical legacy. Two, in particular, stand out: the Baikal–Amur Mainline (BAM) railway, running 3,200km from Novokuznetsk to the Pacific, and the Chernobyl Atomic Energy Station (AES).

Conceived in the same tradition as the great construction undertakings of the Stalin era, the BAM was heralded as 'the project of the century' when construction began in 1974. Its threefold purpose was to facilitate the export of raw materials to Asia, to shift the main Soviet Asian railway line away from the Chinese frontier and to provide the basis for the creation of a 'mighty industrial belt' along the BAM's route through Siberia. The history of its construction was a litany of delays, cost overruns, corner-cutting and environmental damage. Many sections of the railway had to be replaced before it was open. The BAM's completion, scheduled for 1983, was announced in 1984, but the line was unfit for the freight traffic for which it was intended until 1989. The now infamous Chernobyl Atomic Energy Station was less exceptional and more typical of major industrialisation projects. Its design reflected, *inter alia*, the authorities' faith in the benefits of scale, which led to the construction of stations with up to half a dozen reactors in one location, as well as their conviction that standardisation made for efficiency. The Atomic Power Ministry's manuals for the assembly-line-style manufacture of nuclear power stations set out detailed instructions governing every aspect of construction that took no account of local conditions such as the groundwater levels, soil and rock formation and the presence of seismic activity (Graham, 1993: 81–93).

POLICY-MAKING IN PRACTICE: THE CASE OF ARMS CONTROL

The case of arms control policy is particularly enlightening with respect to the relationship between the top leaders and the wider elite in policy-making, thanks to the publication of a joint work on the subject by two former Soviet officials who participated in arms-control policy-making at a very high level (Savel'ev & Detinov, 1995). Aleksandr Savel'ev served as deputy director of the Central Committee's Department for the Defence Industry, and Lieutenant-General Nikolai Detinov was involved in arms control in a number of posts at the Ministry of Defence, serving later with the Soviet delegation to the talks on Intermediate Nuclear Forces. Together, Savel'ev & Detinov have provided an extraordinary glimpse inside Soviet policy-making processes at the highest levels and in a highly sensitive sphere. It is therefore an account worth considering at some length.

According to Savel'ev & Detinov, a Politburo Commission was formed at the end of the 1960s to oversee the Strategic Arms Limitation Talks (SALT). It included Gromyko, Andropov, Ustinov (then the CC Secretary responsible for the defence industry) and Ustinov's predecessor as Defence Minister, Andrei Grechko. They were joined by Leonid Smirnov, the deputy head of the Military-Industrial Commission (VPK), and, initially, by Mstislav Keldysh, the President of the USSR Academy of Sciences. Keldysh was soon dropped. In the early stages of the talks, when relatively little technical expertise was required, the so-called 'Big Five' met rarely and took little external advice. The instructions they gave to Soviet negotiating teams seldom changed. Despite the political capital he personally had staked on détente in general and arms control in particular, Brezhnev's role was largely passive: he accepted expert advice and the conclusions of the Big Five. As Brezhnev's health failed, Gromyko increasingly took the lead. Grechko's influence was limited by his opposition to the entire SALT process, which sometimes led him to adopt obstructionist positions that left him isolated among the Big Five. However, Grechko's misgivings notwithstanding, the Big Five generally sought consensus and unanimity was the rule for most decisions.

When outside expertise was required, the Big Five tended to consult officials and experts on an *ad hoc* basis. These were usually selected by Ustinov, as head of the VPK. Ustinov's role here was critical, since he was broadly in favour of SALT, unlike Grechko, who regarded it as an imperialist ploy to lock the Soviet Union into a strategic disadvantage. As the talks grew increasingly technical, this reliance on experts increased and was at last institutionalised with the formation in November 1974 of the 'Little Five' – a working group consisting of officials from the departments represented by the Big Five: the VPK, the KGB, the foreign and defence ministries and the Department for the Defence Industry of the CPSU Central

Committee. (Savel'ev & Detinov were among the Little Five.) The available expertise on which the Little Five could draw was, initially at least, very limited. When the SALT talks began, Soviet specialists had actually done remarkably little research into notions of deterrence, strategic stability or the relationship between offensive and defensive weapons, which were central to much Western thinking about arms control.

This was not an unusual problem. While the physical sciences were highly developed and policy-makers could turn for advice to some of the world's leading mathematicians and physicists for input, there was far less expertise available in many other policy-relevant fields. Lysenkoism had retarded the development of many branches of biology and related fields, while the social sciences were struggling to establish themselves as something more than an arm of the ideological apparatus. In this, Soviet social sciences made considerable progress during the Brezhnev era, particularly empirical sociology. However, this progress was uneven and heavy-handed official intervention remained a fact of life (*chap.* 9).

Thus, while decision-making was – not surprisingly – highly centralised, especially in such a sensitive field as arms control, the process was designed to facilitate a certain amount of expert advice and input. Nevertheless, the authors themselves conclude that the Big Five/Little Five system was more of a bargaining forum for powerful institutional interests rather than a mechanism for reaching strategic decisions. Its aim was 'not so much to meet the American position head-on as to find a balance among various national interests, which were concerned and were represented by all their representative agencies' (Savel'ev & Detinov, 1995: 52). This sometimes made for self-defeating decisions, such as the construction of an anti-ballistic missile radar at Krasnoyarsk that constituted a violation of the ABM Treaty (Savel'ev & Detinov, 1995: 97–100). The siting of the radar in violation of the treaty was the product not of a military-strategic decision but of a process of haggling among the departments involved over construction costs and logistical difficulties.

CHAPTER FOUR

FOREIGN POLICY FROM CUBA
TO HELSINKI

In most respects, Khrushchev's successors shared his foreign policy aims: rapprochement with China on terms acceptable to the Kremlin; acknowledgement by the United States of the USSR's status as an equal superpower; ratification of the post-war *status quo* in Europe; a reduction in East–West tensions; and the extension of Soviet influence in the developing world. Underlying it all was the determination to establish the Soviet Union as a truly global power. Where the new leaders differed from Khrushchev was in their readiness to pursue these aims patiently and without running too many risks. He had often run very high risks in an attempt to achieve his aims quickly and cheaply, relying on bluff, bluster and deception; Berlin and Cuba were the classic examples of this approach. The new leaders, by contrast, were prepared to take their time and yet also to pay a higher price than he to achieve their ends. Khrushchev's heirs were thus more cautious but they were no less ambitious.

THE DEFENCE BUILD-UP OF THE 1960s

For Khrushchev's successors, the key lesson of the Berlin and Cuba crises was that the USSR must not allow itself to be drawn into a direct confrontation with the United States in which it would have to operate from a position of strategic inferiority. They therefore undertook a major military build-up, aiming for more than the minimum deterrence sought by Khrushchev (Kennedy-Pipe, 1998: 125; Tompson, 1995: 253). Much of the research and development underlying this build-up had, in fact, been done in the Khrushchev era, and many of the key production decisions had been taken in the last two years of Khrushchev's rule, in the wake of the Cuban crisis. But it was in 1965 that the mass deployment of SS-9 and SS-11 heavy Intercontinental Ballistic Missiles (ICBMs) began. By the end of the decade, the USSR had achieved substantial equivalence in long-range nuclear forces. Nor were conventional forces neglected. The modernisation of Soviet and Warsaw Pact militaries accelerated. In pursuit of its global role, the Brezhnev leadership gave particular attention to the navy, which for the first time established a permanent presence in both the Indian Ocean and the Mediterranean. In 1970, the Soviet navy conducted the *Okean* manoeuvres, involving every ocean in the world. Globally, the Soviet Union was still the challenger and the United States the leading power. The United States still retained an edge in several categories of strategic weapons, and Soviet conventional power-projection capabilities remained inferior to those of the United States in every area except sealift capability (Menon, 1982: 270–1). Nevertheless, the shift in the military balance was palpable and affected the outlooks of both sides. By 1969 Washington had accepted the changed military balance: at his first press conference as president, Richard Nixon spoke of 'strategic sufficiency', thereby effectively renouncing any claim to strategic superiority and acknowledging the rough parity achieved by the USSR. The following year, Brezhnev felt able to declare that 'No question of any importance in the world can be solved without our participation, without taking our economic and military might into account' (Kohler *et alii*, 1977: 228).

The changed military balance established the basis for the two most important developments of the 1970s: superpower détente and the extension of Soviet influence in the developing world. The achievement of a rough overall military equivalence enabled Brezhnev and his colleagues to seek a new understanding with Washington from a position of equality rather than weakness. Until 1968–69, the Brezhnev leadership had been wary of arms control talks in particular, fearing that the Americans would try to use any negotiations to freeze the USSR into a position of inferiority; by 1969, this was no longer a danger. Yet even as military parity gave the Kremlin the confidence to seek a better relationship with the United States, it also enabled Soviet leaders to pursue an agenda in the Third World that the United States would see as fundamentally incompatible with détente.

MANAGING THE BLOC

Whatever its global ambitions, the Brezhnev leadership's top priority in foreign affairs was Eastern Europe. Indeed, one of its main aims in dealings with the West was to secure western recognition of existing borders in Europe and of Soviet hegemony in East-Central Europe. Soviet dominance in the region rested largely but by no means exclusively on military power. It also depended on economics and, in particular, on the use of implicit price subsidies in Soviet energy exports to East European states to secure their compliance in other areas. As Reissinger (1992) has argued, economic relations between Moscow and its clients were characterised by bargaining and compromise; the bargaining was asymmetrical, to be sure, but the USSR made concessions as well as demanding them (Marrese & Vanous, 1983).

The Soviet position within the bloc also depended on the loyalty and reliability of key members of East European elites. This was difficult to ensure in the case of local Communist leaders like Mao and Tito, who had come to power independently of the USSR. Events in Hungary in 1956 had illustrated a second danger: a conflict in the local Communist leadership in which less than reliable (from Moscow's perspective) forces gained the upper hand. A third source of trouble stemmed from leaders installed with Soviet assistance who then secured their positions at home to such an extent that they felt able to assert greater independence from Moscow (Kennedy-Pipe, 1998).

For the Brezhnev leadership, Romania increasingly came to represent a case of the third type. After securing Khrushchev's agreement to the withdrawal of Soviet troops from his country in 1958, Romanian leader Gheorghe Gheorghiu-Dej came to act with increasing independence, a trend that grew more pronounced from the early 1960s. Romania adopted a neutral stance in the Sino-Soviet dispute. It rejected Soviet proposals for greater economic integration within the bloc, as these would have impeded Romania's industrial development. Romanian leaders also adopted a steadily more strident nationalist stance, even speaking publicly of Romania's 'lost provinces', a reference to territories taken from Romania by the Soviet Union in 1940. Gheorghiu-Dej's successor, Nicolae Ceaucescu, attacked the concept of military blocs and moved to develop ties to the West rather faster than Moscow would have liked. Domestically, however, he maintained a tight Stalinist regime, and Romania's small population and strategically peripheral location meant that such deviations from the Soviet line were tolerated.

In 1968, Czechoslovakia presented the Kremlin with a far more serious challenge – a crisis of the second type, involving conflict among local Communists in which 'unreliable' elements seemed to be prevailing. There were few, if any, regrets in Moscow when Czechoslovak leader Antonin Novotny was forced to resign first the presidency of the country and then the leadership of the Communist Party of Czechoslovakia (CPCS). The conservative Novotny had mismanaged the country and impeded an economic reform process that the USSR itself favoured. It soon became clear, however, that Novotny's removal had not resolved the split in the Czechoslovak leadership between reformers and conservatives and that the former were gaining the upper hand. By March 1968, the Soviet Union was expressing its concerns to Czechoslovak leaders, pressing Novotny's Slovak successor, Alexander Dubček, to bring the situation under control. This he failed to do. On the contrary, the reformers, with public opinion on their side, took matters further. Press censorship was discontinued from March, and unauthorised political activity was permitted. Moscow began to fear that the CPCS's monopoly of power was being surrendered. No less worrying for Moscow was talk of a trade deal with West Germany and the extension of a West German loan to finance economic reform. The reformers' drive to build 'socialism with a human face' appeared to threaten both Communist power in Czechoslovakia and Czechoslovakia's place in the Soviet bloc (Williams, 1996 and 1997).

The pressure on the Czechoslovak leaders to halt the liberalisation process was intense. Brezhnev met Dubček six times during January–August, twice at meetings of Warsaw Pact leaders, and spoke to him frequently by telephone. Although there were no longer Soviet forces stationed permanently in Czechoslovakia, Warsaw Pact units conducted military exercises in the country in the late spring in an effort to intimidate the CPCS reformers. After the exercises ended, many of these forces remained deployed on the country's borders, a clear if tacit threat to Prague. This threat was reinforced by the demands made in the so-called 'Warsaw Letter' of 15 July, directed by the Warsaw Pact leaders at the Dubček leadership following a summit which the latter had refused to attend. The letter reminded the Czechoslovak leaders that the fate of socialism in their country was a matter of concern to all their 'fraternal' allies and demanded a crackdown on political activity outside the CPCS and the reimposition of unity and ideological orthodoxy within it. A final Soviet-Czechoslovak summit took place at Cierna nad Tisou on 29 July. This was intended to be the prelude to invasion: the Kremlin expected to provoke a split in the CPCS leadership, following which a 'healthy' (i.e. pro-Soviet) core could form a new Presidium and invite Warsaw Pact military assistance to maintain order [*Doc. 4*]. An address to the Czechoslovak people explaining the intervention was drafted after the Warsaw meeting and approved by the Soviet Politburo on 26–27 July. In the event, the CPCS leadership did not split under pressure, and the summit instead resulted in a deal between the Dubček leadership and the Kremlin which delayed the invasion.

It soon became clear, however, that the CPCS leadership was not carrying out its part of the agreement, and Warsaw Pact forces occupied the country on August 20–21, bringing the 'Prague Spring' to an end. Dubček was left in place for the time being but forced to concede the maintenance of Soviet troops in the country, to tighten political controls and to remove reformers from sensitive posts while retaining conservatives who had backed the Soviet intervention. However, a number of incidents in the months that followed fuelled anti-Soviet sentiment in the country, including the self-immolation of the student Jan Palach in Prague and disturbances following the Czechoslovak victory over the USSR in the world hockey championships. In response to these developments, Moscow dispatched Defence Minister Andrei Grechko to Prague to oversee the removal of Dubček and the installation of the conservative Gustav Husak. Husak presided over the 'normalisation' of the country and remained in power until the Velvet Revolution of 1989.

The invasion of Czechoslovakia was widely condemned, particularly in the West, but its impact on East–West relations was relatively short-lived. The intervention's most lasting legacies were the splits it provoked in the world Communist movement (some western Communist parties condemned the intervention) and the chill effect it had on reformist thinking both within the Soviet Union and in the bloc. In the aftermath of the crisis, Moscow, through the newspapers *Pravda* and *Krasnaya zvezda*, enunciated what came to be known as the 'Brezhnev doctrine' or the 'doctrine of limited sovereignty'. In essence, it stated that the interests of the socialist common-wealth transcended those of individual socialist states and that socialist states were duty-bound to come to the aid of socialism wherever it was threatened. In other words, it was an explicit declaration of the limits of Moscow's tolerance for doctrinal deviation.

WAR IN VIETNAM AND US-SOVIET RELATIONS

The Brezhnev leadership's accession to power coincided with the escalation of US involvement in the Vietnam conflict. Soviet backing for North Vietnam and the South Vietnamese National Liberation Front in their drive to unite all Vietnam under Communist rule was not initially assured. Soviet–North Vietnamese relations had cooled noticeably in the early 1960s, largely owing to Hanoi's failure to take Moscow's side in the Sino-Soviet quarrel and to the USSR's desire, in the wake of Cuba, for better relations with the United States (Gaiduk, 1995/96: 232). Khrushchev, shortly before his removal, had indicated his acceptance of a US proposal – rejected by both Hanoi and Beijing – to take the US–North Vietnamese quarrel to the UN Security Council. Motivated in large measure by the rivalry with China, his successors quickly reversed this position and in November 1964 pledged their support for the Communist government of North Vietnam in the event of US attack. Brezhnev and his colleagues feared losing influence in Hanoi to Mao Zedong, and relations with the United States were in any case deteriorating, a fact that reduced the opportunity cost of backing North Vietnam. Nonetheless, Kosygin, at least, hoped to extricate the Americans from their Vietnamese entanglement, which would certainly have facilitated an improvement in the superpower relationship. An attempt by him to defuse the escalating conflict in early 1965 failed, and the USSR quickly signalled that it would stand by its commitment to support Hanoi against the Americans.

This proved to be a tremendous windfall for the Kremlin. As the war dragged on and the US involvement deepened, Vietnam became a major drain on US resources, the focal point of bitter political conflict within the United States and a major blot on Washington's international reputation, particularly in the developing world. Soviet support for Vietnam, by contrast, was relatively inexpensive and was never allowed to compromise Moscow's pursuit of more important interests. In 1972, for example, Nixon received a warm welcome in Moscow, despite the fact that he had just ordered the mining of seven North Vietnamese ports and launched aerial attacks on supply routes from China to Vietnam.

There were, nevertheless, perceived dangers in the Soviet commitment to Hanoi. Soviet leaders found their North Vietnamese allies to be ungrateful, unpredictable and unmanageable, and were frequently irritated by their 'parochial' outlook – that is, by their failure to sacrifice their own interests to the USSR's larger global strategy. The Soviets found their lack of influence over their Vietnamese clients frustrating in the extreme: instead of weaning Hanoi away from Beijing, Soviet support merely enabled the Vietnamese Communists to maximise their own independence by playing off the two Communist giants against each other. (Sino-Vietnamese relations were, of course, equally difficult, especially after Hanoi in 1968 decided to begin direct talks with the United States.) The Kremlin also feared that US desperation to secure a successful outcome to the conflict could lead to uncontrolled escalation (Gaiduk, 1995/96: 250–3). Many Soviet and American policy-makers therefore shared the hope that the USSR would help broker a deal between Washington and Hanoi.

Soviet leaders were reluctant to assume this mediating role directly, mainly because Soviet officials in Hanoi did not believe they really had much power to shape North Vietnamese behaviour. Soviet hard-liners in any case saw little reason to help the United States escape its costly involvement in Indochina. The USSR did, however, convey US proposals to Hanoi and it encouraged Polish mediation efforts in the mid-1960s, while pressing Hanoi to enter into direct talks with Washington. Thus, the Vietnam War was, paradoxically, a stimulus to both superpowers' pursuit of détente (Nelson, 1995; Gaiduk, 1995/96).

THE ROAD TO SUPERPOWER DÉTENTE

Vietnam notwithstanding, there was considerable evidence in the mid-1960s that East–West relations were entering a new phase. Differences over the war did not prevent the two superpowers from agreeing the outlines of the nuclear Non-Proliferation Treaty (NPT), which was signed by the US, the USSR and the United Kingdom in July 1968, just weeks after the Soviet Union had accepted the invitation extended by President Lyndon Johnson in early 1967 to enter what became the SALT process.

Developments in Western Europe were also encouraging to the Kremlin. French President Charles de Gaulle's vision of a Europe extending from the Atlantic to the Urals and his pursuit of a special Franco-Russian relationship were as gratifying to Moscow as they were irritating to Washington. Far more important, however, was the gradual shift in West German policy. In January 1965, the leading Social Democratic politician Willy Brandt called for increased East–West trade and cooperation on joint projects on a European scale, although he stopped short of advocating recognition of the GDR. In 1966, Brandt became Foreign Minister and began to implement the new *Ostpolitik*. West Germany dropped the Hallstein doctrine of 1955, which stipulated that Bonn would not enter into diplomatic relations with any state that recognised the GDR, except the USSR. While the USSR, Poland and the GDR were quick to denounce this change, Romania moved to establish diplomatic relations with the Federal Republic of Germany in April 1967, and Moscow itself grew markedly less wary of negotiations with Bonn during 1968–69. Neither de Gaulle's search for a special relationship with Moscow nor Brandt's *Ostpolitik* amounted to the 'decoupling' of the United States from its West European allies that Moscow sought. However, Europe's pursuit of an East–West thaw did reflect an underlying fear about where the superpowers' own management of their relationship might lead (Jain, 1993).

The pace of change in East–West relations accelerated markedly from 1969, as both superpowers staked ever more political capital on the achievement of a substantial reduction in tensions between the two blocs. For the Soviet leaders, this shift reflected a number of changes in the international environment. The first was the achievement of strategic parity with the United States, which enabled Soviet leaders to negotiate with their American counterparts as equals. At the same time, other international developments made it imperative· that they do so. The US opening to China raised the dangerous possibility of Sino-American collusion against the USSR, while growing awareness of the destructiveness of nuclear weapons meant that 'nuclear logic' itself dictated that the superpowers seek to bring the arms race under control and stabilise the strategic balance. For the United States, the desire to wind down its involvement in Vietnam was an important motive in seeking a new, more cooperative relationship with Moscow. In Europe, western anger over the Czechoslovak intervention quickly dissipated, and the election of Willy Brandt as West German Chancellor in October 1969 gave a renewed impetus to Bonn's pursuit of *Ostpolitik*. Finally, the desire for increased trade and technology transfer provided a further motive for engagement with the United States.

Although economic performance in the late 1960s was still quite satisfactory, there was already a growing awareness within the Soviet elite that the USSR, while overtaking America in the output of some traditional industries, like steel, was falling behind in computers, petrochemicals and other rapidly advancing sectors. Trade and technology imports seemed to offer at least part of the solution to this problem. The economic interest in détente was not one-sided. West European states were eager to increase trade, and the United States was feeling the costs of superpower competition and the after-effects of Lyndon Johnson's determination to have both guns and butter, pursuing his Great Society agenda at home while financing the war in Vietnam. The rise of Western Europe and Japan, moreover, meant that the United States no longer enjoyed the unchallenged economic leadership of the capitalist world that it had possessed during the first post-war decades.

CHINA

The pursuit of détente with the West stood in marked contrast to, and was partly prompted by, the deterioration of Soviet relations with the People's Republic of China (PRC). The potential of the Sino-Soviet Cold War to turn hot was vividly demonstrated on the day of Khrushchev's removal, as the Chinese conducted their first successful atom bomb test. It is thus hardly surprising that the Soviet Union's new leaders were anxious to secure a new *modus vivendi* with Beijing. It soon became apparent, however, that the price of accommodating China would be too high. Beijing remained un-willing to accept unquestioned Soviet leadership of the world Communist movement, and the two states clashed over a number of regional and global issues. The Soviet government's 1965 decision to sign the NPT provoked Chinese opposition, as had Moscow's decision two years earlier to sign the Test Ban Treaty, which forbade nuclear weapons tests in the atmosphere, under water and in outer space. Beijing had long resented Moscow's lack of enthusiasm for China's own nuclear weapons programme. The Indo-Pakistani War of August–September 1965 found the two on opposite sides, although the Soviet Union did attempt to mediate the conflict in the hope of gaining the support of both against China (Malik, 1994). In Vietnam, the two great Communist powers backed the same side, but this did not prevent conflict between them, since support for Vietnam was an arena of com-petition rather than a basis for cooperation. Soviet aid deliveries to North Vietnam during 1965–71 were about triple those of China, and Moscow repeatedly accused the People's Republic of delays in transhipment and other disruptions in the flow of aid to Hanoi. Mao's Great Proletarian Cultural Revolution added to Soviet distrust of China, while Beijing was quick to see a threat to itself in the invasion of Czechoslovakia and the enunciation of the 'Brezhnev doctrine' (Jian and Wilson, 1998).

Relations between the two Communist powers deteriorated markedly in late 1968, culminating in a serious crisis the following year. Clashes along the disputed Sino-Soviet border had occurred at intervals since 1962. The March 1969 Chinese ambush of a Soviet patrol on Damanskii Island in the Ussuri river provoked a Soviet retaliation in which Chinese casualties exceeded 800 and Soviet losses reached about 60. This was the first of a series of incidents culminating in a major action by Soviet forces near the Dzungarian Gate in mid-August. Moscow raised the stakes by signalling to the Chinese that it was considering a nuclear strike, a threat which provoked a major war scare in China. The Soviets put out feelers to the United States about possible cooperation in the prevention of, or retaliation for, provocative acts by the PRC, and reportedly took informal soundings in Washington concerning the likely US response to a major Soviet attack on China (Shevchenko, 1985: 165–6). Both Moscow and Beijing were aware of the dangerous ground they were on, and steps were taken to defuse the situation. The immediate threat of war passed, but little else was achieved. Tensions along the frontier remained high, and the number of Soviet divisions deployed along the 4,000-mile Sino-Soviet border was doubled to 46 during 1967–72.

Both Moscow and Beijing turned their attention increasingly towards Washington. The USSR had been actively pursuing a new accommodation with the United States since the election of Richard Nixon in 1968, and Beijing had been quick to follow suit. Mao signalled his interest in removing Sino-American relations from the deep freeze as soon as Nixon took office, ordering the publication of Nixon's inaugural address in major Chinese papers. This interest was reinforced by the Sino-Soviet border clashes that erupted in March (Jian and Wilson, 1998: 155). It is not clear how aware Soviet leaders were of Nixon's pursuit of an opening to China, but the July 1971 announcement that Nixon was to visit Beijing early the following year appears to have been as great a surprise to the Kremlin as it was to the rest of the world. In October, the Soviet leadership invited Nixon to visit Moscow the following May. However, because the ensuing reduction in tensions with Washington was never matched by a parallel détente with Beijing, the triangular diplomacy that dominated superpower relations for the rest of the Cold War kept Moscow at a significant disadvantage [*Doc. 9*].

THE SOVIET UNION AND THE DEVELOPING WORLD

The Brezhnev leadership continued Khrushchev's efforts to extend Soviet influence in the developing world, although until the mid-1970s it remained wary of large-scale commitments too far from Soviet borders. Vietnam, of course, was one exception to this rule, and Cuba was another, albeit not always a happy one for Moscow – the post-crisis decade was a difficult one for Soviet-Cuban relations. The cost of Soviet financing of the Cuban economy mounted steadily but did not prove sufficient to prevent Cuban leader Fidel Castro from criticising Soviet aid to North Vietnam as insufficient, nor did it check Castro's promotion of armed revolutionary struggle in Latin America. Havana only reluctantly backed the invasion of Czechoslovakia in 1968. So strained did relations become that the Kremlin in 1967–68 considered ending its support for the Cuban revolution and abandoning Castro to his fate (Pavlov, 1994: 89). However, the principal object of Moscow's attentions in the Third World during the late 1960s was the Middle East; US support for Israel offered the USSR an easy opportunity to court support in the Arab world. The anti-Islamic propaganda of the Khrushchev era was dropped in favour of an emphasis on the revolutionary and anti-imperialist potential of Islam (Kennedy-Pipe, 1998: 134). Egypt, in particular, became the focus of Soviet ambitions, not least because it could offer the USSR naval facilities in the Mediterranean, something the Soviet navy had not enjoyed since the break with Albania in 1961.

The results of these efforts were decidedly mixed. Soviet support failed to prevent the Arabs' humiliating defeat in the Six-Day War of June 1967, which, given the Arabs' reliance on Soviet arms, was a significant embarrassment to Moscow. Moreover, the USSR's decision to break off ties to Israel in order to show its solidarity with its Arab clients meant that Moscow was largely frozen out of the post-war diplomacy. This was a decision for which the Soviet Union would pay a diplomatic price for more than 20 years. Defeat at the hands of Israel forced Egypt to withdraw from its involvement in the civil war in Yemen, where it had been supporting the Republican side since 1962. The Royalist forces lost no time in exploiting the Egyptian withdrawal and a royalist victory seemed imminent within weeks of the Egyptians' departure in early October 1967. This prompted direct Soviet intervention in support of the Republicans, which turned the tide by year-end. The participation of Soviet pilots in combat in Yemen marked an important departure in Soviet policy. This was followed by an even more extensive direct military involvement in the 'War of Attrition' waged between Israel and Egypt over the Suez Canal in 1969–70. The deployment of Soviet air defence units and the commitment of Soviet pilots to combat went far beyond the commitment the Kremlin initially envisaged, but the Soviets appeared to be in control of their escalatory steps and the conflict was contained. The result was a success for the Kremlin: a confrontation with the United States was avoided, the cease-fire terms were not un-favourable to Cairo, Egyptian air defences were restored, and President Gamal Abdel Nasser remained in power.

Nasser's death a month later rendered this last achievement transient, however, as his successor, Anwar Sadat, proved an extremely troublesome client, expelling 17,000 Soviet advisers in 1972, depriving the Soviets of use of Egyptian airfields and reducing their naval facilities on Egypt's Mediterranean coast. Nevertheless, Sadat's military ambitions left him dependent on Soviet support, which was crucial in saving him from catastrophic defeat in the Yom Kippur War of October 1973. In the short term, at least, the Brezhnev leadership could also be pleased with its handling of the October War. The Soviets' extensive logistical support prevented a disastrous Arab defeat, and Brezhnev's threat to intervene directly at the height of the crisis helped force the United States to pressure Israel into complying with the ceasefire resolutions. The Americans, facing a domestic political crisis as well as a crisis of superpower relations, responded to the intervention threat by issuing a 'DefCon 3' military alert worldwide and taking other steps to prepare for intervention. They thereby signalled their determination not to be swayed by Soviet threats. However, the United States also exerted maximum pressure on Israel to halt its advance and allow the resupply of the Egyptian Third Army, which had been facing annihilation. The military outcome of the conflict was thus sufficiently ambiguous to allow the Arabs to claim victory. Soviet arms received favourable publicity, and the projection of Soviet power in the crisis impressively demonstrated the USSR's ability to exert its military power in distant regions at short notice. Moscow's support for its clients and its continuous negotiations with Washington established its equality with the United States as a global power. Finally, the crisis also realised another Soviet aim: the Arab oil embargo demonstrated for the first time the potential of oil as a weapon in international diplomacy.

These immediate successes, however, were counterbalanced by long-term costs. The war re-established the psychological parity of Egypt with Israel and put an end to the state of affairs that had occasioned the massive Soviet entry into Egypt after 1967. This reduced Egypt's reliance on Soviet support and made Sadat more inclined to negotiate, feeling that he could now do so from a position of strength. As Sadat had hoped, the war also prompted the United States to take steps towards a diplomatic resolution of the Arab-Israeli conflict that it had previously rejected. The ultimate outcome of the conflict was thus the Egyptian-Israeli peace treaty of 1979 and the defection of Egypt to the American camp. The Kremlin also lost ground in Syria and Iraq as Kissinger's shuttle diplomacy opened them up to US influence, leaving the USSR cut off from the post-war disengagement process by virtue of its having severed diplomatic relations with Israel six years earlier.

In hindsight, it seems clear that, given Sadat's ambitions, any outcome of the October War that left Egyptian forces on the East Bank of the Suez Canal was destined to work against Soviet interests. This highlighted a larger problem: while its support could limit, and sometimes prevent, Arab defeats, the Soviet Union could deliver for its clients neither a decisive victory nor a negotiated peace. Indeed, some observers saw in Soviet behaviour in the Middle East a calculated strategy designed to ensure Arab dependence on the USSR by supporting the Arab states only enough to prevent their defeat. Given the US commitment to Israel, the consequences of a major Arab victory were indeed potentially serious, so a prolonged stalemate might have been seen as the only acceptable goal of Soviet policy, whatever the aims of its clients. However, Wehling (1997) points to a less Machiavellian conclusion. He finds that Soviet policy was largely a product of the Brezhnev leadership's inability or unwillingness to recognise the tensions between its regional and global aims and to confront the trade-offs facing them.

India remained, as it had been under Khrushchev, one of the USSR's closest friends in the developing world. Though democratic and non-aligned, India was in many respects closer to the Soviet Union than some of the Kremlin's more revolutionary clients. Delhi and Moscow shared a common dislike of America's client, Pakistan, and a common fear of China. During the 1970s, India was the largest non-Arab recipient of Soviet arms, and Soviet arms constituted 90% of its inventory (Webber, 2002). Elsewhere in the developing world, the Brezhnev leadership adopted a far more cautious line. Latin America remained largely a 'no-go' area for the USSR, and Cuban attempts to promote armed revolutionary struggle there were a major source of irritation to the Kremlin. Soviet activities in Africa were likewise fairly limited. From about 1970, however, the KGB did actively promote an 'African strategy' for the USSR, seeing it as an arena offering opportunities to score relatively inexpensive victories in the global contest with the United States. The continent's liberation movements were searching for international allies and were more likely to turn to the USSR than to the former colonial powers or the United States. Moreover, one early KGB analysis rightly pointed out that the United States was not expecting any broad Soviet offensive in Africa (Westad, 1996/97a: 21–2). Nevertheless, until the middle of the decade, direct Soviet involvement in the continent's affairs south of the Sahara was limited. Cuba, by contrast, became involved in a number of African conflicts and Cuban forces were more or less continuously engaged in Africa from 1959. Moscow looked with favour on these activities – unlike Havana's activities in Latin America – in large part because they did not seem to antagonise the United States in the way that similar efforts in Latin America did (Gleijeses, 1996/97: 6–7).

There were several reasons for this early caution on the part of the Kremlin. First, the Soviets found most of the liberation movements to be difficult allies: with the exception of the African National Congress, they tended to be disorganised and internally divided. Secondly, ideological concerns were especially sensitive in this area, in large part because the competition with the PRC for influence in post-colonial Africa made Moscow sensitive to any signs that its local allies were leaning towards Beijing. The deep involvement of the CPSU Central Committee's International Department in Africa policy probably also contributed to the greater concern with ideology (Adam, 1989). Finally, despite the military build-up described above, Soviet power-projection capabilities continued to be limited in important ways. From roughly 1975, however, Moscow increasingly shed its inhibitions about involvement in Africa south of the Sahara, a shift that was to contribute to the souring of East–West relations that characterised the late 1970s.

THE ERA OF HIGH DÉTENTE

The period from 1970 to 1975 marked the high point of superpower détente. This was arguably the most successful period for Soviet diplomacy since the end of the Second World War. Ironically, its very success sowed the seeds of much subsequent failure. Yet this was scarcely evident to most observers in 1985, let alone to the Brezhnev leadership in 1975. Moscow's aim was nothing less than the final settlement of the Second World War in Europe, on terms that would secure the post-war position of the Soviet Union in perpetuity. Thirty years in the making, this final peace agreement for Europe was to be all that Moscow desired – and was to last not much more than a decade.

The first major milestone of the 1970s was the conclusion in August 1970 of the Treaty of Moscow between the USSR and the Federal Republic of Germany. The treaty included a mutual renunciation of the use of force and, crucially, the recognition of all existing borders, including the inner German border and the Oder–Neisse frontier between Poland and the GDR. Germany also signed the Non-Proliferation Treaty, which had finally entered into force in March 1970. The next step in the resolution of the German question was the signing of a quadripartite agreement on Berlin in September 1971. It was agreed that Berlin would be represented by West Germany in all international matters but would not form a part of the Federal Republic. The USSR retained responsibility for western access to Berlin. The normalisation of the two-Germanys settlement proceeded further with the conclusion of a basic treaty between the two German states in December 1972, an agreement which led to the exchange of permanent missions between the two and to the accession of both Germanys to the United Nations.

Earlier that year, Richard Nixon had become the first US president to visit Moscow, where he and his hosts signed a pair of arms control agreements, a trade agreement and a 'Basic Principles Agreement' committing the two sides to a relationship based on equality, reciprocity, mutual accommodation and mutual benefit. To judge from the Soviet press coverage, this last agreement was of particular importance to the Kremlin (Kennedy-Pipe, 1998: 152). Thereafter, superpower summits became, for a few years, a regular feature of the international scene. Brezhnev paid a return visit to the United States in 1973, and Nixon travelled again to Moscow in June 1974, in the dying days of his presidency. His successor, Gerald Ford, met Brezhnev in Vladivostok just a few months after taking office. This activity was in sharp contrast to the record of the quarter-century after 1945, during which Khrushchev had met US presidents on three occasions (including a brief encounter at the failed Paris summit of May 1960), and his successor as prime minister, Kosygin, on just one, in 1967.

The 'nuclear logic' driving the broader superpower rapprochement was evident in the emphasis placed on arms control. The centrepiece of the US-Soviet relationship was the treaty limiting deployment of anti-ballistic missile (ABM) systems [*Doc. 5*]. The prospect of a race in defensive arms was worrying to both sides. The technologies involved were uncertain and expensive, and a race in ABM systems was bound to fuel a parallel race in offensive systems as well. Moreover, if the partial success of one side raised questions about the ability of the other to retaliate following a nuclear strike, the strategic balance would be destabilised, potentially leaving the weaker party to choose between a pre-emptive strike and capitulation (Lee, 1997). The treaty limited each side to two ABM deployments of not more than 100 launchers, one around its capital city and a second at another location containing some part of its ICBM force. The launchers so deployed were to be static and land-based, limited to one missile with one warhead per launcher. Restrictions on associated radar systems were also agreed. The ABM Treaty outlasted the USSR by just over a decade, remaining in force until the United States withdrew from it in order to pursue plans for national missile defence.

The ABM Treaty was accompanied by a five-year Interim Agreement on the Limitation of Strategic Arms (SALT I), which was to set the basis for a second round of SALT talks [*Doc. 6*]. In terms of both numbers of launchers and total megatonnage, this agreement confirmed the marked Soviet superiority that had emerged in the preceding years. However, it failed to cover strategic bombers, in which the United States enjoyed a substantial advantage, nor did it cover US aircraft based at sea or on the territory of US allies close to the USSR. The United States also enjoyed an edge in both accuracy and the deployment of missiles carrying multiple, independently targetable warheads, which were not identifiable by satellite and were therefore excluded from the agreement. In June 1973, Nixon and Brezhnev signed an agreement on the prevention of nuclear war during the latter's visit to Washington.

Symbolically, at least, the high point of détente came with the Helsinki summit of the Conference on Security and Cooperation in Europe (CSCE) in August 1975. The Helsinki Final Act, the culmination of a decade of diplomacy and two years of negotiation in Helsinki, was signed by 33 European statesmen as well as leaders of the United States and Canada. The Final Act contained three 'baskets'. The first, pertaining to security in Europe, confirmed the inviolability of post-war frontiers (including the division of Germany) and the inadmissibility of attempts to revise them other than by peaceful negotiations conducted in accordance with international law. For Brezhnev, this multilateral ratification of the post-war order was a major achievement. In short, basket one was the long-overdue peace treaty confirming the fruits of the Soviet Union's victory over Nazi Germany. It was not, however, without its awkward points: paragraph 14 committed the signatories to non-intervention in the affairs of other states, a commitment difficult to square with the Brezhnev doctrine. Basket one also provided for a range of confidence-building measures designed to reduce the risk of conflict. Basket two was dedicated to cooperation in the fields of science, technology and the environment, while basket three committed the signatory states to protect a range of human rights, many of which were routinely ignored by the Soviet authorities.

Some have presented this as a major mistake by the Brezhnev leadership, since it gave domestic and foreign critics a legal instrument to use against it. However, the subversive impact of the Final Act's human rights provisions should not be exaggerated. Basket three was no more extensive than the UN Covenant on Human Rights, which Moscow had signed in September 1973, or the USSR Constitution adopted in 1977, neither of which meant much in practice. Nevertheless, human rights issues were prominent in subsequent CSCE review conferences, and 'Helsinki Watch' groups emerged as leading critics of the human rights abuses of Communist regimes in Europe.

Ironically, the CSCE process stalled soon after Helsinki. The follow-up conference in Belgrade in 1977 ended in deadlock, and by the time of the 1980 Madrid conference Afghanistan and Poland had put East–West relations under their greatest strain in a generation. The next CSCE summit of real importance was the Paris meeting of 1990, which ratified the end of the Cold War. Brezhnev, had he lived to see it, would have viewed it as the surrender of everything he had sought to secure in Helsinki and, indeed, of everything the Soviet Union's post-war European policy had been intended to achieve.

CHAPTER FIVE

FROM HELSINKI TO THE SECOND COLD WAR

Few could have realised in the summer of the Helsinki summit that the 1970s would end with tensions between the superpowers at a level not seen since the early 1960s and that the early 1980s would come to be regarded as a second Cold War (Halliday, 1986). Yet even as the leaders of 35 states gathered in the Finnish capital to finalise what amounted to the formal political settlement of the Second World War in Europe, the pressures on both sides that would lead to the ultimate failure of détente were making themselves felt. As the 1970s progressed, Moscow and Washington clashed with increasing frequency, over everything from emigration and human rights in the USSR to civil wars and international conflicts in Asia, Africa and Latin America. The invasion of Afghanistan at the end of 1979 and the US response to it put the last nails into the coffin of détente and in-augurated a new period of US-Soviet tensions. Brezhnev's legacy to his immediate successors was nothing less than a new Cold War.

ARMS CONTROL AND TRADE

Progress on arms control slowed markedly after 1975, although there were negotiations along a number of tracks. The SALT talks continued, with a view to following up the interim SALT I agreement with a SALT II treaty. This was to be based on a preliminary agreement reached by Brezhnev and Ford at Vladivostok in November 1974. Though widely criticised in America and ultimately repudiated by Ford's successor, Jimmy Carter, the Vladivostok accords involved significant concessions on the Soviet side. In particular, Brezhnev agreed to leave US forward-based systems out of the equation, a concession some of his colleagues strenuously opposed (Savel'ev & Detinov, 1995: 41; Kornienko, 1995: 142). In late 1973, seven NATO states and five Warsaw Pact members entered into talks on conventional arms control in Europe. This issue was to prove even less tractable than nuclear arms control, and a major conventional arms control treaty was not in fact signed until the Conventional Forces in Europe Treaty of 1990 sealed the end of the Cold War.

The failure of the two superpowers to make greater progress on arms control reflected a number of factors. First, the easy decisions were taken with the ABM Treaty and SALT I, under which the two sides agreed to forego weapons systems they did not particularly want anyway and to avoid a defensive arms race that neither welcomed (Rathjens, Chayes and Ruina, 1974). Secondly, many key players in both states' security establishments remained fundamentally suspicious of the whole process. Thirdly, the two sides did not share a common understanding of the aim of the talks. While American negotiators sought a rough US-Soviet parity in strategic systems, the Soviet side focused on 'equal security' rather than equal arsenals. This meant that Moscow always negotiated with an eye on the British and French arsenals, which the US regarded as outside the negotiations. The Soviet commitment to equal security also meant that the Soviet view of what constituted a 'strategic' weapon differed from the US view: for Soviet negotiators, any nuclear system capable of hitting the USSR was a strategic weapon. Finally, developments in other areas of policy soured the relationship more generally and made it more difficult for advocates of arms control on either side to press for the compromises needed to reach agreement.

The economic fruits of détente were even more disappointing, particularly to Soviet leaders. Nixon and Brezhnev did manage to settle the issue of the USSR's wartime lend-lease debt, and a three-year trade agreement signed in July 1972 envisaged Soviet purchases of at least $750m worth of US grain. However, these and other less high-profile deals agreed with West Germany and other western states did not meet Soviet expectations of détente. The Joint Trade Commission set up by the US and the USSR in 1972 achieved little, and western restrictions on technology transfers to the East remained in place. Moscow was extremely irritated by two amendments to US legislation that affected US-Soviet trade. The Stevenson amendment aimed to cap US credits to the USSR at $300m, which would have severely restricted the scope for expanding trade, while the Jackson–Vanik amendment tied US trade policy towards the USSR to Soviet policy with respect to emigration [*Doc. 8*]. The Soviet Union actually accepted the terms of Jackson–Vanik in practice – Jewish emigration from the USSR rose rapidly, reaching a peak of 35,000 in 1973. However, it found the form of the US trade bill finally adopted in December 1974 and the publicity surrounding the issue too much to swallow. Moscow cancelled the 1972 agreement in January 1975. Although a new five-year grain agreement was signed the following October, the whole episode marked a major setback to proponents of détente in both countries. Indeed, some observers have seen the December 1974 Central Committee meeting, which ratified the cancellation decision, as a crucial turning point in Soviet foreign policy (Gelman, 1984).

DÉTENTE UNDER STRAIN

The fall of Richard Nixon, who resigned the US presidency on 9 August 1974 as a result of the Watergate scandal, proved to be a greater blow to détente than was apparent at the time. It initially appeared that the foreign policy of the new Ford Administration would be characterised by continuity. Ford retained Nixon's Secretary of State, Henry Kissinger, and within a few months of taking office met Brezhnev in Vladivostok to press forward with the conclusion of a SALT II agreement. However, by mid-1975, Ford was retreating from the pro-détente positions of the early 1970s. The increasing activism of the Democrat-controlled Congress in foreign affairs, the final defeat of US clients in Indochina in the spring of 1975 and the eruption of the Angolan crisis put Ford on the defensive over foreign policy. By the time of the 1976 presidential election campaign, he was eschewing the word 'détente' in his public pronouncements.

The most surprising source of tension was Angola. After the fall of the Caetano regime in April 1974, Portugal, the colonial power in Angola, set 11 November 1975 as the date for Angolan independence. As that date approached, competition intensified among the three liberation movements in the country: Jonas Savimbi's Union for the Total Liberation of Angola (UNITA), Agnostino Neto's Popular Movement for the Liberation of Angola (MPLA) and Holden Roberto's National Front for the Liberation of Angola (FNLA). Historically, Moscow had backed the MPLA, a weak, factionalised and unpopular movement that the Kremlin found a difficult and unreliable client. The Nixon Administration in July 1974 had authorised CIA financial support for the FNLA and UNITA, while China had begun supplying arms and other assistance to the FNLA. The USSR's main concern at this stage appears to have been curtailing Chinese influence on the continent. Nevertheless, Moscow initially showed little enthusiasm for intervening on behalf of its clients in the conflict. Even the normally bold Cuban leadership moved cautiously, not least because its relations with Washington had warmed somewhat in late 1974 and early 1975. The Soviet Union did agree to an MPLA request for aid in March 1975, a request supported by Cuban lobbying. However, Moscow moved cautiously, anxious not to aggravate African sensitivities about external intervention, and the aid was mainly delivered through the Cubans.

Three things changed Soviet calculations over the summer. First, the FNLA and UNITA joined forces, which threatened to eliminate the MPLA altogether as a force in Angola. Secondly, Moscow in August received intelligence concerning a planned South African intervention. The subsequent introduction of South African troops into Angola enabled Moscow to move decisively without upsetting other African governments. Thirdly, Congress rejected the Ford Administration's request to authorise increased assistance to the FNLA/UNITA in response to growing Soviet involvement in the conflict and even cut the aid already being channelled through the CIA. Aid to the MPLA was stepped up; the number of Cuban troops in Angola rose from 12,000 to 19,000. By March 1976, the military tide had turned in favour of the MPLA, and the Neto government had been recognised by most African and European governments. The Brezhnev leadership had good reason to be pleased with its handling of the Angolan crisis. After its initial hesitation, it had challenged the United States and its regional clients in a theatre far from Soviet borders and had prevailed. In delivering Cuban troops to Angola, the USSR had demonstrated the ability to project military power across the globe. And it had shown African liberation movements that it was a more effective patron than China. The failure of the United States to act decisively in the crisis, a legacy of both Watergate and US defeat in Indochina, appeared to augur well for such operations in the future.

Soviet leaders were both surprised and disturbed by the souring of relations with the Ford Administration, and they were pleased when Ford's Democratic challenger, Jimmy Carter, narrowly won the presidency in November 1976. Carter's rhetoric on human rights was a source of concern, but Moscow nevertheless preferred him to Ford. On 18 January 1977, just before Carter took office, Brezhnev delivered a speech in which he rejected the pursuit of military superiority or first-strike capability by the USSR, declaring that victory in a nuclear war was impossible and that the aim of Soviet defence policy was to deter aggression. This was the clearest statement yet of a Soviet position roughly equivalent to the US doctrine of 'mutual assured destruction'. The speech had been carefully drafted with a view to impressing the incoming US president with the USSR's peaceable intentions (Kornienko, 1995: 141). Carter responded with a clear commitment to pursue the speedy conclusion of a SALT II treaty.

The honeymoon did not last. On 14 February, after less than a month in office, Carter indicated that he did not wish to continue the SALT negotiations on the basis of the Vladivostok accords, aiming instead for actual *cuts* in the superpowers' arsenals. This shift in US policy was a most unwelcome development from the Kremlin's perspective and a blow to Brezhnev personally. The Soviet leader had faced internal opposition to the Vladivostok agreement that Carter was now disavowing (Kornienko, 1995: 142–3). Carter seems not to have had any idea what a shock his new line would be to Soviet leaders. It soon became clear that there was little prospect of concluding SALT II by late 1977 or early 1978, as initially hoped. By the time SALT II was signed in June 1979 [*Doc. 7*], the relationship had deteriorated to such an extent that the Carter Administration chose not to submit it to the Senate for ratification. The Soviet intervention in Afghanistan at the end of that year put paid to any lingering hopes for its ratification that Carter may have harboured.

The shift on arms control was not the only disappointment to Moscow. Carter's emphasis on human rights antagonised the Soviet leaders, as did his response to the crisis in the Horn of Africa and his handling of the Middle East peace process. This last was seen by the USSR as a betrayal of trust. On 1 October 1977, the two superpowers issued a joint declaration committing themselves to work together towards a comprehensive settlement of the Arab-Israeli conflict. Seven weeks later, Egyptian President Sadat made his surprise visit to Jerusalem, setting in motion the process that resulted in the Camp David Accords in September 1978 and an Israeli-Egyptian peace treaty in March 1979. In the wake of Sadat's trip, the Carter Administration shelved the joint declaration and devoted its energies to brokering an Egyptian-Israeli deal. This was doubtless Sadat's intention. He had terminated the Soviet-Egyptian Treaty of Friendship and Cooperation in 1976, thereby completing Egypt's exit from the Soviet orbit, and had little interest in a peace process in which Moscow played a leading role. His dramatic flight to Jerusalem helped ensure that no such process ever got under way.

By the end of 1977, another military crisis in Africa had dealt a further blow to US-Soviet relations. Moscow had long been interested in the Horn of Africa, on account of its strategic location and the perceived opportunities for promoting an anti-imperialist agenda there. However, it had little by way of a foothold in the region until 1969, when General Mohammed Siad Barre came to power in Somalia and adopted a policy of close alignment with Moscow. The alliance with Somalia, which was engaged in a long-running territorial dispute with Ethiopia, meant that Moscow was slow to seize the opportunity offered by the overthrow of Ethiopia's Emperor Haile Selassie in 1974. Despite the Marxist orientation of the Provisional Military Administrative Council, or Derg, that replaced the Emperor, the USSR did not immediately embrace the new Ethiopian regime. However, the emergence of the strongly pro-Soviet Mengistu Haile Mariam as the Derg's leader led to the development of closer ties between Addis Ababa and Moscow. This led the Kremlin to hope that it could engineer a rapprochement between its rival clients. However, the Somali-Ethiopian conflict over the Ogaden continued to escalate, and by July 1977 it was clear that (Siad Barre's denials notwithstanding) Somali regular forces had invaded Ethiopian territory. Moscow thus agreed to Mengistu's request for assistance. The USSR mounted a massive airlift in support of Ethiopia in November–December, and by March 1978, Ethiopian forces, supported by 16,000 Cuban troops, Soviet supplies and East Bloc advisers, had expelled the Somalis from the Ogaden.

The chief cost of the operation to Moscow was the loss of Somalia: Siad Barre expelled Soviet advisers from the country and deprived Soviet forces of the use of the naval facilities at Berbera. This was entirely predictable and a price worth paying for the much richer prize of Ethiopia. Nevertheless, Henze (1996/97: 45–7) notes that Moscow was reluctant to make the choice and continued to seek a negotiated solution that would allow it to keep both allies long after it had become clear that this was impossible and that the Kremlin would, ultimately, support Addis Ababa. The success of the Ethiopian operation was in part made possible by US reluctance to intervene, of which Moscow was well aware. However, while unable to prevent Ethiopia's shift into a Soviet alliance or the defeat of Somalia, the Carter Administration reacted angrily to the Soviet-Cuban operation. Growing Soviet and Cuban activism meant that, by 1979, Angola, Ethiopia, Benin, Congo (Brazzaville), Guinea, Guinea-Bissau and Mozambique had all declared Soviet-style socialism to be their aim, while some other African states were on friendlier terms with Moscow than with Washington.

CHINA

The death of Mao Zedong in September 1976 raised hopes in Moscow of a change in Chinese policy. By the end of the decade, however, it was clear that these hopes were to be disappointed and that the Sino-US rapprochement would continue. Initially, Chinese leaders were too preoccupied with the struggle to succeed Mao to give much attention to a major reassessment of foreign policy. Sino-Soviet relations remained extremely cold. The end of the war in Indochina left them backing rival clients: Beijing supported the Khmer Rouge government that had taken power in Cambodia, while Moscow supported the newly united Vietnam. When Vietnam invaded Cambodia in support of opponents of the Khmer Rouge in 1979, China responded with an invasion of northern Vietnam. Moscow's reaction was remarkably moderate, perhaps owing to fear that retaliation would strengthen the Sino-American axis. The danger of escalation was avoided when China withdrew its troops, having made its point. On balance, the episode was a success for Moscow, inasmuch as China soon pulled out of Vietnam, while Vietnamese forces remained in Cambodia in support of the pro-Vietnamese government Hanoi had installed there.

　　The early 1980s saw renewed attempts to reduce tensions in the Sino-Soviet Cold War. Despite differences over Soviet involvement in Afghanistan (see below), there were signs of a thaw. Soviet proposals for confidence-building measures were rebuffed by Beijing in early 1981 but did lead to meetings between foreign ministry officials. Moscow also began pressing for a resumption of border negotiations from late 1981, with Brezhnev himself calling for talks in March 1982, in a speech in which he acknowledged that China was indeed a socialist state – a major ideological concession. China continued to remain publicly cool towards the idea, but private contacts continued and trade began to grow. Foreign Minister Huang Hua was dispatched to Brezhnev's funeral in November 1982. While this represented some improvement on the worst days of the Cultural Revolution, the USSR continued to feel itself vulnerable to a Sino-US axis. The three-way relationship among the world's largest military powers was clearly working to Moscow's detriment.

AFGHANISTAN

Ironically enough, the Soviet Union's problems in Afghanistan began with the April 1978 overthrow of Mohammad Daoud, an unreliable non-Communist client, by Afghanistan's Communist party, the People's Democratic Party of Afghanistan (PDPA). The coup surprised the Soviets (Kornienko, 1993: 107), and it soon became evident that it was not such good news for them. The new PDPA regime was internally divided and incompetent as well. By early 1979, it had alienated much, if not most, of Afghan society and was facing serious armed opposition. In March, a major rising in Herat, the economic and administrative centre of western Afghanistan, first prompted Soviet leaders to consider intervening, not least because they believed Iran to have fomented the disturbances there (Kornienko, 1993: 108). At this stage, the Kremlin was adamant that it would not deploy troops in Afghanistan in support of the regime [*Doc. 10*]. As the year wore on and the situation deteriorated, however, the pressure for action grew. In September, Prime Minister Hafizullah Amin, the hard-line leader of the PDPA's Khalq ('People's Party') faction, overthrew his rival, President Nur Mohammad Taraki, the leader of the Parcham ('Banner') faction. Amin's policies were even more radical than Taraki's and intensified opposition to the regime [*Doc. 11*]. That the PDPA government was in deep trouble was evident to all: it made 19 requests for Soviet military aid between March and December. On the other hand, Amin, uncertain of Soviet support, was putting out feelers to the United States, prompting fears that he was about to defect to the western camp (Andropov *et alii*, 1995; Westad, 1996/97b: 130).

The Soviet General Staff continued to resist intervention, believing that it would increase rather than subdue opposition to the Afghan regime. Nevertheless, it began preparations for an invasion in October under pressure from Defence Minister Dmitrii Ustinov, who had emerged as the Politburo's leading advocate of intervention. Suslov, too, was hawkish in his views, while CC Secretary Kirilenko was the strongest opponent of military action. By December, the tide was running in favour of the hawks. Amin was proving unmanageable, and Brezhnev and his colleagues were becoming convinced that the alternative to intervention would be the emergence of a pro-American Afghanistan (Kornienko, 1993: 111). At the same time, relations with the West had already deteriorated to such a degree that damage on this count did not loom large in the Kremlin's calculations. Indeed, NATO's 12 December Euro-missile deployment decision (see below) prompted Andropov and Ustinov to cite the parallel danger they saw to the south – the possible deployment of US nuclear weapons in Afghanistan. On 8 December, Brezhnev, Gromyko, Andropov and Ustinov agreed on the need to intervene, a decision ratified by the Politburo four days later.

The long-requested military 'assistance' was deployed during 24–27 December. Ten thousand paratroopers were deployed to Kabul while Soviet ground forces crossed the Afghan border. By 27 December, when Amin was killed and replaced by the Parchamist Babrak Karmal, there were 70,000 Soviet troops in the country. Even then, it was not clear what they were to do there. The KGB had favoured a limited operation while the Ministry of Defence aimed to overthrow Amin and guard Afghanistan's borders with Pakistan and Iran (Westad, 1996/97b: 131).

The West's harsh reaction to the invasion surprised Soviet leaders, who saw it as a defence of the brutal Amin and hence a confirmation of their own fears about the consequences of leaving him in power. They did not take seriously the West's claim that Soviet forces might move further south than Afghanistan. The then head of the KGB's analytical service has since claimed that Soviet forces in Afghanistan were under orders not to cross the frontier under *any* circumstances, even under fire. However, he acknowledges that the decision to deploy the 40th army with all its equipment – including tactical rockets – was bound to arouse fears that Soviet forces might move still further south (Leonov, 1995: 67).

Initially, at least, the operation went reasonably well. The Soviet forces met limited resistance, agricultural procurement prices were raised and other concessions were made to shore up support for Karmal. By February 1980, however, it was clear that Soviet forces could not soon leave. On the contrary, their numbers began to grow, reaching 100,000 by the end of that year. Yet there remained a basic lack of clarity about their mission. Some commanders on the scene insisted that it was simply to seal Afghanistan's borders, arguing that they did not have the forces needed to resolve the country's internal problems by military means (Shubin, 1997: 20). Neither Brezhnev nor the Politburo had clearly specified the aims to be achieved before a withdrawal could take place. The USSR was stuck with the Karmal regime, with little choice but to increase its commitment at each decision point. The more it intervened, the more difficult it became to extricate itself. By late 1981, even the Politburo recognised that it could not resolve the Afghan conflict by military means, but neither could it find an acceptable diplomatic solution (Kornienko, 1993: 112). The result was a war the USSR could not win and, for almost nine years, would not lose.

POLAND

It is likely that the costs of the Afghan operation influenced Soviet leaders' attitudes to the next major foreign policy crisis that confronted them – the rise of Solidarity in Poland, which presented the biggest threat to Soviet interests in Eastern Europe since 1968. When labour unrest erupted in Poland in July 1980, the Kremlin seems to have favoured a tough response. However, mindful of Poland's history of worker protests, Moscow also recognised the need for some flexibility. Thus, while maintaining the pressure on the Polish leadership to bring the situation under control, the Soviet leaders endorsed the replacement of Polish leader Edward Gierek with Stanislaw Kania, a man associated with a conciliatory line. They tried to bolster Kania's position with an economic agreement signed a few days later. By November, the inability of Polish leaders to resolve the crisis was apparent, and the USSR began to hint at, and then to prepare for, a military solution. This was prompted in part by the fear of a general transport strike in Poland, which would have been a major threat to Warsaw Pact logistics.

For more than a year thereafter, the Soviet leadership raised and lowered the political and military pressure in response to developments within Poland. Invasion plans reached an advanced stage and military manoeuvres were carried out at times and places intended to pressure the Poles (Gribkov, 1992; Garthoff, 1998: 231). However, it is now clear from declassified Politburo documents that the Soviet leadership was extremely anxious to secure an internal solution ([Doc. 12]; Kramer, 1995; Shubin, 1997: 24–8). Even a hardliner such as Suslov, who headed the Politburo commission formed in response to the crisis in August 1980, regarded invasion as an unacceptable option (Gribkov, 1992: 52, 56). In the end, the crisis was resolved by a military coup within Poland itself. General Wojciech Jaruzelski, who succeeded Kania as party leader in October 1981, almost immediately began deploying special military detachments around the country to maintain order. This process culminated with the declaration of martial law on the night of 12–13 December and the transfer of governmental power to a Military Council of National Salvation.

While it is clear that the success of Jaruzelski's coup came as a great relief to the Brezhnev leadership, controversy still rages about Moscow's role in bringing it about. For years after the event, it was widely reckoned that Jaruzelski had acted under Soviet pressure and that the alternative to martial law would have been a Soviet-led intervention by the Warsaw Pact armies. Jaruzelski himself still defends this version of events (Jaruzelski, 1998), but others have cited Politburo documents suggesting that Jaruzelski actively lobbied for Soviet support and that he pressed Moscow to guarantee that it would intervene if the coup failed ([Doc. 13]; Kramer, 1998a: 5–6; Machiewicz, 1998: 40–2). There may be some truth to both versions: Boretskii (1993: 34) finds that some documents show Jaruzelski pleading for Soviet help (read: intervention), while others suggest that he thought matters could and should be sorted out by the Poles themselves. Historians also disagree about what Moscow would have done if the coup had failed. Mastny (1999) believes that it would have accepted a Solidarity government, provided that Soviet security interests were respected. Kramer (1995: 123) rejects this view, arguing that Moscow would have intervened to prevent Solidarity from taking power.

Whatever the truth surrounding the decision, Brezhnev and his colleagues could reasonably regard the outcome of the crisis as a success. While the Polish situation remained a drain on Soviet resources and a propaganda weapon for the West throughout the 1980s, Moscow had succeeded in achieving its principal aims with respect to the crisis. Moscow's chief concerns were to protect the integrity of the Warsaw Pact, to maintain Poland's pro-Soviet foreign policy alignment and to prevent the spread of the Solidarity 'infection' to neighbouring socialist states. Jaruzelski's coup enabled the USSR to avoid direct intervention in Polish affairs while achieving each of these aims (Kramer, 1995). If there was a price to be paid for this success in terms of western condemnation and new sanctions, the Kremlin could at least take comfort from the fact that the Reagan Administration's harsh response to martial law was creating tensions in the western camp.

CONFLICTING EXPECTATIONS AND THE FAILURE OF DÉTENTE

Support for détente had never been universal among US or Soviet elites. From the beginning, there had been stalwart opponents of the process in both capitals. They stood ready to use the conflicts of the mid-1970s to bolster their case. For many Americans, Soviet activism in Angola, the Horn and Afghanistan highlighted Moscow's determination to exploit American weakness and pursue its expansionist aims. The American reactions, in turn, provided their Soviet counterparts with further evidence of US commitment to the 'containment' policies of the Cold War. The activities of hawks on both sides were often mutually supportive: hardliners in each country pointed to the statements and actions of their counterparts in the other as evidence of aggressive intent. In any case, the anticipated economic benefits of détente for the USSR had failed to materialise, while US arms control policies were, in the opinion of Soviet hawks, designed to keep Moscow at a strategic disadvantage (Savel'ev & Detinov, 1995). As the decade wore on, the opponents of détente grew more vocal, the advocates more defensive and the waverers more inclined to scepticism about the viability of conciliatory policies.

The failure of détente was largely the product of the two superpowers' very different ideas about the nature and scope of détente itself. For Washington, the 'linkage' that existed between greater cooperation in East–West relations and Soviet policies in the Third World was crucial. Moscow, by contrast, never accepted that there was any contradiction between a reduction in East–West tensions and continuing competition for influence in the developing world. The Soviet Union sought to combine US-Soviet détente in bilateral and European issues with intervention in the Third World, a continuing military build-up and the exclusion of western influence from Eastern Europe. This policy, dubbed 'offensive détente' by Snyder (1991: 246–50), was ultimately self-defeating. Although by no means the only factor involved in the shift in American policy, it contributed to a hardening of the US stance vis-à-vis the Soviet Union and to the further rapprochement between Washington and Beijing. It also saddled the Soviet economy with a steadily growing defence burden at a time of declining economic performance, and it led to increasingly expensive geopolitical commitments abroad. By the early 1970s, the signs of 'imperial overstretch' were increasingly evident (Kennedy-Pipe, 1998: 166). Yet Brezhnev would have found it politically difficult to pursue a less ambitious policy. As Anderson (1993) argues, the specific matrix of policies that constituted 'offensive détente' was the outcome of a bargaining process among key leaders and institutional interests. The tensions and contradictions that characterised these policies were not simply the result of Brezhnev's inability to face painful trade-offs among competing goals; they were the product of the tactical compromises that emerged from this process of elite bargaining.

The differing Soviet and US perceptions of détente reflected their different positions in the international system. Although the structure of that system was basically bipolar, it was essentially an asymmetrical bipolarity (Wohlforth, 1994/95). The United States had emerged from the Second World War as a global hegemon: in economic, political and military terms, it faced no rivals on a *global* scale. Soviet policy represented a challenge to this hegemony. This reality was not always evident to all the participants. Both US and Soviet policy-makers in the 1970s tended to exaggerate both the extent of American decline and the strength of the Soviet challenge. In the wake of Watergate, Vietnam and 'stagflation', the United States neither looked nor felt like a hegemon, especially when faced with apparent Soviet advances in the Third World and the growing economic challenge from its own allies in Europe and Asia. Yet even during the mid-1970s, the global superpower competition was unequal. The United States was the richer power and it had the richer allies. It was the prime beneficiary of the three-way balance that had emerged with China's opening to the West. Militarily, its power-projection capabilities exceeded those of its rival, and it enjoyed the benefit of forward basing all around the periphery of the Soviet bloc.

This difference in relative position was reflected in a corresponding difference in the two powers' ambitions. The United States was a *status quo* power, committed to maintaining the established international order. The USSR, by contrast, was a *revisionist* state globally but a *status quo* state with respect to Europe, where its principal aim was to secure the post-war settlement. For Moscow, therefore, East–West détente reflected the commitment of both powers to preserving the post-war order in Europe but did not preclude competition elsewhere. To US policy-makers the Soviet distinction between East–West détente and competition elsewhere appeared arbitrary and self-serving – an attempt to reap the benefits of superpower cooperation without paying a price for it. For the Kremlin, the distinction was neither arbitrary nor without historical precedent. In the decades prior to the First World War, the European great powers had likewise drawn a distinction between Europe and the rest of the world. Alliances contracted in Europe did not commit the parties to support each other in colonial crises, and the management of colonial disputes in the pre-war period highlighted the unwillingness of the powers to provoke a European war over conflicts in Africa or the Orient (Martel, 1986: 53–67; Joll, 1992: 174–98). Moscow was not alone in drawing a distinction between Europe and the rest of the world: so did many of Washington's European allies.

For Soviet leaders, this distinction was entirely consonant with their understanding of the causes of détente. They believed détente to be irreversible, because it reflected 'a fundamental shift in the balance of forces in the Soviet Union's favour' (Roberts, 1999: 64). This shift was both cause and consequence of the USSR's growing global role. In other words, Soviet leaders were convinced that both détente in East–West relations and the Soviet Union's increasing activism in the Third World were products of the growth of Soviet power, mainly military power. The achievement of strategic parity with the United States and the expansion of Soviet power-projection capabilities had established the Soviet Union as an equal partner of the United States in managing world affairs. This made it only natural that the USSR would become increasingly active in the Third World and that the United States would have to seek an accommodation with it. Soviet leaders expected détente to survive as long as the Soviet military power that they believed to underpin it was undiminished. They reasoned that the United States, having lost its military superiority, could not risk a return to confrontation. They were wrong.

AFTER DÉTENTE

The failure of détente and the onset of the 'second Cold War' thus came as an unwelcome surprise to Brezhnev and his colleagues. In Roberts's (1999: 64) view, their faith in the irreversibility of détente 'blinkered Moscow's perception of the contribution made by its own actions to [its] gradual erosion'. To some extent, this faith was justified: the second Cold War never matched the bitterness of the early phases of the first, nor did the USSR find itself as vulnerable in the early 1980s as it had been in the early 1960s. However tough his rhetoric, Ronald Reagan did not possess the strategic superiority that Truman, Eisenhower and Kennedy had enjoyed. While the rhetoric of the Reagan Administration did indeed worry the Kremlin, prompting genuine fears of American aggression, the United States continued to abide by the still unratified SALT II agreement. Despite talk of 'rollback', no serious attempt was made to challenge Soviet hegemony in Eastern Europe, and Washington's most provocative actions were reserved for areas of secondary importance to the USSR, such as Grenada and Nicaragua. In the Middle East, where the vital interests of the two powers intersected and where a serious confrontation would have been extremely dangerous, both states acted with a measure of restraint. In any case, the Soviet leadership never really acknowledged that détente was dead. Brezhnev himself was too closely identified with the policies of détente for it to be seen to have failed. Faced with what seemed to be the unremitting hostility of the new administration in Washington, Moscow turned its attention increasingly towards Europe, seeking both trade opportunities to offset the effects of the sanctions imposed by the United States over Afghanistan and Poland, and support for its efforts to moderate the US stance on arms control issues.

With respect to the latter, the focus shifted from strategic to the intermediate-range nuclear forces deployed in Europe, as the terms of SALT II continued to set the parameters for the two superpowers' development of their strategic arsenals. The key Soviet concern here was NATO's December 1979 decision to deploy 108 Pershing-2 missiles and 464 'Tomahawk' ground-launched cruise missiles in an effort to offset the Soviet deployments of SS-20 intermediate-range missiles. Prior to the decision, Brezhnev had indicated to German Chancellor Helmut Schmidt that Moscow might limit its future SS-20 deployments if NATO did not proceed with the Pershing-2/ cruise deployment. Indeed, at one point he had even offered to destroy some SS-20s. The United States insisted that *all* the SS-4s, SS-5s and SS-20s be withdrawn in return for dropping the new deployments – the so-called 'zero option'. This was more than Moscow could accept. Many in the Soviet leadership doubted whether Soviet restraint in this area would be reciprocated; at best, they reckoned, the West was trying to secure the removal of Soviet missiles in return for nothing more than the abandon-ment of a planned future deployment (Kornienko, 1995: 241–2). With the talks stalemated from late 1981, the USSR devoted increasing attention to the growing peace movement in Western Europe, which opposed the new NATO deployments. The successful campaign against the neutron bomb in the 1970s gave some grounds for hoping that the anti-INF campaign, which Moscow covertly supported, would succeed. The protests did place a number of European governments under considerable pressure and prompted them in turn to press the United States to adopt a more conciliatory stance, but they were ultimately unable to prevent the deployments.

When Brezhnev died in November 1982, US-Soviet relations were at their lowest ebb in twenty years, with no sign of a thaw in sight. Brezhnev's détente policies had come to nothing. Yet hindsight should not now obscure the fact that, at the time of his death, Brezhnev and his colleagues had little reason to regard his foreign policy record as a failure. While a few observers were already then beginning to detect signs of serious imperial overstretch on the part of the USSR (Collins, 1981), the USSR's international position still looked strong. Poland was once again under control, and the Solidarity phenomenon had not triggered any 'contagion' effect within the Bloc. Afghanistan remained a drain on Soviet resources, but Soviet leaders do not seem to have doubted that they could engineer a satisfactory outcome. To the West, there was evidence of mounting tension between the United States and its European allies, and, with the US economy deep in recession, Ronald Reagan looked like a probable one-term president. Brezhnev died believing he and his colleagues had made the Soviet Union a world power. Few imagined then that this achievement would be wiped away within a decade.

CHAPTER SIX

ECONOMIC POLICY UNDER BREZHNEV AND KOSYGIN

The early achievements of the Soviet command economy were impressive, especially if one overlooks the costs involved – as the Soviet leaders themselves in fact did. For decades, official Soviet growth rates outstripped those of the West, and even independent estimates suggested that the USSR's was a very fast-growing economy. The system's resilience during the Second World War, the speed of post-war reconstruction and the obvious successes of such priority sectors as space exploration were enough to convince Soviet leaders of its essential soundness. For a time, these achievements – especially the apparent technical edge demonstrated by the Soviet space programme's early triumphs – even convinced many in the West that the system might be capable of producing superior performance.

Such perceptions may now appear absurd. Viewed from a post-Soviet perspective, the failure of the Soviet economic system looks like a foregone conclusion, and it is easy to forget how differently things looked in the early 1960s. Yet the essential conservatism of the Brezhnev leadership with respect to the institutional architecture of the centrally planned economy can only be understood in light of the economic successes of the early post-war decades. Throughout the Brezhnev era, the basic institutions of the Stalinist economic system were left untouched, although there were numerous attempts to refine them. The initial reform package launched by Kosygin in 1965 was followed by a steady stream of reorganisations and *ad hoc* measures that prompted Gertrude Schroeder (1979) to write of 'the Soviet economy on a treadmill of "reforms"'.

SOVIET INDUSTRY UNDER THE KOSYGIN REFORMS AND AFTER

Stalin's successors were not unaware of the defects of the command economy. There was real concern about its inefficiencies and, in particular, its tendency to stifle innovation. Academic economists debated possible reforms more or less continuously from the mid-1950s. Khrushchev's preference for administrative reorganisations and party activism meant that economic reform, though much discussed, was not attempted until after his removal (Tompson, 2000). In September 1965, the new leadership reversed the most significant of Khrushchev's economic innovations, the so-called *sovnarkhoz* reform of 1957. Khrushchev had abolished the centralised branch ministries that had dominated the Stalinist economic system and replaced them with a system of territorially based 'Councils of the National Economy', or *sovnarkhozy*. The ostensible aim of the reform was to improve the coordination of planning among different economic sectors and to eliminate waste and duplication that arose from the branch ministries' pursuit of *de facto* autarky – known in Soviet parlance as 'departmentalism'. Instead of managing individual branches on a national level, as the ministries had done, the *sovnarkhozy* were organised along territorial lines. It soon became apparent that the 'localism' of the *sovnarkhozy* was a bigger problem than the departmentalism of the ministries – in some cases, neighbouring provinces became involved in 'trade wars' with one another.

It was thus no surprise that Khrushchev's successors moved relatively swiftly to return to something like the ministerial system of the Stalin period. The only major difference between the structure created in 1965 and the pre-1957 system was the role assigned in the post-Khrushchev period to the State Committee for Material and Technical Supply (Gossnab), which assumed functions previously assigned to ministerial supply departments. Planning functions, which had been dispersed among a number of agencies, were reconcentrated in a powerful USSR State Planning Committee (Gosplan).

The resurrection of the ministerial system coincided with the so-called 'Kosygin reforms', which aimed to give enterprise managers greater independence from the newly reconstituted ministries while encouraging them to pay more attention to cost and profit. Managerial powers were enhanced and the number of compulsory plan indicators was reduced. The reform package included the introduction of payment for capital, bonus funds for enterprises, sales targets (to counter the accumulation of excessive stocks of unsold goods) and the decentralisation of some investment decisions. Enterprises were also to be amalgamated to form larger units. Prices were recalculated on the basis of cost plus a percentage of the value of capital assets, a formula intended to correspond to Marx's price of production (Schroeder, 1979: 324–9). Over time, 'trade in the means of production' among enterprises was to emerge, a gradual elimination of the administered system of allocating supplies (Nove, 1989: 367). Unfortunately, the reform package was from the outset fraught with contradictions and many of the changes were never implemented. These were the inevitable outcome of the political compromises the reformers had had to reach with more conservative elements in the leadership. Thus, the traditional emphasis on basic plan indicators was retained alongside attempts to increase the role of value indicators such as profit in the regulation of enterprise behaviour. As Mau observes, the fundamental ideas behind the reform were put forward by economists of a strongly reformist orientation, but the drafting of the actual measures fell to rather more moderate officials, and implementation was left to officials who were generally unenthusiastic about reform and often hostile to it (Mau, 1996: 23).

Not surprisingly, therefore, the Kosygin reforms had come to nothing by 1970. They fell victim not only to bureaucratic resistance but also to the underlying logic of the system as a whole. Bureaucratic resistance reflected both the self-interest of officials involved in industrial management and a basic inconsistency of the reform itself: ministerial and party functionaries were still responsible for plan fulfilment in their domains. They were thus expected to accept a reduction in their authority over enterprises for whose results they would nevertheless be held accountable. This they under-standably resisted (Hoffman & Laird, 1982: 44–5). The opposition of party officials, moreover, reflected Brezhnev's own views: he remained strongly committed to party activism in economic management and was sceptical of Kosygin's reforms (Shelest, 1995: 248; Suny, 1998: 423). Some of his former colleagues argue that Brezhnev effectively tried to sabotage imple-mentation of the reforms (Baibakov, 1991; Voronov, 1991).

The reforms were inconsistent in other ways as well. Schemes devised to link managerial bonuses and other incentive funds to indicators like profitability and sales were ineffective, largely because bonuses still depended above all on plan fulfilment, and in particular on the fulfilment of gross output targets, which were often defined in quantitative rather than value terms. Kontorovich (1988) argues that many of the microeconomic effects of the reform were perverse. The greater weight attached to the profit target, together with the reduction in the number of products covered by output targets, encouraged managers to increase profits by inflating prices and producing a more limited range of more expensive products. The result was a worsening of the mismatch between product mix and consumer demand. Technical innovation may also have fallen victim to the defects of the reforms. 'Innovation bonuses' were dwarfed by the bonuses awarded for 'the main results of economic activity' (i.e. output targets), and the pro-portion of bonuses awarded for innovation actually fell sharply after the reform was introduced.

In Kontorovich's view, these specific problems reflected a more fundamental problem with the Kosygin reforms: their fundamental incompatibility with the logic of the centrally planned economy. For all its flaws, the Soviet system had an internal logic of its own, which the reforms contradicted. In a system in which supply and demand were regulated by planning, input/output balances were crucial, and any reform that removed resources from planners' control created uncertainty and jeopardised the central balancing of inputs against outputs. The proposal to develop a demand-driven wholesale trade among enterprises was thus bound to fail. The amalgamation of enterprises into larger economic units, by contrast, made balancing easier. It was thus entirely compatible with the dominant logic of the system and became a permanent feature of it. Indeed, the next major attempt to reform industrial management, in 1973, involved the consolidation of many industrial enterprises and R&D institutions into larger production associations and scientific-production associations. The formation of such multi-enterprise complexes had first been mooted as part of the Kosygin reforms in 1965. The principal aim of this initiative was to accelerate technological progress by better integrating research and development with actual production and to rationalise production by concentrating responsibility for the production of specific goods. It was also expected that such multi-enterprise corporations would be more financially independent and thus reduce the drain of subsidies from the state budget. Some associations did in fact improve production within their domains, but the gains from elimination of duplication and increased concentration and specialisation were largely of a one-off character.

Sustained improvement would have required a new style of man-agement altogether, which mergers alone could not provide, as well as measures to reduce autarky and eliminate the incompatibility of incentives at different levels of economic administration (Gorlin, 1976: 187). However, economic policy was moving in the opposite direction. A package of 'reforms' adopted in 1974 increased centralisation, with the imposition of a multiplicity of obligatory targets and indicators from above, including 'normed value added' (Nove, 1989: 368). Normed value added was intended to focus attention on an enterprise's own processing of its inputs; its effect in practice, however, was to encourage over-processing and the overuse of labour and capital. In any case, the system remained oriented to gross output, with little regard for cost or quality. Further tinkering followed in 1979, but the effect of these changes – which were intended to simplify measures of success – was to increase the number of indicators managers faced and the administrative burdens on both managers and bureaucrats in the ministries and planning organs (Bornstein, 1985).

THE LIMITS OF REFORM

One of the major weaknesses of the original Kosygin reforms was the failure to tackle the issue of price formation, without which no attempt to introduce market efficiencies into the Soviet system could get very far. The 1965 reforms were accompanied by a wide-ranging recalculation of producer prices, which was intended to eliminate some obvious absurdities and free some sectors, like timber, from the systematic losses imposed by a structure of prices that discriminated against them (Nove, 1989: 367). However, Kosygin flatly rejected any tinkering with the actual *mechanism* of price formation: prices continued to be set centrally and did not reflect relative scarcities (Nekrasova & Degtev, 1994: 589–90). Yet it made no sense to use profits as an indicator of efficiency when prices reflected neither demand nor need. In the absence of economically meaningful prices, concepts such as cost and profit were statistical artefacts, devoid of real economic significance. Relaxing administrative controls and encouraging managers to act on the basis of price and profit signals, therefore, was as likely to reduce allocative efficiency as to increase it. Moreover, to the extent that the price changes adopted in 1965 had any economic content at all, their cost-plus basis gave firms no real incentive to cut costs (Nekrasova & Degtev, 1994: 592). On the contrary, since profit was often calculated as a percentage of costs, the pursuit of profit encouraged higher costs.

The second reason for the ultimate failure of reform efforts was the failure to apply the ultimate economic penalties for poor performance: closure, in the case of enterprises, and unemployment in the case of workers. This reflected the regime's fear of the social and political consequences of breaking its implicit social contract with its subjects. As White (1986), Hauslohner (1987) and Cook (1992, 1993) have argued, the regime's accommodation with the populace rested on an implicit bargain: the state provided such economic benefits as job security, relative income equality, free housing, free medical care, and generous social welfare provision in return for quiescence and compliance. The economic system performed poorly for Soviet citizens as consumers in part because it demanded so little from them as producers. As one common saying put it, 'we pretend to work, and they pretend to pay us'. Over time, deteriorating economic performance eroded the regime's ability to sustain its side of the bargain and thus undermined popular support for it. Yet the reverse was also true: as Hauslohner observes, the regime's commitment to maintaining the contract was a major contributor to declining economic performance. The economic reforms which might over the long term have corrected this situation would have required the authorities to renege on elements of the contract. So although radical proposals for reform were debated, they were never adopted.

Nowhere is this more evident than in the search for a solution to the problem of redundant labour. The Soviet system presented managers with numerous incentives to hoard labour – just as they hoarded any other inputs. As labour force growth slowed, managers' tendency to keep more workers on the books than they really needed became an increasingly serious problem. Solving this problem required creating incentives for managers to reveal – and part with – their 'reserves' of excess labour. Such attempts foundered on the regime's unwillingness to countenance open un-employment and on planners' readiness to withdraw the rewards extended to enterprises which sought to reduce employment and boost productivity. In 1967, the Shchekino Chemical Plant was allowed to retain its full wage fund while reducing its workforce (by voluntary means). The result was a 15% decline in employment and a doubling of productivity. However, attempts to extend the Shchekino system failed to produce substantial or durable improvements. As Harrison (2002) points out, the key problem was that the bargain involved was time-inconsistent. Enterprises were promised that they would retain their wage funds intact provided they fulfilled their output plans. However, once enterprises had acted to reduce labour and increase productivity, planners had an incentive to renege on this promise. Continuous changes to the rules governing the system generally enabled planners to do exactly that; the plants were left to carry on at peak productivity levels, meeting plan targets without benefit of their former labour reserves.

While it is easy to condemn the Brezhnev leadership's commitment to the maintenance of the 'contract', it is now clear that its successors were not notably successful in their attempts to revise its terms. Soviet leaders in the late 1980s ultimately proved unwilling or unable to abrogate the social contract. Faced with the consequences of making good on its threat to close chronic loss-makers and reduce job security, the Gorbachev leadership retreated, choosing bailouts over bankruptcy. The only major element of the contract that it did abandon was price stability, but this was, as Cook notes, an unintended consequence of reformist policies rather than the result of a comprehensive, rationalising price reform (Cook, 1992: 37–52).

SOVIET AGRICULTURE IN THE BREZHNEV ERA

Like Khrushchev, Brezhnev sought both to enhance the performance of the perennially weak agricultural sector and to give the country's long-suffering peasantry a better deal. The need to address the plight of the peasantry was clear: despite the steps taken by Khrushchev, roughly three-quarters of collective farm workers lived below the officially defined poverty line in the early 1960s and about one-quarter were also below the officially defined subsistence minimum. Rural poverty presented a practical as well as a moral problem, moreover, since it encouraged the flight to the towns of the most productive elements of the rural workforce (McCauley, 1998: 376). The new leadership therefore continued the process of integrating peasants into the wider economy and society. Farm workers were given internal passports, which had been taken from them in 1938, and other forms of discrimination imposed under Stalin were removed, making peasants on collective farms eligible for the same social security and pension arrangements as urban workers [*Doc. 14*]. By the 1970s, rural wages were only slightly below those of urban industrial workers and were often supplemented by small-scale private agricultural activity – although differences in the availability of consumer goods meant that rural workers often had less opportunity than their urban counterparts to spend their earnings.

Soon after coming to power, the new leaders overturned a number of Khrushchev's pet schemes in the sector. In March 1965, the Territorial-Production Associations (TPAs) Khrushchev had created in agriculture in 1962 were abolished and the old network of district-level party and soviet bodies in rural areas was reconstituted. The Ministry of Agriculture was given back many of the managerial functions that Khrushchev had stripped from it. The TPAs, which had generally encompassed several districts, had been intended to consolidate and rationalise the middle level of agricultural management. In fact, they had irritated district-level officials, on whose prerogatives they had encroached, while duplicating the work of a number of other central and provincial bodies, with which they were often at cross-purposes. For the farms, the resulting tangle of jurisdictions and lines of authority simply reduced what little autonomy they still enjoyed. The abolition of the TPAs was thus good news for state and collective farms, especially as it was allied to a number of other measures, including sharp increases in procurement prices, the fixing of procurement plans for longer periods, and the reduction of planned assignments to manageable levels. Farms were granted more freedom to organise their affairs within the framework of plan assignments. There were limits on the number of plan indicators imposed from above, and payment for above-plan production was increased (Nekrasova & Degtev, 1994: 587–8). Khrushchev-era restrictions on private livestock were eased, and the general attitude towards peasant households' private economic activity softened.

The Brezhnev leadership made a deliberate break with Khrushchev's approach to agriculture in two important ways. First, the new leaders accepted the need to invest heavily in agriculture. Khrushchev's constant search for quick, inexpensive solutions to agricultural problems had underlain a number of ill-advised initiatives – not least those advanced by the charlatan Lysenko. Secondly, Khrushchev's successors promised an end to the hurried, 'campaignist' approach that had marked his agricultural policies. Khrushchev's desire for quick, cheap, spectacular results had made for tremendous instability in policy, as one scheme after another was launched with inadequate preparation and then abandoned as soon as it failed to produce the hoped-for miracles. Data on Soviet investment patterns bear witness to the new leaders' commitment to agriculture. Its share in total investment rose from 19.6% in 1961–65 to 23.2% in 1966–70 and 26.2% in 1976–80. Allocations to agro-industrial sectors such as fertiliser production accounted for a further 5% or so of investment in 1961–65, rising to 8% in 1976–80. In absolute terms, investment in the agricultural sector nearly tripled over the period, rising from Rb48.6bn in the first half of the 1960s to Rb131.5bn a decade later (Nove, 1989: 363).

The initial results of the new policies looked encouraging: despite large fluctuations from year to year, the basic trend in agricultural output was steadily upwards, and the rate of increase, while falling over time, was faster in the USSR than in most other countries, both developing and developed. Indeed, the Soviet Union became the world's largest wheat producer in the 1970s (though not the largest producer of all grains combined). Massive grain purchases abroad were dictated principally by the desire to increase supplies of animal feed, and thus enhance Soviet diets, rather than by problems with the supply of grains for primary human consumption. Nevertheless, agricultural performance was far from satisfactory, as the sector proved unable to use efficiently the massive investments being made in it. Indeed, Easterly and Fischer (1995) concluded that the rate of productivity growth in Soviet agriculture averaged around –4% per annum during 1970–90. Even the official data show a steady decline in productivity growth and return on investment. The failure to raise agricultural production in line with household incomes, which were increasing rapidly, led to a growing gap between free market and state prices for food and, consequently, to the unavailability of an increasing range of basic foodstuffs through state outlets at state-determined prices. Prices in the collective farmers' markets in 1965 were about 35% higher than in state retail outlets; by 1970 they were 54.5% higher; by 1978 they were double the official state prices; and by 1984 they had reached a level 120% above the prices in the state retail network (Nove, 1989: 372).

A further overhaul of agricultural administration was launched in the context of the much trumpeted 'food programme' of 1982, but it did not involve any serious break with central planning or administrative allocation. In an effort to reduce the wasteful use of resources by service organisations which were supposed to support agricultural production, the regime created new District Agricultural-Production Associations (RAPOs), which brought together state and collective farms with up- and down-stream enterprises linked to agriculture, including food-processing enterprises and wholesale trade organisations. This crude attempt at greater vertical integration in the sector was a failure, as it did little more than render the already unwieldy structure of agricultural management still more complex. Farms still complained that they had too little control over their own affairs and too little leverage vis-à-vis organisations that were supposed to 'serve' them (Nove, 1989: 366). More promising, in theory at least, was the attempt to introduce collective work groups (brigades) with work-sharing and revenue-sharing arrangements. The decision to link pay to results for smaller groups of peasants working autonomously within the brigade system was intended to improve peasants' incentives to produce. The shift to the brigade system had little success, however, largely because local party officials feared the reconstitution of family farming within the framework of the brigades.

Brezhnev's rural policies extracted a high and steadily growing price from the rest of the economy. The regime's inability to achieve substantial long-term improvements in agricultural productivity, coupled with its unwillingness to adopt food price increases to offset the rise in procurement prices, meant that the gap between retail supply and demand for food widened, leading to increasing reliance on imports. Imports, in turn, increased the costs to the state of holding down food prices. The price of a bushel of US Hard Red Winter Wheat imported into the USSR rose from $1.54 to $4.45 between 1970 and 1980, while the price of a kilo of bread remained unchanged, at its 1955 level of 20 kopecks (Moody, 1991). By 1979, direct subsidies to agriculture had topped the Rb23bn mark; a further Rb4bn was paid to suppliers of industrial inputs to the farm sector, to offset the low prices they were required to charge for their output. Yet gross agricultural output during 1976–79 averaged less than Rb100bn per annum (Nove, 1989: 362–3). Nevertheless, food-price increases and local-ised supply problems remained a source of hardship for ordinary Soviet citizens, occasionally giving rise to riots and other disorders in major industrial centres such as Sverdlovsk, Dnepropetrovsk and Gorkii.

BLIND SPOTS IN ECONOMIC POLICY AND THE 'OBSESSION WITH GROWTH'

The economic policies of the Brezhnev era reflected the leadership's con-tinuing focus on what had been the central economic policy priority of both Stalin and Khrushchev: rapid output growth. The Stalinist command economy, after all, had been created to facilitate the rapid industrialisation of the Soviet Union, and the desire to overtake the developed capitalist economies was a major priority. This reflected both the perceived need to demonstrate the superiority of the socialist model and the conviction that rapid growth was needed to ensure Soviet security in a world dominated by hostile capitalist powers (Gros & Steinherr, 1995: 56–76). Growth also provided planners with a relatively clear, simple indicator on which to focus their efforts. Soviet growth, however, was defined in terms of physical quantities rather than value. Efficiency and quality, both more difficult for planners to assess adequately, were therefore sacrificed to quantitative growth. It could hardly have been otherwise, given the rejection of scarcity prices and consumer sovereignty, which alone could have provided mean-ingful information about quality and cost. Managers, subject to neither the profit motive nor competition, were free to pursue the bonuses awarded for plan fulfilment with little regard for quality, cost or the potential for innovation and improvement.

What was true for enterprise managers was also true for national-level planners and administrators: the obsession with growth led to a disregard for costs, while the price system blinded policy-makers to the true opportunity costs of their choices. This meant that the system coped rather badly with environmental degradation and other externalities, which, in theory, it should have been able to address far better than a decentralised market system. The result was the development of industries that were spectacularly wasteful in their use of resources. Shubin (1997: 75) argues that the Kosygin reforms actually made the situation worse, since managers often used their new freedoms to cut environmental corners.

This obsession with the growth of physical output caused Soviet leaders to neglect those activities which could not be easily measured in terms of discrete units of output, such as the infrastructure for transportation, distribution and storage, as well as the services sector as a whole. Insufficient account was taken of the provision of resources for repair, maintenance and project completion (Skidelsky, 1996: 107). This was true, too, of the Soviet Union's attempts at greater integration with the international economy. Soviet leaders attached a very high priority to importing advanced western production technologies but, with few exceptions, they seem to have been oblivious to the need to import western management techniques. Not for the first time in Russia's history, its rulers sought to import western achievements without importing the institutions and values that had made such achievements possible – institutions and values that were, to their minds, dangerous. Ironically, these blind spots reduced output growth as well as quality and efficiency. Lack of concern with distribution contributed to hoarding behaviour by managers anxious to ensure that supply bottlenecks did not threaten plan fulfilment. Thus stocks consistently grew faster than output, immobilising ever larger quantities of resources for longer and longer periods. Failure to pay more attention to project completion lay at the root of the notorious problem of *dolgostroi* (literally 'long-build') – the proliferation of large, unfinished construction projects, often running a decade or more behind schedule (Nove, 1989: 373). In 1972, Kosygin reported that the volume of investment immobilised in unfinished construction projects had trebled in the preceding four years (Edmonds, 1983: 83). Over time, this lack of attention to distribution, repair and project completion was cumulative and reduced the marginal productivity of investment spending (Skidelsky, 1996: 107).

Many of these projects would have made no economic sense even if completed, for, as Graham (1993) has shown, the authorities continued to invest heavily in economically inefficient, environmentally damaging megaprojects like the BAM. At a more prosaic level, the blindness to cost and the obsession with increasing physical output were in large measure responsible for both the increasingly dangerous methods employed in the expansion of nuclear power generation and the 'crisis amid plenty' described by Gustafson (1989) as characteristic of the Soviet energy sector as a whole. The supply-driven approach of the Brezhnev era led to steadily declining returns on investment, while the lack of attention to costs and demand led to high costs, spectacular waste, the premature depletion of many fields, and periodic (albeit sometimes localised) crises that could not be solved but instead had to be suppressed through crash programmes of investment in the coal, oil and gas sectors. Nor were the country's hydrocarbons sectors unique. As growth slowed in the 1970s and early 1980s, their story was all too typical of what was happening to the system as a whole.

CHAPTER SEVEN

ECONOMIC PERFORMANCE

The image of the Brezhnev era as a 'time of stagnation', which came to dominate Soviet and western perceptions of the period in the late 1980s, was above all rooted in the Brezhnev leadership's failure to deliver satisfactory economic performance. The economic conservatism of Brezhnev and his colleagues was blamed for steadily declining growth rates, falling productivity of both capital and labour and a growing gap between the regime's ever-more-modest five-year plans and actual economic performance.

The causes of this slow but steady decline in economic performance are still far from completely understood. Brezhnev's critics claimed that his unhappy economic legacy was largely a product of his foreign policy agenda. Strategic parity with the United States and the projection of Soviet power to such far-flung corners of the globe as Angola came at a high economic price. This 'burden-of-empire' hypothesis was becoming the conventional wisdom in many quarters even before Brezhnev's death and it remains the most common view today. It is also seriously incomplete. While there is no denying that Brezhnev's ambitious foreign and military policies imposed high costs on the economy, the poor performance of the later Brezhnev years was rooted in systemic weaknesses that grew more pronounced over time. It was Brezhnev's misfortune to be in power as the Soviet economic system was outliving its usefulness. It was the misfortune of his subjects that neither Brezhnev nor his colleagues knew how to arrest the process of economic decline. Nor, we now know, did his successors.

GROWTH PERFORMANCE UNDER BREZHNEV AND KOSYGIN

Although the USSR was never subject to the business cycles which afflicted western economies – a point Soviet officials were fond of making – it experienced something at least equally disturbing: a long-term secular decline in growth rates. On the official Soviet data, the average rate of growth of net material product[1] fell from 10.2% in the 1950s to 7.0% in the 1960s, 4.9% in the 1970s and just 3.6% in the 1980s (see Table 7.1). Moreover, these estimates were clearly very high of the mark, probably by a factor of at least two; growth rates for the 'priority' sectors of most concern to the Brezhnev leadership were over-stated by a factor of more than three (Eydelman, 1998: 76). External analyses differ as to details but agree that the divergence between official and actual performance *increased* over time, not least because the effects of many of the system's information problems were cumulative. In particular, price increases were systematically under-recorded, so that as much as 50–60% of the apparent increase in goods production during 1976–80 was actually the result of price inflation, not rising output (Nekrasova & Degtev, 1994). This was not an entirely unwelcome development, since it enabled the regime to conceal to some degree the real extent of the slowdown by focusing on the 'rouble value' of output. This showed a 75% increase over 1976–83, as against a mere 9% increase in gross production (McCauley, 1998: 373). The slowdown in growth was thus far more dramatic than it appeared. By the end of the 1970s, growth seemed to have stopped, and some estimates suggest that it was actually negative during 1978–82 (Khanin & Selyunin, 1987; Khanin, 1991; Harrison, 1993; Aganbegyan, 1988; Schroeder, 1995; Steinberg, 1990).

Table 7.1   Estimates of average annual growth

Period	Soviet estimates[a]	CIA estimates[b]	*Khanin[a]
1950–60	10.2%	5.2%	7.2%
1960–65	6.5%	4.8%	4.4%
1965–70	7.7%	4.9%	4.1%
1970–75	5.7%	3.0%	3.2%
1975–80	4.2%	1.9%	1.0%
1980–85	3.5%	1.8%	0.6%

[a] Net material product. [b] Gross national product at 1982 factor cost

Source: Harrison (2002: 40)

*G. I. Khanin is a leading Russian economist whose alternative estimates of Soviet growth performance played a crucial role in shaping Soviet debates on economic reform during the late 1980s.

[1]   Soviet growth was calculated in terms of 'net material product' (NMP) rather than 'gross domestic product' (GDP), which is commonly employed in the rest of the world. Since NMP omitted most services, and since Soviet planners likewise tended to neglect the service sector, this had the effect of exaggerating growth rates.

At the same time, it was becoming increasingly evident that the techno-logical gap between the USSR and the most advanced Western economies, which for a time seemed to have been narrowing, had begun to widen again. As the dissident physicist Andrei Sakharov (1968) argued, the USSR was only overtaking US production levels in traditional industries that were, in fact, of declining importance. In fields such as petrochemicals, computers and automation of production, it was falling further behind [*Doc. 18*]. Sakharov was not alone in worrying about this: official concern was expressed to the Central Committee and, in suitably watered-down form, even to the Soviet public (*Pravda*, 13 January 1970). The Soviet system was proving incapable of coping with the challenges of the so-called 'third industrial revolution' – the move into computers and other high-tech areas. Gustafson (1981: 138–9) crystallised the problem as follows. The Soviet economic system was best at delivering a small number of large-scale, customised projects and/or a large number of highly standardised systems. It was worst at producing a large number of custom-made systems adapted to their settings – whether in the field of architecture, engineering or computer software. Hence the absurdity of nuclear power plants built according to manuals specifying every detail of construction and operation, without reference to groundwater levels, population density, seismic activity or local topography (Graham, 1993: 89–93).

While the long-term decline in growth rates pre-dated Brezhnev's accession, it was during the Brezhnev era that it became so pronounced as to cause real concern in the Soviet Union. As Harrison (2002) observes, Soviet national income and consumption rose in *per capita* terms by roughly 50% and 70% during the 18 years of Brezhnev's rule, but around three-quarters of the improvement in both indicators was achieved in the first half of the period. Up to about 1973, Soviet growth rates more or less kept up with West European rates of growth. Soviet output per capita from 1964 to 1973 remained at about half the average level for Western Europe, and both the USSR and the major West European states were growing faster than the United States. The declining trend in growth rates was no more pronounced than in Western Europe and could easily be explained in terms of a return to trend following the high growth rates characteristic of the post-war recovery in both East and West. In this, Harrison follows Janossy (1971) in regarding the high growth rates of the 1950s and 1960s as the products of a prolonged post-war recovery that gave way gradually to a return to the pre-war trend. After 1973, Soviet growth rates fell below West European levels; the country ceased to close the output gap with the United States and began to fall further behind Western Europe.

THE FAILURE OF THE CENTRALLY PLANNED ECONOMY

This is not the place to attempt even a cursory summary of the voluminous literature on the defects of the Soviet economic system (for a good overview see Gros & Steinherr, 1995: 7–76). These were well known to western observers of the Soviet economy before October 1964, and Soviet economists and officials were aware of many of them as well. What requires explanation is not the system's imperfection, which was nothing new, but rather the steady and apparently irreversible deterioration in its performance over time.

Many western and Russian observers have cited the defence burden (Rowen & Wolf, 1989; Skidelsky, 1996), and there is little doubt that the cost of Brezhnev's ambitious foreign and defence policies was indeed a factor. It would appear that, by 1980, the USSR was spending more on defence than the United States, despite the fact that its economy was perhaps one-third the size of its rival's. Even the lowest recent estimates suggest that the USSR was devoting 15–17% of its GDP to defence (Schroeder, 1995), with some assessments pointing to a figure of 25–30% (Gros & Steinherr, 1995: 57). Because so much Soviet military expenditure was hidden and because the system of fixed prices served to understate the consumption of resources by the defence sector, Brezhnev and his colleagues are unlikely to have appreciated fully the economic cost of their policies. Nevertheless, they were not oblivious to the problem: as early as 1971 the General Secretary publicly admitted that economic growth would be faster were it not for the burden of defence expenditure. The 'defence-burden' explanation is 'morally' appealing, since it implies that, if Soviet leaders spent less on guns and more on butter, performance would have been better. However, this is only a part of the explanation and by no means the most important part. Indeed, several recent assessments find that the defence burden's contribution to declining growth performance was relatively modest (Easterly & Fischer, 1995; Harrison, 2002). The deeper causes must be sought in the system of central planning.

This system had two major strengths: it was an effective mechanism for the rapid, large-scale mobilisation of unutilised factors of production (raw materials, capital and labour), and it was reasonably effective when directed at a limited number of fairly basic goals (Gustafson, 1981: ch. 10). It was at its best when directed towards a single overriding goal, to which all other concerns were clearly subordinate – hence its fairly impressive performance during the Second World War. Its major weaknesses mirrored these strengths. While relatively successful as an engine of 'extensive' growth, based on factor mobilisation, the system was singularly ill suited to 'intensive' growth, based on increasing the efficiency with which the factors of production were employed. Yet after the initial mobilisational stages of

Soviet development were completed, further growth depended on just such gains in efficiency. Kosygin estimated that 80–85% of the increase in net material product envisaged by the Ninth Five-Year Plan would have to come from increases in productivity (Edmonds, 1983: 6). The pursuit of efficiency, however, was impeded by the system of fixed prices, which blinded economic agents to the true costs of their activities and rendered the pursuit of efficiency in any economically meaningful sense extremely problematic. The incentive structure facing managers, workers and economic administrators at every level continued to privilege quantitative targets over efficiency, quality or future value. Even those obvious inefficiencies that were evident in the Soviet context were often ignored. Thus it was that Soviet industry by the 1980s was consuming two to three times as much energy and raw materials per unit of output as the developed western states were, while producing goods of substantially lower quality.

The second major weakness of the system is implicit in what has just been said about the focus on quantitative targets: if it was useful for directing effort to the pursuit of a single overriding goal, it was extremely poor at coping with multiple goals and the trade-offs between them. Planners tried to deal with a multiplicity of goals by increasing the number of performance indicators, but however many performance indicators they might attempt to assign, the structure of bonuses and other incentives meant that economic agents could easily see which ones were worth pursuing and which were not. Moreover, the absence of scarcity prices meant that it was often impossible to make economically meaningful choices between alternative goals. The prices of apples and oranges, for example, were arbitrarily assigned and did not send any signal about the supply of, or demand for, either fruit and therefore gave no indication of whether it would be more profitable to produce one or the other. Since prices were arbitrary, the rouble could not function as a proper measure of value. In the absence of some such composite standard of value, it is impossible to compare things that are not fundamentally alike. Concepts like profit and return on investment were sometimes employed, but they were devoid of any real economic content.

In view of these weaknesses, it is hardly surprising that growth slowed as the system matured. In a real sense, Soviet central planning was at least partly a victim of its own success, unable to cope with the management of the increasingly complex economy that it had created. The Russian economist Vitalii Naishul' has argued that, as the number of commodities, technologies, enterprises and even hierarchies increased, planning 'from above' began to fail. The need to plan the production and allocation of millions of different products simply overwhelmed the information-processing capacities of the system. Increasing complexity was therefore mitigated via use of greater aggregation and more synthetic indicators. This made plan construction easier, but it made plan implementation harder, as inconsistencies and bottlenecks multiplied (Naishul', 1991; Zaslavskaya, 1984).

A third major problem was chronic short-termism. This was somewhat ironic, since the system's apologists viewed this as one of the major weaknesses of capitalism. In principle, planning was supposed to favour a focus on long-term developmental goals, since planners were free from pressures to generate a quick profit at the expense of long-term performance. In practice, managerial bonuses and other incentives all favoured the fulfilment of current plan targets. Economic agents therefore operated with short time horizons. This generated such behaviours as 'storming' – the habit of running equipment round-the-clock in the run-up to the end of the planning period so as to ensure plan fulfilment. In practice, storming meant raising costs, reducing quality, damaging equipment and wasting inputs, but it was nevertheless a rational strategy for Soviet managers. Planning deadlines also constituted a major barrier to innovation: any attempt at innovation, whether successful or not, was likely to disrupt production for a time, thereby putting the current plan at risk. Moreover, even a successful innovation would bring no more than a one-off reward to the enterprise – and it would thereafter result in tougher plan targets (Berliner, 1976). This was as much a deterrent to the diffusion of new technology and methods as to their development. Technologies imported from the West to Soviet plants generally remained confined to those plants and were rarely upgraded. These problems were nothing new in the Brezhnev era, but they mattered far more as economic growth came to depend more on efficiency and innovation, as opposed to the mobilisation of unutilised or under-utilised land, labour and capital.

These and other problems of the system were aggravated by the lack of any adequate feedback mechanism. The planning process created incentives at all levels for agents to conceal their true capabilities and exaggerate their resource requirements, while the price system meant that financial data provided no meaningful information about economic performance. At the same time, press censorship ensured that other channels for the airing of societal demands were severely constrained. The media and the economic system were both constructed to function chiefly as transmission belts for policy-makers' instructions and priorities and left little scope for any effective feedback. Perhaps the best analysis in this vein was that of von Beyme (1975), who examined the system in cybernetics terms, looking at the relationships among three major elements: inputs of information; outputs in the form of commands, policies and legislation; and a feedback loop to transmit information about the impact of outputs back to the core of the system. The system, von Beyme concluded, favoured outputs over inputs – what in cybernetics would be called 'oversteering'. In practical terms, this meant that Soviet leaders were victims of their own propaganda. While not unaware of the system's basic defects, they failed to grasp the depth of these problems, because they were in fact extremely ill informed about actual economic performance. They did not simple-mindedly believe official propaganda, but they did fail to grasp the extent to which even those indicators they thought reliable were systematically biased. Taken together with the fact that the gap between real and recorded growth seems to have been widening, this meant that the statistical information at the Soviet leaders' disposal was growing worse over time.

The maturity of the system posed a further problem for Brezhnev and his colleagues: by the 1980s much of the industrial capital stock was very old; most of it was technically out of date, and much of it was physically worn out as well. This was just one aspect of a larger problem, which also grew worse over time: the Soviet economy was an economy without exit. Plants were rarely closed, the service lives of machinery and equipment were far too long, and too little attention was paid to obsolescence. Reported scrappage rates (a proxy for replacement rates, which were not published) were so low for so long that many western economists believed them to be substantial under-estimates. Scrappage rates declined along with growth rates, reaching a post-war low in the early 1980s (Harmstone & Patackas, 1997). The lack of exit also impeded structural change, since it meant that established sectors, even in decline, continued to soak up investment and other resources that might have been devoted to the development of new industries. To the extent that it was capable of generating growth at all, the system tended to produce more of the same from year to year. The result was the over-development of basic industrial sectors and the under-development of most others. In structural terms, therefore, Soviet planners by 1980 had arguably created the world's largest and most advanced nineteenth-century economy.

The failure to replace ageing equipment was especially detrimental because labour-force growth was also rapidly declining (McCauley, 1998: 375). Since nothing could be done about labour-force growth except in the very long term, there was an acute need to substitute capital for labour. Easterly and Fischer (1995) argue that the inability to do this was the Achilles' heel of the Soviet economy. Indeed, they find that, if investment and human capital are controlled for, Soviet growth performance during the period 1960–89 was the worst in the world and that its relative performance grew worse over time. In other words, high rates of investment were required to sustain even declining rates of growth, because the problem of diminishing returns to capital was so acute. This led to a paradox. Although the basic industrialisation of the country had long been completed, growth rates for investment goods remained well above those for consumer goods and for services well into the 1980s (Hauslohner,

1987). The inefficiency of investment spending reflected, in part, the lack of exit mechanisms. Failing enterprises were subsidised rather than closed, and poor performance was seen as evidence of a need for investment, which meant that it was often rewarded.

DÉTENTE, FOREIGN TRADE AND THE 'SCIENTIFIC AND TECHNICAL REVOLUTION'

One of the main motives for the leadership's pursuit of détente with the West was economic. The Brezhnev era witnessed an unprecedented increase in the USSR's foreign trade activity. This was facilitated by two external developments that greatly increased Soviet export earnings – the tenfold rise in the price of gold in the early 1970s and the subsequent take-off of oil prices following the first 'oil shock' of 1973. This increase, however, was from such a small base that the USSR in the 1980s still came last in a ranking of 126 states by the contribution of exports to national income (Samuelson, 1990: 154). Nevertheless, the gold-and-hydrocarbons windfall, together with the revenues from rapidly rising arms sales to Arab states (a secondary effect of the oil price increases) and the western credits that became available as a result of the thaw in East–West relations, enabled the USSR to quadruple its imports of western capital goods from 1972 to 1976. However, in the absence of changes in the resource-allocation mechanism and managerial incentives, the utility of such imports was limited. Kotkin (2001: 16) argues that the oil windfall was ultimately damaging to economic performance, as it enabled the Soviet leadership to avoid needed economic reforms while sustaining a superpower competition it could ill afford.

The largely autarkic character of the Soviet system was, of course, nothing new, and the Brezhnev leadership did at least take the first halting steps to increase the country's engagement with the international economy. However, the USSR was ill equipped to profit from international economic links. The rejection of market prices and market relations meant that Soviet planners effectively had no economically meaningful way of assessing the actual or potential gains from trade. Nor were policy-makers interested in the gains from trade in the sense that an economist in a market system would understand the term. On the contrary, self-sufficiency remained a key value. Trade with the Soviet Union's satellites and allies was pursued chiefly with a view to fostering greater integration for political reasons, while trade with the West was largely about securing goods and technologies that the USSR could not produce on its own – especially investment goods that would further increase self-sufficiency in the long run. Exports were simply the price paid for such imports. Planners could not identify the most efficient bundle of goods to export in order to finance needed imports. Moreover, the cumbersome bureaucratic arrangements established to manage the state's foreign trade monopoly created numerous disincentives to export (Evangelista, 1996: 116–17; Shmelev & Popov, 1989: 221). The decision to forego the gains from international trade cost the USSR in terms of both static efficiency (the efficient allocation of resources at any given time) and dynamic efficiency (maximising growth over time). Soviet planners were largely blind to these losses, however, since they could only be comprehended in terms of scarcity prices. The institutional features that insulated the Soviet Union from the rest of the world economy effectively prevented both domestic agents from fully appreciating the costs of autarky (Evangelista, 1996).

The high priority attached to technology imports reflected Soviet policy-makers' belief in the potential of the so-called 'scientific and technological revolution', or STR – the term used in Soviet parlance to describe those phenomena associated in the West with such concepts as the 'third industrial revolution', the 'informational revolution' and 'post-industrial society'. Many Soviet observers confidently expected the STR to deliver sharp increases in both productivity and quality. Soviet observers had, since the late 1950s, paid increasing attention to the STR and the growing internationalisation of the world economy (Hoffman & Laird, 1982). However, Soviet discussions of the STR focused on the technology itself rather than on the social institutions that gave rise to it. Yet it was not *production* technologies that the USSR needed to acquire from the West so much as what Woodruff (2000) calls *transaction* technologies – ways of doing business, of managing economic relationships and enterprises. These, of course, are social constructs. Transplanting them into any society is far more complex than merely importing advanced machinery, and in the Soviet context such transplants were politically out of the question. As a result, the Soviet economy proved extremely poor at using and diffusing the technologies it imported, let alone developing them further. Thus, the confusion between the fruits of the third industrial revolution and the forces driving it meant that the hopes Soviet planners pinned on foreign trade and technology transfer were not, and could not be, realised.

LIVING STANDARDS AND HOUSEHOLD WELFARE

Despite deteriorating economic performance, living standards continued to rise steadily, if not spectacularly, throughout the Brezhnev era. The standard of living in the Soviet Union at the end of the Brezhnev era has been variously estimated at between one-fifth and one-third of the contemporary American level (Schroeder, 1987: 15; Birman, 1989: 2–3) but it does appear to have been rising, however slowly. Real wages rose steadily throughout the period, increasing by some 50% during 1967–77 alone. However, income data provide a poor indicator of living standards in the Soviet system, since a great deal depended on the availability of goods, which was highly variable, and there is considerable evidence to suggest that inflation during the Brezhnev years, while never acknowledged, was significant. Data on consumption patterns thus provide a better guide to real living standards.

These, too, point to a substantial and sustained rise in household welfare, albeit one that slowed markedly from the mid-1970s. Millar (1991: 191) estimates that the average Soviet household's standard of living roughly doubled between 1945 and 1970, while Harrison (2002) reckons that average consumption rose by some 70% during the Brezhnev era, although around three-quarters of this growth took place during 1964–72. Personal consumption growth in 1976–80 averaged less than half the rate recorded in 1966–70 and halved again after 1980, with the slowest growth recorded in such key areas as food, housing and recreation. Even Soviet sources acknowledged in the early 1980s that the food supply situation had worsened in comparison with the 1960s (Colton, 1986: 35). Nevertheless, while the rate of improvement in living standards slowed markedly, it did not stop altogether: even the 'alternative' statistics of Khanin (1996) show personal consumption rising during 1975–85, albeit at slow and falling rates – Khanin's estimate for 1981–85 is below 1% per annum.

Soviet diets, in particular, improved during the Brezhnev years. *Per capita* consumption of meat rose 40.5% between 1965 and 1980, while consumption of fish, vegetables and fruits rose by 39.7, 34.7 and 35.7% respectively. By contrast, the consumption of grain products and potatoes – long the staples of Soviet diets – fell by 11.5 and 23.2% respectively, as a wider range of products became regularly available. While the percentage increases in consumption of major food products during 1950–65 were very much higher than in 1965–80, this reflects the very low levels of consumption of the immediate post-war period. In absolute terms (kilogrammes *per capita* per year), the gains of the latter period are no less impressive. Soviet consumption of major consumer durables also rose impressively. The proportion of households owning a television rose from 24% in 1965 to 85% in 1980 and 96% in 1984. Some 86% of households owned a refrigerator by the end of 1980 (rising to 91% in 1984), up from just 11% in 1965. The corresponding figures for washing machines were 21% in 1965 and 70% in 1980 [*Doc. 14*]. Similar patterns can be observed with respect to other major consumer durables. The major exception was automobiles: only 9% of households owned their own cars by the end of the Brezhnev era (TsSU, 1976 and 1985).

These data, while subject to the same problems that afflict all Soviet economic data, broadly correspond to Soviet citizens' own perceptions of their circumstances. As Shlapentokh (1998) has argued forcefully, the notion that *perestroika* and the revolutionary upheavals that followed it were caused by popular dissatisfaction with living standards does not withstand serious scrutiny. On the contrary, it was the political opening of the late 1980s that generated the discontent, by changing Soviet consumers' frame of reference when evaluating their living standards and by arousing unrealistic expectations about how fast their standard of living would or could rise. This is not to say that Soviet people were uncritical of the system or satisfied with all aspects of their daily lives. Shortages of basic goods, queues for everyday necessities and the low quality of consumer goods were all sources of dissatisfaction – indeed, local food shortages triggered small-scale disturbances in a number of major cities. Nevertheless, such data as are available for the period to about 1987 suggest that the great majority of Soviet citizens, while not uncritical, were broadly satisfied with their lives, considered their living conditions 'normal' and accepted the regime's claims about the superiority of the Soviet way of life. These claims did not deny the higher levels of personal consumption found in the West but rather stressed the Soviet system's guarantee of greater equality and material security. Soviet people were constantly reminded that, in their society, unemployment was virtually unknown and crime far lower than in the developed capitalist countries. Broadly speaking, they believed that the Soviet way of life, while perhaps materially poorer, was morally and culturally superior to that found in the West [Doc. 22].

Shlapentokh's argument rests chiefly on survey data collected by Soviet researchers in the 1970s and 1980s and may therefore reflect respondents' fear of voicing discontent more than their true feelings about their circumstances. However, the picture they paint differs little from that found in western surveys of Soviet emigrés. These might naturally be expected to give a much less favourable evaluation of their life in the USSR. Yet surveys conducted in the late 1970s found very high levels of satisfaction with respondents' pre-emigration standard of living (Millar, 1987: 33). Moreover, the Soviet data do show that ordinary citizens were prepared to express discontent with particular issues, such as inadequate housing. They also tend to support Shlapentokh's views about rising expectations: discontent with housing, for example, actually began to rise in the post-Stalin period even as the authorities mounted a major residential construction drive (Shlapentokh, 1998: 36). Altogether, it is difficult to avoid the conclusion that, even as growth and technical change were slowing, Soviet citizens in the mid-1970s were enjoying a level of material well-being such as they had never known before and would not soon experience again.

CHAPTER EIGHT

SOCIO-ECONOMIC AND DEMOGRAPHIC CHANGE

Looking back on the preceding decades, the western journalist Martin Walker (1986: 175) wrote in the mid-1980s that the Soviet Union 'went through a social revolution while Brezhnev slept'. While this is undoubtedly an exaggeration, it rightly draws attention to the contrast between continuing social change and political conservatism that characterised the Brezhnev years. Soviet society was undergoing major socio-economic and demographic changes under Brezhnev, changes that would to a great extent determine the political and economic dilemmas his successors would face. The modernisation of Soviet society that the regime itself had engineered came to maturity against a backdrop of political sclerosis and declining economic performance. The result was both mounting frustration on the part of much of the population, as career aspirations and expectations of a continuing rise in living standards were frustrated, while the cultural gap between rulers and ruled grew ever wider.

URBANISATION AND EDUCATION

By comparison with the decades that preceded it, the Brezhnev era was fairly tranquil with respect to social change and development. Viewed in terms of 'objective' indicators of social change like urbanisation, the 'social revolution' to which Walker refers was in fact largely the continuation of trends already under way when Brezhnev came to power in 1964. Yet while the Brezhnev era was free of the sort of large-scale social upheavals that had punctuated the first half of the twentieth century, the cumulative effect of these changes over the 18 years of Brezhnev's rule was considerable.

Among the trends that continued through the Brezhnev era were rising levels of urbanisation and educational attainment. The USSR had become a predominantly urban society only in 1961, and the urban population share at the end of 1964 was just 53%. By the time of Brezhnev's death, more than 64% of Soviet citizens lived in urban areas (TsSU, 1985: 7). This figure would have been even higher had it not been for deliberate efforts to check the flight of peasants from the countryside to the cities. Increases in education levels were even more rapid. Between 1959 and 1984, the proportion of Soviet adults with a full higher educational qualification more than tripled, to 8.2%. A further 1.6% had incomplete tertiary education, while 36.4% had completed secondary education (specialised or general), as against 10.9% in 1959. Excluding pensioners, students and others outside the workforce reveals that 58.5% of the labour force in 1984 had at least a complete secondary education, as compared with just 15.8% in 1959 (TsSU, 1985: 29). In 1965, only 57.5% of pupils completing their eighth year of school continued their secondary education; the others went straight into the workplace. By 1980, 99.5% went on in school, with only 0.5% leaving formal education for a job (Rutkevich, 1984: 24). The number of graduates being turned out by Soviet universities and other institutions of higher education each year rose from 343,000 in 1960 to 631,000 in 1970 and close to a million a decade later. The result of these two trends was, in Daniels' (1993: 67) words, 'a population that was more mobilisable but less manipulable' by the regime. It was also, increasingly, a population that was better educated than its rulers and thus less willing to accept their judgements without question. The authority of the poorly educated former peasants and workers who dominated the top elite suffered as an ever larger segment of society gained the benefits of the much more extensive educational opportunities available.

Ironically, although the quality of both basic schooling and higher-level research was very high, much of this education was of questionable economic value. This was particularly true of technical subjects like engineering, which accounted for a very large proportion of higher and specialised secondary education. Soviet technical specialisations were among the narrowest in the world, largely as a result of individual ministries and even large industrial enterprises training individuals for their current needs. Thus, mechanical engineering was split into several dozen fields, with individuals specialising in mechanical engineering for tractors, machine tools, and so on. Metallurgical engineers specialised in specific metals and their alloys. There were even degrees in engineering ball-bearings for paper mills. This pattern applied to many vocational courses and much on-the-job training as well. The result was a workforce characterised by a very high level of enterprise- or even job-specific skills. At the same time, for political reasons, Soviet technical specialists were given no introduction to broader socio-economic issues that were, in many cases, intrinsic to their work. Engineers, for example, received no training in economics, cost-benefit analysis or human psychology. Issues like working conditions or the environmental impact of engineering work were not addressed in their training (Graham, 1993: 67–75).

The more immediate problem for the authorities, however, was not the quality of education being provided but the overproduction of engineers and other specialists. The economy simply could not absorb them as fast as the educational system was producing them. The result was a steadily growing population of graduates who could not be employed in the sort of jobs for which they were trained and to which they aspired. This over-abundance of highly trained specialists was matched by a shortage of workers, particularly skilled workers (Daniels, 1993: 69; Andrle, 1998: 257). This was not without its advantages for the regime. First, it made it far easier to hold down the salaries of white-collar professionals in line with the leadership's wage policies. Secondly, the production of 'surplus' special-ists meant that they were more readily expendable should they step out of line politically. Nevertheless, the major impact of the glut of over-educated specialists was the emergence of a growing number of individuals who were well educated but frustrated in their careers and increasingly alienated from the prevailing order.

This was part of a wider problem of declining inter-generational social mobility (Andrle, 1998: 257). The enormous opportunities for upward social mobility created by the regime's policies were crucial in generating support for the Soviet system during its early decades in power. By the 1960s, however, the social structure had settled and the better off elements of society were increasingly preoccupied with passing their advantages on to their offspring. One western study estimated that 60–70% of the entry-level appointees to the 'bottom rungs of the elite occupations' were offspring of individuals already belonging to the elite (Yanowitch, 1977: 30). Colton (1986: 46) argues that there was an ethnic dimension to this problem, as the economic slowdown 'shrivelled career opportunities just as the expansion of higher education for late-modernising groups, especially Muslims, produced larger graduating classes of native cadres'. Progress in reducing inter-ethnic differences in educational attainments was thus a decidedly mixed blessing (Jones & Grupp, 1984: 179).

THE 'SOCIAL CONTRACT' UNDER STRAIN

Social policy was largely dictated by the requirements of the tacit social contract identified by Hauslohner (1987) and Cook (1992, 1993), under which the state provided material security in return for political quiescence and compliance. The implementation of fairly egalitarian wage policies was also an element of the contract and ensured that income differentials remained extremely low by comparison with those found in western countries. Under Brezhnev, these wage policies were particularly geared to benefit the industrial working class (Ellman, 1980; Nove, 1982). Blue-collar workers, particularly skilled workers, tended to earn more than their white-collar counterparts, with the gap between them growing from about 1968

[*Doc. 14*]. Even doctors were relatively poorly paid, and engineers in industrial plants often earned less than the workers they supervised. By 1985, managerial and technical personnel earned just 110.1% of the average manual worker's wage, down from 148% in 1960 (Lane, 1990: 144). This was in part a result of the regime's tendency to value 'productive' work – which in Soviet parlance meant work generating measurable physical output – over 'unproductive' work in spheres such as services and trade.

The blue-collar bias of wage policy was more than just a product of ideological preferences for low income differentials or the advancement of the proletariat. It was also a response to a widespread flight from manual labour. Many educated young people chose poorly paid white-collar work in preference to better paid blue-collar jobs. This preference for status over income reflected the fact that money incomes were far from the sole determinant of material well-being in the USSR. Power in the Soviet system rested to a very great extent on the administration of privilege and much therefore depended on status, connections and location rather than wages and salaries. The system of privileged distribution, whereby members of the elite enjoyed preferential access to goods unavailable or only rarely available to the rest of the population, is well known. Moreover, despite its relatively egalitarian wage policies, the Brezhnev leadership actually expanded such closed networks of elite distribution substantially, in spheres ranging from medical care to catering. Yet as Andrle (1998: 255–6) observes, this was just the tip of the iceberg. Similar, if poorer, channels of closed distribution existed at every level in Soviet society. There was a well understood, if entirely unofficial, hierarchy of cities based on how well supplied they were with food and consumer goods. Workers in some industrial sectors, such as heavy industry and defence-related production, enjoyed better access to so-called 'deficit commodities' (foodstuffs and goods in short supply) than did those in light industry or services sectors. Social mobility thus depended on more than education, professional attainment or salary. It was often about crossing administrative boundaries – obtaining clearance for work in a sensitive industrial sector or a residence permit for a major city.

By the late 1970s, all the major elements of the social contract were under strain. The slowdown in growth meant that all social groups' expectations of a continued rapid rise in living standards – such as they had experienced in the 1950s and 1960s – were disappointed. The state's ability to deliver on its most fundamental economic commitment – to ensure adequate supplies of basic goods and foodstuffs at official prices – was steadily eroded. Shortages, queues and, in many areas, rationing were increasingly a part of everyday life. At the same time, the social welfare elements of the contract suffered from chronic underfunding. This was particularly evident in the healthcare system. Despite a doubling in the number of hospital beds and doctors per capita between 1950 and 1980, there was good reason to believe by the beginning of the eighties that the quality of care was in decline (Schroeder & Denton, 1982: 325). Under-investment meant that the quality of medical facilities was, in many areas, comparable to that found in developing countries. There were severe shortages of drugs and medical supplies. Furthermore, poor pay reduced the quality of entrants into the medical profession while increasing the incentives for practitioners to 'privatise' much of their work. This they did either by moonlighting when not on duty (which was strictly illegal) or by accepting, if not demanding, bribes to perform their basic duties (Davis, 1984). Nor was the medical system unique in failing to make good on the regime's promises to Soviet citizens. The authorities' refusal to acknowledge the price rises that were taking place from year to year condemned a growing number of pensioners to poverty. Pensions were determined by life-time earnings; they were not raised to keep up with wages nor were they increased to reflect the rising cost of living (George, 1991: 48).

The slowdown in the growth of living standards, the slow unravelling of the social contract and declining social mobility all contributed to an increasingly widespread social malaise, a growing sense of pessimism and cynicism. These feelings both contributed to and were fed by pervasive corruption at all levels (Simis, 1982). Popular frustrations were also aroused by increased awareness of living standards abroad, as a growing portion of the population gained a glimpse of life in the West and even more – around one million Soviet citizens a year in the 1970s – travelled to the fraternal socialist countries of Central Europe, where living standards also tended to be higher. As Colton (1986: 50–4) observed, ordinary citizens increasingly responded to the regime's failure to meet their expectations by partially withdrawing from authorised public life. This search for 'private solutions' led citizens in a variety of different directions, from religion to the vodka bottle to the second economy. The literature of the period turned increasingly from public concerns to private ones, and an increasing number of people, particularly young people, turned away from official culture altogether, usually in favour of a counter-culture largely imported from the West.

Much of this was possible only because of the regime's willingness to tolerate a great deal of deviant behaviour that would previously have been punished. Lax policing of the second economy and the turning of blind eyes to report-padding and corruption on the part of managers constituted a part of the regime's 'Little Deal', a tacit accommodation between the regime and its increasingly acquisitive subjects. In return for political quiescence, the latter were given increasing scope to pursue private material gain, even at public expense (Millar, 1985). This is not to suggest that Soviet people were turning from socialism or withdrawing their allegiance from the regime. However, they were increasingly aware of the regime's failure to make good on the promises of socialism, and resentful of the elite's nakedly self-interested pursuit of privilege for itself [*Doc. 22*].

EMERGING DEMOGRAPHIC PROBLEMS

The most disturbing evidence of the regime's declining ability to deliver prosperity and material well-being to its subjects is to be found in the USSR's performance on basic indicators of human welfare, such as life expectancy and infant mortality. During the Brezhnev era, these began to show a dramatic deterioration relative to other developed and developing countries, and even some absolute deterioration on certain indicators. Until about 1960, the USSR had seemed to be rapidly reducing the gap between itself and the West on indicators of human well-being (Wheatcroft, 1999). Infant mortality rates, for example, were by 1960 below the levels found in Austria and Italy, and were expected to converge with West German levels by the 1970s. In the 1960s, however, this progress went into reverse and the gap between the USSR and the West began to widen again.

The crude death rate climbed from a low of 6.9 per 1,000 in 1964 to 10.3 in 1980. Death rates for every age group except 11–20-year-olds rose steadily throughout the period. Soviet infant mortality was triple the West German rate by 1981. Infant mortality actually rose from 1967 to 1980, falling back to the 1967 level only in 1985, by which time it was roughly equal to the infant mortality rates found in Panama or Tonga – despite the fact that Soviet statistical methods reduced the reported figure. Use of World Bank methods would have raised the figure by around 15–25%. Male life expectancy also went into decline, an unprecedented development in an industrialised country in peace-time. On the official data, life expectancy for men and women combined in the late 1980s fluctuated around 68–69 years, down from a peak of 70 in 1971–72 (Eberstadt, 1988: 6–7). Feshbach and Friendly (1995: 3) paint an even gloomier picture, estimating that life expectancy at birth fell from 66.1 years in the mid-1960s to just 62.3 in 1980. The extent of this deterioration became generally known only in the late 1980s, as the regime's initial response to the problem was simply to stop publishing data on some of the more embarrassing indicators, such as infant mortality, in the mid-1970s. Publication was not resumed until after 1985.

These trends cannot be attributed solely to the economic system. The long-term secular improvement in human welfare indicators which stalled in the 1960s actually began well before the revolution, and the subsequent deterioration continued after the collapse of communism. Nevertheless, it seems clear that deteriorating economic performance was a contributing factor, if only because of the resulting decay of the country's under-funded health system.

Alcohol consumption was also a major contributor. According to Nemtsov (2001), by 1982 the average Soviet adult was consuming the equivalent of almost 18 litres of pure spirit per year, nearly double the figure for 1970 and far above that for the mid-1960s. In a careful study of the data on alcohol-related deaths, including both direct (alcohol poisoning, alcoholic psychosis, cirrhosis of the liver, severe alcoholic pancreatitis) and indirect effects (alcohol-related road accidents, suicides and murders, and diseases complicated by alcohol or drunkenness), Nemtsov concludes that alcohol in the early 1980s contributed significantly to well over one-quarter of all deaths among Soviet citizens. The impact of alcohol and the environment was also evident in data showing that over 10% of infant deaths were the result of congenital defects (Shubin, 1997: 79).

Lax enforcement of environmental regulations and the authorities' obsession with output growth contributed to the mortality crisis through their impact on air and water quality. By the late 1980s, an estimated one-third of adults and two-thirds of children suffered from respiratory disorders, and one-quarter of all deaths in 1980 were related to lung disorders and malignant tumours. While these deaths were often a result of tobacco use, they also reflected rising levels of air pollution (Shubin, 1997: 79). Soviet industrial enterprises routinely dumped industrial waste into rivers and reservoirs that found their way back into household water supplies, with the worst such dumping around large industrial cities like Leningrad, Irkutsk, Sverdlovsk and Chelyabinsk. Such practices were also common in Transcaucasia and Central Asia (Sidorenko & Krut'ko, 1990: 765–6). Nor were rural areas always much better: mismanagement of irrigation and pesticide use poisoned water supplies in many areas; around the Aral Sea, the impact was so great that mothers could not breastfeed their children for fear of poisoning them (Shubin, 1997: 76). In many areas, enterprises deposited industrial waste onto household rubbish tips, which were often used by local people for composting. This resulted in extremely high concentrations of heavy metals and other toxins in people's diets (Sidorenko & Krut'ko, 1990: 771–2).

Mortality trends were not the only demographic development to cause the authorities serious concern. Birth rates presented the Brezhnev leadership with two grounds for concern. First, the rate of population growth declined from around 1.6% per annum in the early 1960s to just 0.8% at the end of the Brezhnev era (Feshbach, 1982: 30). This sharp slowdown in natural population increase meant that labour force growth virtually ground to a halt, while the country's pensioner population continued to grow rapidly. Equally worrying to the leadership was the evidence that the country's ethnic make-up was changing rapidly and in problematic ways. Birth rates in urban areas of European Russia fell to below replacement levels, while the USSR's non-European peoples, particularly its Muslim nationalities, continued to grow rapidly. The natural rate of population increase in the Russian Soviet Federated Socialist Republic in 1980 was just 0.49%, while Kazakhstan and the three Transcaucasian republics registered increases of 0.8 to 2.0%, and the rapidly growing republics of Central Asia all posted increases of between 2.0 and 2.9% (TsSU, 1991: 86). Altogether, the Muslim population of the USSR was growing at around 2.5% per year, more than quadruple the rate of population growth registered by Great Russians.

These differential growth rates were cause for concern on a number of grounds. First, the simple prospect that the Russians would lose their majority position was disturbing to Brezhnev and his (overwhelmingly Russian) colleagues in the Kremlin. Secondly, the Muslim peoples of Central Asia appeared to be the least assimilated, culturally and linguistically, in the USSR. This complicated a third problem, which was economic. The efforts of the authorities to foster the relocation of workers from labour-surplus regions such as Central Asia to ease labour shortages in the industrial cities of Europe and Siberia were never very effective, partly because Central Asians were reluctant to relocate and partly because attempts to persuade them to do so were never more than half-hearted – the centre had too many doubts about the desirability of engineering a large-scale migration of non-Europeans to these places. Yet the alternative solution of redirecting industrial and infrastructure investment to Central Asia would be both extremely expensive and politically difficult. Since neither strategy was implemented, the rapid accumulation of surplus labour in Central Asia led to the stagnation of per capita incomes there, despite the large-scale transfer of resources from more developed republics as part of the regime's attempt to reduce inter-republican income disparities. Finally, Soviet leaders were also increasingly concerned about the potential influence of Islam in the region, particularly after the Afghan war began at the end of 1979. Concern about the rapid growth of the Muslim population was serious enough to prompt calls for the use of differential family allowances to encourage higher birth rates in some regions (i.e. among Slavs) and the inclusion in the 1981 Party Programme of a proposal (never implemented) for 'birth incentives' differentiated by regions.

NATIONALITIES POLICY UNDER BREZHNEV

The Brezhnev leadership's handling of nationality issues remains extremely controversial. Nahaylo and Swoboda (1990) present the Brezhnev era as one of steadily advancing policies of Russification, which generated increasing resistance and contributed to the national upheavals of the late

1980s that eventually destroyed the USSR. Brubaker (1996: 23) is not alone in believing that Brezhnev's handling of this issue served to 'prepare the way for the demise of the Soviet state'. Yet much of this argument is based on hindsight and a degree of *post hoc* reasoning. Fowkes (2002: 68) challenges this view, describing Brezhnev's nationalities policy as 'a policy of corporatist compromise, ethnic equalisation and masterly inactivity' that 'was sufficient to allow the Soviet way of dealing with the national question a few more years of calm, unthreatened existence'. He suggests that the Brezhnev regime's mix of accommodation and repression probably extended the life of the Soviet multinational state longer than might otherwise have been the case.

Fowkes's 'corporatist compromise' was largely reflected in Brezhnev's acceptance that the national republics would be led by members of the titular nationalities – a principle that had been increasingly, if inconsistently, observed under Khrushchev – and in his readiness to cede considerable authority to local elites. Institutionally, of course, the Brezhnev leadership took a number of early steps to reverse Khrushchev's decentralisation of economic management, and the practice of placing ethnic Russians in important but less visible posts in the republics was continued. However, the appointment of Russians to monitor local leaders on Moscow's behalf was never very effective – there were simply too many incentives to 'go native' – and the institutional recentralisation of 1965 was substantially counterbalanced by Brezhnev's commitment to stability of cadres. During his 18 years in office, there were only four cases in which the Kremlin intervened to replace the leadership of a union republic. Local leaders enjoyed a security of tenure about which they could only have dreamed under Stalin and Khrushchev. Long terms of office offered national leaders unprecedented opportunities for corruption and the creation of local political machines that would make any attempt by Moscow to check their power even more problematic. The result was a process of what Simm (1991: 265) calls 'inconspicuous decolonisation', as political patronage, corruption and the growth of the shadow economy all combined to erode central control over the non-Russian republics.

With hindsight, it is clear that the Brezhnev leadership's political compromise with native elites undermined the cohesion of the system, in large measure because it was limited to republican affairs. The composition of all-union party and state bodies grew progressively more Russian during Brezhnev's leadership. The proportion of Russians in the Central Committee elected at the Twenty-third Congress of the CPSU in 1966 was around 57%; the corresponding figure for the Committee elected at the Twenty-sixth Congress in 1981 was 68%. The 1966 Politburo included six Russians among its 11 full members; by 1981, ten of the 14 full members were Russian, and the CPSU Secretariat consisted exclusively of Russians.

Moreover, the non-Russian members of the Politburo were generally leaders of union republics, based outside Moscow and therefore not fully involved in the Politburo's deliberations. Real decision-making at all-union level was increasingly concentrated in the hands of sub-groups of the Politburo that most often consisted wholly of Russians (*chap. 2*). This combination of trust in cadres at republican level and Russian dominance at union level reinforced the incentives for non-Russian officials to identify with their nations and regions and to pay relatively little attention to all-union concerns, over which they had little if any control anyway (Gleason, 1990).

The second element of Brezhnev's nationality policy, ethnic equalisation, was implemented much more evenly than the first. In economic terms, it enjoyed limited success in the late 1960s and early 1970s, as the regime worked to reduce inter-republican differences in productivity and income by means of inter-republican transfers and the allocation of investment to less developed regions. Disparities in *per capita* income declined, albeit modestly, in the 1970s but began to increase again towards the end of the Brezhnev era (Bond *et alii*, 1990). Other strands of economic policy served to aggravate inter-regional inequalities, including policies aimed at regional specialisation, which were supposed to facilitate both efficiency (via economies of scale) and political cohesion (by binding the Soviet republics together in a web of economic interdependence). The most striking example of this was the cotton monoculture imposed on much of Central Asia. Whether they emphasised equalisation or not, the regime's development policies created numerous grievances in the non-Russian areas. The ecological effects of Central Asia's cotton monoculture were catastrophic, while more 'favoured' regions gained the dubious benefit of industrial investments that were also environmentally harmful. Investment projects for which local elites lobbied aggressively subsequently became sources of grievance on account of their environmental costs or their impact on local peoples' traditional ways of life. Russian as well as non-Russian regions suffered the disastrous side-effects of Soviet industrial development, but in non-Russian regions it was difficult to overlook the ethnic issue, since the key decisions were usually taken by Russians in far-away Moscow.

Far more successful was the regime's attempt to reduce inequalities in educational attainments (Fowkes, 2002), but this was a decidedly mixed blessing for the Soviet leadership. Rising levels of education among the non-Russians reduced the willingness of the minority populations to accept Russian dominance of political, economic and cultural life and increased the self-confidence of indigenous elites. Moreover, the non-Russians' educational attainments were rising at a time when career opportunities for those with higher education were declining.

The third element of the policy mix identified by Fowkes, 'masterly inactivity', is easily the most controversial. There is clearly something to be said for it. The Brezhnev leadership quickly backed away from the provocatively assimilationist official rhetoric of the late Khrushchev years and turned a blind eye to the corruption and incompetence of many local elites. Proposals to alter or abolish the USSR's ethnically based federal system, though long debated, were rejected (Hodnett, 1967). Whether the issue was the institutional architecture of the Soviet state or the behaviour of republican elites, Brezhnev's approach was cautious, preferring the ills of the *status quo* to the political risks and potential side effects of any serious attempt at change. This caution reflected an awareness of the sensitivities surrounding nationality issues, which were about the only thing other than food shortages that triggered large-scale popular disturbances in the Brezhnev era. Mass protest meetings and large-scale demonstrations in defence of national rights occurred in Armenia, Abkhazia, Georgia, Uzbekistan and Lithuania. At times, street protesters and dissident defenders of national rights enjoyed the tacit backing, if not the active connivance, of local elites, and when central initiatives affecting national rights met resistance, they were often abandoned. Concern about the future of non-Russian languages and cultures also fuelled the growth of dissident movements in a number of republics from the 1960s onwards.

Against this view, Nahaylo and Swoboda (1990), among others, argue that the Brezhnev era was a period of steady Russification. They also emphasise the regime's hard line on nationalist dissent, particularly in Ukraine and the Baltic states, and the evidence of growing minority resistance to linguistic Russification in particular. In fact, the picture varied widely from place to place. Linguistic Russification seems to have been pushed hardest in the western union republics, particularly Ukraine and Belorussia, and official sensitivity to any hint of nationalism was greater in the western republics. This was due in part to the late entry of the Baltic states and western Ukraine into the Soviet Union and, after 1968, to the evidence of sympathy for the Prague Spring in the western parts of the USSR. There was one notable exception to the regime's general intolerance of any hint of nationalist feeling, an exception that reinforced concerns about the Russifying elements of its nationalities policies: the Brezhnev leadership's attitude towards Russian nationalism was extremely indulgent (Dunlop, 1983; Yanov, 1978).

Yet while they were most keenly sensitive to the activities of nationalist dissidents in the far west of the country, the Soviet authorities during the Brezhnev era appear to have seen Central Asia as the area of greatest long-term concern. If any ethnic grouping posed a long-term threat to the integrity of the Soviet Union, it was reckoned to be the rapidly growing and apparently unassimilable population of Central Asia. Growing evidence of net out-migration of Russians from the Central Asian republics further reinforced concerns about the potential for ethnic unrest in Central Asia.

Numerous western specialists shared this view (e.g. Rywkin, 1982; Bennigsen and Broxup, 1983). Such worries were also reflected in cadres policy. Moscow consistently accepted a greater 'indigenisation' of local leaderships in the European republics and Transcaucasia than in Central Asia. The irony is that both the Kremlin and the western observers were quite spectacularly wrong about Moscow's 'Muslim challenge'. When the USSR finally collapsed, separatist movements were strongest in the Baltic States, Transcaucasia and, to a lesser extent, Ukraine. These were also the republics in which Communist elites were quickest to defect and identify with the cause of national independence. By contrast, Kazakhstan and Central Asia did not leave the Union; they were cast adrift by the Slav leaders who finally liquidated it. The terminal crisis of the Soviet state thus found that the centre had been preparing all along for a struggle on the wrong front.

It is clear that the Brezhnev leadership did not in any sense *solve* the national question, despite frequent claims to the contrary. However, it is far from clear that any 'solution' to it existed at all. The USSR was a multi-national empire, created by force and held together by a mixture of coercion and inducements. While most of its citizens accepted its legitimacy and few sympathised with the aims of radical nationalists at this time, tensions among ethnic groups were widespread and the ethnic diversity of the country remained, as it had been since the nineteenth century, a potential threat to its cohesion. The speed with which centrifugal forces asserted themselves as political controls were relaxed in the late 1980s suggests that the Brezhnev policy mix had much to recommend it, at least to an authoritarian elite committed to retaining power and holding the state together. For all its apparent contradictions and ambiguities, it represented a reasonable strategy for coping with a problem that did not admit of any ultimate solution.

CHAPTER NINE

CULTURE AND IDEAS

Cultural de-Stalinisation came to an abrupt halt with Khrushchev's removal but the steps taken to reverse it were halting and incomplete. This half-hearted retreat from de-Stalinisation disappointed those who hoped that Khrushchev's fall would bring its continuation under a steadier, less volatile leadership but failed to satisfy the neo-Stalinists in the anti-Khrushchev coalition. However, it represented a politically viable middle course and it does appear to have suited Brezhnev himself. Stalin's reputation was gradually and quietly repaired in some respects, especially as a war leader, but this stopped short of a full-scale rehabilitation. Many aspects of his rule were simply passed over in silence. Neither Brezhnev nor Kosygin appeared anxious to put Stalin back on his pedestal alongside Lenin; indeed, their reluctance to repudiate the whole process of de-Stalinisation was one of the impediments to a rapprochement with China (Shelest, 1995: 243–4). At the same time, Khrushchev's leadership and all that was associated with it – above all, the de-Stalinisation campaign – rapidly disappeared from official history.

This handling of the Stalin question was typical of the new administration's approach to the sphere of culture and ideas, which reflected the new leaders' search for order and stability rather than ideological purity. While the Brezhnev leadership's cultural policies were decidedly more conservative than Khrushchev's, they stopped far short of a return to the strict enforcement of socialist realism that had characterised the thirties and forties. The acceptable boundaries of artistic expression were narrowed and the regime came down hard on dissident intellectuals, but the conservatism of the Brezhnev years did not bear comparison with the repression and enforced conformism of the pre-1953 period. Moreover, the regime's harsh treatment of any overt manifestation of dissent sometimes obscured the fact that it allowed a great deal of heterodox thought within the confines of the established order. A growing number of writers and scholars found themselves able to work in the grey area that existed, however precariously, in the space between the stultifying orthodoxies of official dogma and the open challenge to the regime that was dissent. It was in this ideological 'twilight zone' that much of the 'new thinking' which later underlay Mikhail Gorbachev's reforms was born.

CULTURE HIGH AND LOW

Hindsight has made it easy for later scholars to present Khrushchev's removal as a sort of Stalinist restoration in the sphere of culture and ideas. During the long years of enforced cultural conformity and repression of dissent that followed October 1964, Khrushchev's record on culture and the freedom of intellectual life came to look rather better than it really had been, and his ouster thus came to seem a decisive turning point. This was not so clear at the time. Much of the liberally inclined intelligentsia welcomed the October coup. Khrushchev had been an inconsistent liberaliser, at best, and most intellectuals seems to have 'expected political, economic and cultural reform to continue under Brezhnev, but without the fits and starts associated with Khrushchev' (Sherlock, 1990: 15). Journalist Anatolii Strelyanyi (1988: 226) recalled later that he and colleagues had thrown a spontaneous party at work on hearing of Khrushchev's removal; some even danced on the tables (for a similar reaction, see Karpinski, 1989). Such expectations were reinforced in January 1965, when the fortieth anniversary issue of the liberally inclined literary journal *Novyi Mir* carried works by a number of writers who had been officially condemned, and in some cases persecuted, under Khrushchev. This suggested that the new leaders would be relatively liberal in such matters.

The first clear indication that these hopes were misplaced came later in 1965, with the arrest of the writers Andrei Sinyavskii and Yulii Daniel, who had produced satirical works critical of the regime and had published them abroad. They were tried, convicted and sentenced to prison in 1966 for 'anti-Soviet propaganda'. Yet even then, it took some time before much of the creative intelligentsia came to appreciate fully the extent to which policy was changing. There were still, after all, some grounds for optimism. Many writers and artists, in particular, seem to have appreciated the quiet, orderly conduct of the Twenty-third Party Congress in 1966, which was free of the sort of public attacks on specific writers that had characterised the Khrushchev era. Even those unsettled by the Sinyavskii–Daniel case were reassured by the fact that there seemed to be neither a return to Stalinism nor a thoroughgoing rehabilitation of Stalin in the offing (Semichastnyi, 1995). Gradually, however, it became clear that the new leadership was much less liberal than Khrushchev had been, particularly after 1968.

Oddly enough, however, the cultural norms enforced by the regime had less to do with Marxism-Leninism than with adherence to older, more conventional 'bourgeois' values. This was nothing new. As Fitzpatrick (1976) has shown, cultural policy from the mid-1930s on was dominated less by the regime's professed revolutionary ideology than by a respect for the established 'classics' of pre-Revolutionary Russian culture and for an almost Victorian sense of propriety. The Brezhnev era was no exception. Writers were as likely to be condemned for writing risqué verse or prose as for touching on sensitive political themes, while composers were more likely to face trouble with the authorities for producing atonal music than for writing music deemed to be insufficiently Leninist. Official Soviet high culture under Brezhnev was something of a conservative, middle-brow version of what Soviet leaders imagined to be the bourgeois high culture of pre-Revolutionary Russia.

It was in some respects entirely appropriate that political-ideological considerations no longer predominated in cultural policy, for they no longer dominated art and literature to the extent that they had. Increasingly, the 'partial withdrawal' from public life and the search for 'private solutions' on the part of ordinary citizens observed by Colton (1986: 50–4) found reflection in the concerns of artists and writers. The movement away from socialist realism that had begun after 1953 continued. It was characterised not so much by any alternative approach to politics as by a focus on the private sphere of individual emotions and relationships. Marxism-Leninism was not so much challenged as ignored. Writers, in particular, turned inward, demonstrating a growing interest in the single individual, quite apart from his place and function in society. Literature shifted away from the 'concerns and master plot of socialism' and towards 'a Chekhovian concern with the venial sin, the petty failings, betrayals and cruelties of ordinary people in day-to-day living' (Terras, 1991: 609). This trend cut across a wide range of approaches and cultural forms. In literature, it was as true of so-called 'urban prose' writers like Andrei Bitov and Yuri Trifonov as it was of the 'village prose' school (the *derevenshchiki*) represented by Valentin Rasputin, Vasilii Belov and others.

In some instances, the drift away from Marxist-Leninist values in art and literature was not only permitted but encouraged from on high. Some members of the leadership gave encouragement to the development of Russian nationalist sentiment, and Russian thinkers whose views transgressed the accepted limits on this issue were treated relatively gently. Brezhnev himself appears to have favoured the *derevenshchiki*, who emerged in the 1960s. Rather like the nineteenth-century slavophiles, the *derevenshchiki* presented the rural community as the last repository of those truly Russian values that might yet save Soviet society from the spiritual bankruptcy of a materialism imported from the West: honesty, simplicity, harmony and close ties to both family and the land. It is ironic that Brezhnev and his colleagues were so enamoured of the village prose writers, for the movement owed much to the man who was probably the regime's least favourite writer, the dissident Aleksandr Solzhenitsyn (Zakulin, 1971; [*Doc. 19*]). Official sympathy for an emerging Russian nationalism found expression in other ways as well, not least in the official favour enjoyed by journals with a decidedly Russian nationalist bent, such as *Molodaya gvardiya* and *Nash sovremennik*. The emergence and rapid growth of the innocuously named All Union Society for the Preservation of Historical and Cultural Monuments was a further sign of official support for Russian nationalism. In sponsoring Russian nationalists, Soviet leaders were taking a serious risk. The views of the so-called 'Russites' both provoked non-Russians and, at times, came perilously close to overt criticism of the Soviet regime. Reddaway (1980: 165–6) argued that the Russites' sponsors in the leadership probably sought to determine whether a 'sanitised' Russian nationalism could be synthesised with Marxism-Leninism to produce an ideology with greater popular appeal and to test how effectively it could be used against the 'generally West-oriented liberal intelligentsia'.

As time went on, Soviet literature began to pay a price for the authorities' conservatism. Increasingly, the country's best writers were either openly at odds with the regime or quietly moving into latent opposition to it. Many ended up in exile: while Solzhenitsyn was the best known literary figure to emigrate, many others were either forced into exile or pressured into choosing emigration, including Iosif Brodsky, Andrei Sinyavskii, Aleksandr Zinoviev, Viktor Nekrasov, Vladimir Voinovich, Vasilii Aksenov and Eduard Limonov. Those who remained within the sphere of official literature tended to use Aesopian language to express themselves, counting on readers to grasp the subtexts that contained their real messages.

For Soviet leaders, many of the most disturbing developments in the cultural arena concerned not the high culture of literature and the fine arts, over which the regime retained fairly tight control, but in the sphere of popular cultural, particularly youth culture. This was largely a continuation of trends already under way by the time of Khrushchev's removal in 1964. Increasingly, younger Soviet citizens were drawn to cultural imports from the West, like rock music, and to the Soviet 'alternative' culture represented by the ballads of such 'guitar-poets' as Bulat Okudzhava, Aleksandr Galich and Vladimir Vysotskii, whose verses challenged the official culture and dealt with the marginal and dispossessed elements of Soviet society. The actor and singer Vysotskii, in particular, became wildly popular with his portrayal of tough-guy anti-heroes, his songs of liquor, sex and delinquency, and his lampooning of much official culture. Vysotskii's funeral in 1980 was one of the largest outpourings of mass emotion of the postwar period, despite the fact that the official media largely ignored his death (Stites, 1992: 157–8). This was more than a matter of taste: there was a growing sense that the rejection of – or, at any rate, indifference to – official culture on the part of young people reflected a broader alienation from the Soviet order. As in the West, much of this alienation appears to have been related to frustrated expectations as a result of slowing economic growth and declining levels of social mobility. Moreover, as Hosking (1994: 607) has observed, Soviet youth in the Brezhnev era no longer had a central role to play, as it had in the decades prior to 1945 – whether in war or in the revolutionary transformation of society.

It would be a mistake, however, to see popular culture as somehow intrinsically antagonistic to official values. The continuing popularity of novels and films about the Second World War, for example, in which national-patriotic themes continued to loom large, represented an important area of convergence of official and popular tastes. The mystery-thriller genre of *detektiv* also grew rapidly in popularity, as did science fiction – much of it highly scientifically literate work written by scientists. As in the West, science fiction was largely concerned with technological development and its potential – whether that potential was life-enhancing or life-denying. Finally, the Brezhnev era witnessed the emergence of historical novels dealing with themes largely ignored by official historiography, such as Valentin Pikul's extremely popular novels about eighteenth and nineteenth century Russia. Many of these new literatures also found their way onto cinema and television screens (Stites, 1992: 151–4).

Other cultural forms gradually won at least reluctant approval from the authorities. Jazz and disco came to be accepted and even rock music was grudgingly allowed some space to develop. Unable to suppress it, the authorities tried to coopt and control this disruptive new musical form. The musical establishment remained solidly conservative and continued to use its control over record production, concert venues and other such resources to impede the development of rock, jazz and the guitar-poets. In this, they found ready allies in both the country's political leaders and the conservative Ministry of Culture. As Stites (1992: 162) observes, this was not so much about ideology as about self-interest. The bosses of the musical establishment did not understand the new music and were threatened by it. Cloaking themselves in the mantle of moral and ideological purity, they sought to marginalise if not destroy it. That they failed so comprehensively owed much to the new affluence of Soviet society: the ubiquity of the tape recorder – used to spread the ballads of Galich, the latest western rock albums or the music of 'underground' Soviet rock groups – highlighted the extent to which youth culture was developing independently of the regime's wishes or plans.

THE CRACKDOWN ON DISSENT

The Sinyavskii–Daniel case was followed by a major crackdown on the circulation of unpublished writings in manuscript form (*samizdat*). The security organs also began to step up the pressure on nationally minded dissent, particularly in Ukraine. This determination not to tolerate intellectual dissent was reinforced by the Prague Spring. The reaction of the Soviet intelligentsia to events in Czechoslovakia was a major shock to the leadership, which found that large numbers of party members in scientific institutes were openly refusing to vote in support of the invasion at party cell meetings (Balakin & Balakina, 1995: 63). Czechoslovakia was thus followed by a sustained anti-dissident campaign that resulted in the internment (in prisons and psychiatric hospitals), internal exile or expulsion from the Soviet Union of a number of leading writers, artists, scientists and others who dared openly to question the regime's course or – more seriously – its legitimacy.

The seriousness with which the regime viewed dissident activity was out of all proportion to the numbers directly involved. According to a KGB report on dissident activity, some 1,292 authors composed over 9,000 'anti-Soviet' documents in 1965, for the most part crudely produced flyers and small posters (Freeze, 1998: 370–1). Many were expressions of protest whose 'anti-Soviet' character was chiefly in the eyes of the authorities. However, dissent and protest had from an early stage in the development of the Soviet regime come to be equated with opposition, an attitude fixed in the 1920s that changed little until the late 1980s. The apparent growth of dissent was thus a major source of concern to the country's leadership, prompting the creation in 1967 of a separate KGB directorate (the fifth) for the struggle with ideological diversions. While the number of active dissidents was never very large, the circulation of their ideas within the country, often facilitated by western broadcasts, meant that they were capable of reaching a much larger audience.

The 'soft repression' of the Brezhnev years (Suny, 1998: 433) was far less arbitrary and unpredictable than the repression of the Stalin period. First, there was greater clarity than ever about what was and was not permissible – not least because individuals were generally warned about their conduct before repressive measures were applied to them. 'Pastoral' chats with representatives of the KGB were usually the first step in dealing with a person who seemed in danger of landing himself in real trouble. The threats standing behind these chats were, of course, unmistakable. This so-called 'prophylactic' approach was more often than not effective [*Doc. 15*]. Secondly, the KGB under Yuri Andropov was less inclined to resort to arrest and imprisonment. While capable of great ruthlessness – including the notorious use of psychiatric hospitals for the incarceration and 'treatment' of dissidents – the security apparatus in the 1970s and early 1980s relied increasingly on measures such as the granting or withholding of promotions, awards and other privileges, or the threat of loss of employment. This served to deter all but the most determined troublemakers (Balakin & Balakina, 1995: 64). Finally, the authorities did make at least some attempt to observe the forms of legality. In this respect, the use of legal processes in the Sinyavskii and Daniel case represented 'progress' of a sort in the eyes of some observers (Alexeyeva, 1985: 277). This attention to 'socialist legality', however, was far from consistent, and the skill with which dissidents sought to use Soviet law against the authorities was a constant reminder to the latter that law was, at best, a double-edged sword.

Much of the regime's anti-dissident effort was, of course, counterproductive, with repressive measures driving many otherwise loyal citizens into dissident activity and arousing sympathy for the dissidents among many more. Thus, the arrest of Sinyavskii and Daniel prompted a demonstration by around 200 students from Sinyavskii's institute, while sixty-three leading intellectuals signed an open letter in support of the two writers, and 200 more sent a letter to the Twenty-third Party Congress asking that the case be reviewed. Nevertheless, by the early 1980s the regime appeared to have crushed the dissident movement. Writing at the end of the Brezhnev era, the leading western specialist on Soviet dissent concluded that the dissident movement was at its lowest ebb in twenty years. Its best-known figures were in prison, in exile or – if they were lucky – under constant KGB surveillance. *Samizdat* publications had fallen sharply, and there was little evidence that the great mass of Soviet people had any sympathy for the handful of troublemakers who were targeted in the regime's post-Afghanistan crackdown on dissent (Reddaway, 1983).

This victory was less important than it seemed, for the real problem facing the regime by the 1980s was not the small number of active dissidents still challenging it but the far larger number of 'good' Soviet citizens, particularly among the intelligentsia, who sympathised with many of the dissidents' aims. As Barghoorn (1983) argues, there was increasing interaction between dissident groups that the regime wished to stigmatise and isolate and certain key social groups 'within' the system, such as the creative and technical intelligentsia. The goals of many dissidents stopped far short of the overthrow of the Soviet system, with many – perhaps most – aiming for its rationalisation and reform. Thinkers like Sakharov linked their concern with intellectual freedom and democratisation to problems of artistic creativity and technical and economic progress [*Doc. 18*], which resonated widely with non-dissident members of the intelligentsia. While the creative intelligentsia had long enjoyed a difficult relationship with the regime, the scientific and technical intelligentsia in the post-war period had, with good reason, tended to view the regime favourably, as it had raised their pay and status and had also seemed to be successfully tackling the problems of scientific and technical development with which they were chiefly concerned. However, mounting evidence that economic performance was faltering turned the attention of the scientific-technical intelligentsia to the causes identified by Sakharov – 'excessive centralisation, party domination, bureaucratic privilege and inertia' (Barghoorn, 1983: 149). This represented a major shift: a regime that had for nearly half a century successfully identified itself with rapid technological progress and economic growth gradually came to be seen as an impediment to both.

THE CHANGING NATURE OF DISSIDENCE

One of the reasons for the regime's heightened sensitivity to any sign of dissident activity during the Brezhnev years was that, while the number of activists remained small, the nature of the dissident challenge changed in a number of important ways. First, the range of dissident activity broadened, as dissident groups formed in defence of national, religious and human rights. Some, like Sakharov's Human Rights Committee and, later, the Helsinki Watch group, focused on broad civil and human rights. Others, like the short-lived Association of Free Trade Unions in the Soviet Union (FTU) and its successor, the Free Inter-professional Association of Working People (SMOT), concentrated on the rights of workers. In the non-Russian republics, national issues tended to predominate, particularly in Ukraine, where individuals like Vyacheslav Chornovil and Ivan Dziuba challenged what they regarded as policies aimed at the Russification of Ukraine. Religious believers constituted a third major group, consisting chiefly of adherents of those religious groups the authorities treated with least tolerance, such as Baptists and Pentecostals – who by 1979 may have accounted for more than one-quarter of all political prisoners (Barghoorn, 1983: 145) – as well as those adherents of more 'acceptable' religions, like Russian Orthodoxy, who refused to practise their faith within the limits set by the regime. Jewish dissidents reacting to official anti-Zionism and anti-Semitism straddled the boundaries between these two tendencies, reflecting both national and religious concerns. The growth of these tendencies meant that fewer and fewer of the dissidents could be described as 'dissident Leninists' like the historian Roy Medvedev, whose chief concern was to bring about a return to what they regarded as 'true' Leninism – the unsullied and democratic socialism that they believed had been destroyed by Stalin [*Doc. 20*].

Secondly, as the regime's critics grew bolder, dissident literature became more overtly political. During the Khrushchev years, many writers had produced stories, novels and poems with unmistakable political content, but there was nothing so explicit in its political agenda as the open letter to

Soviet leaders drafted by Sakharov, Medvedev and the computer scientist Valentin Turchin [*Doc. 18*], or the appeals addressed to western trade unions and the International Labour Organisation by the FTU and SMOT. This change was reflected in the character of the growing volume of *samizdat* being circulated within the USSR: while much dissent was still expressed through *belles-lettres* forms, the KGB was reporting by 1970 that most of it consisted of 'political programmatic' materials [*Doc. 16*].

Thirdly, the dissidents developed new strategies for advancing their causes. One of the most important was the use of the foreign press. In the late 1960s, Soviet dissidents began to make contact with foreign journalists posted to Moscow, on occasion even convening press conferences with them, as Sakharov and Solzhenitsyn did in August and September 1973. At times, this put the plight of embattled dissidents before western publics and thus onto the agenda of East–West relations. During the period of détente this did help restrain the authorities at key moments. The regime's tolerance of Sakharov's activities was directly linked to concerns about the international repercussions of any move against him, particularly after US President Jimmy Carter wrote to the dissident physicist in February 1977. It was therefore no coincidence that Sakharov's exile to the city of Gorky was ordered soon after the invasion of Afghanistan. The intervention and the West's reaction to it had eliminated détente as a factor in the leadership's calculations. Contact with the western media also helped secure a wider audience for *samizdat* literature within the USSR, since dissident writings that reached the West were often covered in western broadcasts to the Soviet Union by organisations like Radio Liberty.

Another strategy consisted of the use of the law against the state. People like Chornovil and Aleksandr Ginzburg began to submit to Soviet prosecutors (and often to foreign journalists as well) documents concerning official actions that violated the Soviet constitution or Soviet laws. Later, the human rights movement also sought to make use of the USSR's international legal commitments, such as the 1948 UN Declaration on Human Rights and, after 1975, 'basket three' of the Helsinki accords. Such appeals to law invariably failed, although they served a purpose in demonstrating the arbitrariness of the regime, which often casually disregarded its own legislation. They also caused the authorities considerable aggravation: the KGB and the party apparatus were both much exercised by the problem of a group of Moscow defence attorneys like Dina Kaminskaya, who regularly acted for citizens accused of anti-social and anti-Soviet acts. The KGB, the courts and the procuracy were ordered to improve the preparation of politically sensitive cases and to seek legal grounds for excluding lawyers like Kaminskaya from such cases ([*Doc. 17*]; Kaminskaya, 1982). Problems such as these seem to have reduced the authorities' appetite for public trials of the kind staged in the Sinyavskii–Daniel case. Instead, many of those trying to use the law against the state found themselves in psychiatric hospitals, often subject to brutal 'treatment' (Bloch and Reddaway, 1977).

GROWING ROOM FOR 'PERMITTED HETERODOXY'

While the regime's attitude towards those who transgressed the acceptable boundaries of political, social or cultural discourse remained uncompromising, those boundaries themselves were, in some spheres, extended. The tightening of cultural policy undoubtedly meant that there was less scope than before 1964 for the expression of heterodox views about aesthetics or morality, but Brown (1996: 8) and others have argued that the scope for other forms of 'within-system' social criticism – what Shtromas (1979, 1981) called 'intrastructural dissent' – actually expanded under Brezhnev. The Brezhnev era witnessed substantial progress in the development of the social sciences, in particular, including the further development of reformist ideas with respect to the economy and the establishment of sociology as an accepted academic discipline. Of course, much of this thinking was inaccessible to ordinary Soviet citizens and circulated only within the confines of certain scholarly journals, academic institutes and high-level conferences. Even then, the most provocative ideas had to be cloaked in a mix of Marxist-Leninist and social science jargon that often served to obscure their real implications. Bright but potentially troublesome scholars were often transferred to specialist institutes – often in decidedly out-of-the-way places – where they would be free to continue their research but would have limited contact with students, whom they might otherwise 'infect' with their heterodox views. This consideration contributed greatly to the strength of the Siberian division of the USSR Academy of Sciences. The purpose-built research city of Akademgorodok, outside Novosibirsk, emerged as the *de facto* capital of 'intrastructural dissent' (Josephson, 1997). It was there that Soviet economists and sociologists like Abel Aganbegyan and Tat'yana Zaslavskaya did much of the scholarly work that laid the foundations for the reforms of the late 1980s.

There were, to be sure, limits on the extent of permissible within-system debate. Thus, the sociological profession underwent a major purge in 1973, although this proved insufficient to prevent Soviet sociologists from exploring sensitive areas (Beliaev and Butorin, 1982). In economics, Mau (1996: 28–32) argues that debates among reform-minded Soviet economists were constrained by the inviolability of certain basic features of the system, such as state ownership of the means of production. The result was their ideas were of limited value as a guide to policy-makers when at last a reformist leadership came to power. Nevertheless, it is important to emphasise that, even within these confines, it was possible to produce and circulate work that was sharply critical of the existing system and that pointed to potentially radical solutions. The most famous of these was the April 1983 'Novosibirsk Report' (Zaslavskaya, 1984), but as Gooding (2002) has shown, scholars like Aleksandr Birman and Nikolai Petrakov were able to produce very sharp critiques of the existing system even in the late 1960s and early 1970s, with Birman, in particular, anticipating Zaslavskaya's attempts to turn the regime's attention to the need to treat workers as human beings rather than cogs in a machine (Birman, 1966, 1969). As Brown. (1996) has shown, among those in the party elite who took an interest in such thinking was Mikhail Gorbachev, one of the youngest men in the Brezhnev leadership. When Gorbachev finally emerged as the country's leader after 1985, it was the work of such 'within-system' reformers that provided the basis for many of his reforms, particularly in the early years of *perestroika*, before the acceptable limits of public political debate had been stretched sufficiently to encompass the ideas of a Sakharov or a Solzhenitsyn.

PART THREE   ASSESSMENT

CHAPTER TEN

BREZHNEV'S LEGACY TO GORBACHEV

The English parliamentarian Enoch Powell is said to have remarked that all political careers end in failure. There are many exceptions to Powell's rule, but it would be hard to argue that Leonid Brezhnev was among them unless mere longevity counts as the standard of success. On the contrary, Brezhnev's longevity is to a great extent the mark of his failure, for he belongs rather to that enormous class of politicians who fail largely because they do not know when to quit. Had he died, retired or been removed in the mid-1970s, he would almost certainly have been seen as a successful leader who had presided over a decade of rising prosperity at home and growing power abroad. Instead, he hung on to power for another six years, during which most of his accomplishments began to come unstuck, while his own mental and physical powers failed. The international environment cooled, economic performance deteriorated markedly, and an array of domestic social problems grew worse. Something had clearly gone wrong. Yet the country's ageing political elite, like Brezhnev himself, was both unable to do anything about this and yet unwilling to retire in favour of a younger generation of leaders. The result was a prolonged succession crisis that was to dominate Soviet politics for half a decade.

BREZHNEV'S TWILIGHT

The problems that were to come together in the late 1980s in the Soviet system's terminal crisis were already emerging by 1976, when Brezhnev reached his 70th birthday: economic growth was slowing, demographic trends were unfavourable and détente was coming under strain. But it was not yet evident to most Soviet or western observers that these were not isolated problems clouding an otherwise sunny political horizon, nor did they yet realise how poorly the system would be able to cope with the demands being made of it. In any case, the evidence of economic advance and increasing international influence was unmistakable. Five years later, the situation looked very different. At home, the economic slowdown was undeniable. Even the

Kremlin's luck seemed to have deserted it, as an unusual run of bad weather contributed to four consecutive years of falling agricultural output. Abroad, the Soviet Union faced a costly and unwinnable war in Afghanistan and unrest in Poland, while relations with the United States were at their lowest point in a generation. Relations with China were no better.

As Brezhnev's own speeches reveal, the country's leaders were well aware that something had gone badly wrong but did not know what to do about it. The sense of frustration and, indeed, of fear, in his public statements was palpable. So great was it, indeed, that in November 1979, after 15 years of adhering to his promise of 'stability of cadres', he launched a bitter public attack on do-nothing officials who could not cope with their assigned tasks, sacking no fewer than eleven members of the government at a stroke. But that was all. Neither Brezhnev nor his colleagues showed any willingness or ability to contemplate more radical solutions to the country's problems than the mild palliatives that they had been applying for a decade.

The sense of drift and decay was reinforced by the state of the country's leaders. Brezhnev's physical decline was increasingly evident to all. He was reliant on both a pacemaker and constant nursing care, and was even then able to function only intermittently. He moved with difficulty and spoke with a slur. Nor was he alone. Many of his colleagues in the leadership were clearly too old and too ill to perform their duties yet were unwilling to yield their posts to younger men. Drift at the top, in turn, meant that the corruption and nepotism that had long been a feature of the regime became increasingly brazen, particularly in and around Brezhnev's own family. The *fin de règne* atmosphere doubtless contributed to this, as Brezhnev's hangers-on, facing an uncertain future without him, sought to extract maximum benefit from their privileged position while they could. Corruption at the top of the socio-political pyramid, moreover, was replicated at every level from ministerial offices to factory shop-floors, contributing to a growing sense of purposelessness and social malaise. The sense that 'everything had gone rotten' felt by Mikhail Gorbachev and other reform-minded officials was widely shared by Soviet citizens at all levels of society concerned about the future of their country (quoted in Brown, 1996: 81).

Brezhnev's failing health meant that the top elite was far more pre-occupied with the coming succession than with tackling the country's economic and social problems. Whoever prevailed, it was clear that one old man would succeed another. The three principal contenders all combined full membership of the Politburo with membership of the Central Committee Secretariat. The oldest was Andrei Kirilenko, the 76-year-old CC secretary who had overseen cadres (personnel) policy for most of the Brezhnev era and was thus reckoned to have a substantial following in the party elite – many senior officials owed their advancement to him. Brezhnev's personal favourite was the 71-year-old Konstantin Chernenko, who had shadowed Brezhnev for almost 30 years. Finally, Yuri Andropov, at 68 the youngest of the three, returned to the Secretariat in May 1982, after 15 years as KGB chief; he was probably the contender whom Brezhnev and his closest associates liked least. Things soon began to go well for Andropov. Kirilenko, who looked like a much tougher opponent than Chernenko, suffered a severe heart attack in May 1982, which effectively eliminated him from contention. He was formally retired in October and died soon thereafter. Chernenko, who continued to manoeuvre for position, found it difficult to establish any kind of independent political identity. He commanded little respect and offered nothing more than continuity with the past and security for those Brezhnev cronies who feared what would become of them when Brezhnev was gone.

From mid-1982, Andropov began to speak to a wider range of themes than he had been able to address as KGB chief, sketching out the outlines of a 'platform' which implied criticisms of the stagnation and decay of the late Brezhnev era – and, implicitly, of Chernenko, the candidate most closely identified with the *status quo*. Secondly, Andropov appears to have been behind moves to undermine Brezhnev and Chernenko by exposing blatant corruption among Brezhnev's family and associates; here, Andropov's KGB links clearly remained of use to him. By the time Brezhnev died on 10 November, Andropov was able to secure the succession relatively quickly.

THE ANDROPOV INTERREGNUM

Yuri Andropov had perhaps the most varied career background of any of the contenders to succeed Brezhnev. He had spent most of the Brezhnev era as KGB chairman, having worked over the preceding thirty years in a number of Communist Youth League (Komsomol), Party and foreign ministry posts (he was ambassador to Hungary at the time of the 1956 Soviet invasion). Whatever the reason for Andropov's transfer to the KGB, there is little doubt that, at the time, it was a demotion from his position as a Central Committee Secretary. Since 1953, security chiefs had been low-profile and not especially influential. Andropov, who headed the KGB for 15 years, succeeded in changing this to some extent. Under his leadership, the power, professionalism and prestige of the KGB grew, while he himself became first a candidate (1967) and then (1973) a full member of the Politburo. His work at the KGB undermined any liberal or reformist credentials he might have possessed, although there is some evidence that he was a more 'enlightened' secret policeman than his predecessors. Dissident activity within the country was crushed and tight political controls were maintained, but this was done without causing a bloodbath. Andropov also devoted considerable attention to developing the KGB's capacity to monitor and to shape Soviet public opinion.

Andropov had little time to make his mark. By the time of his accession, his health had already been poor for some time, and he had only 15 months to live. He had suffered a mild heart attack as early as 1965–66, his kidneys had long been a problem, and he had suffered over the years from hypertension, pneumonia, colitis, arthritis and other problems. In early 1983, Andropov's health took a turn for the worse, and he received haemodialysis for the last year of his life. While he remained mentally acute, he moved with increasing difficulty and found public appearances hard to manage. His last public appearance was in August 1983, although he did not die until the following February. Andropov's ill health was sharply at odds with the image he projected on taking power, which was one of vigour and energy after the decrepitude of the dying Brezhnev.

Despite his health problems, Andropov consolidated his position rapidly. By early summer, he had managed to assume the additional posts of chairman of the State Defence Council and chairman of the Presidium of the USSR Supreme Soviet. He moved cautiously but steadily to renew the party and state elite: 20% of regional party secretaries were replaced by the end of 1983. High-profile anti-corruption campaigns were launched, which facilitated the removal of close associates of Brezhnev and Chernenko and opened the way for the promotion of new men into high positions. The anti-corruption drive also demonstrated to the public at large that things were changing and that even the highest-ranking offenders were not immune from punishment. More broadly, Andropov mounted a campaign to increase labour discipline and thereby to raise efficiency and productivity. This highly visible campaign, which included police patrols of shops designed to discover 'truant' workers, also appears to have been welcomed by the public. Its economic benefits, however, were both limited and subject to the law of diminishing returns. By mid-1983 it had begun to slacken. Little else was done to invigorate the economy. Limited experiments involving greater enterprise autonomy and more flexible management were conducted, but these did not represent radical departures from the *status quo*.

Continuity with the Brezhnev era was far more evident in foreign policy. His grasp of foreign affairs was more sophisticated than that of Brezhnev, but he was no dove. Relations with the United States remained extremely strained, with Soviet policy towards the West focused on the need to forestall the deployment of Pershing-2 and Cruise missiles. East–West relations reached a low ebb with the Soviet withdrawal from nuclear and conventional arms control talks, and attempts to improve relations with China made only limited headway. The Soviet commitment in Angola deepened, and the Afghan war continued. The most memorable foreign policy episode of the brief Andropov era began on 1 September 1983, when Soviet forces in the Far East shot down a Korean airliner which had strayed into Soviet air space. Some 269 passengers and crew were killed. The downing and the unapologetic Soviet response to it provoked international condemnation and tarnished the country's image. Ironically, it was at this time that Andropov, his health failing, ceased to chair Politburo meetings. He was not even present when his colleagues, guided by brief written instructions from him, first discussed the issue.

Policy thus changed little during the 15 months of Andropov's brief reign. Such changes as did take place did not suggest that the new leader was contemplating political liberalisation or anything more than a relatively limited economic reform. Nevertheless, the Andropov period was important in setting the stage for the more radical reforms of the Gorbachev era. Economic problems were discussed with greater candour than before, and more attention was given to the study of economic reform experiences in Eastern Europe. Perhaps most important of all, Andropov advanced the careers of a number of men who were to play key roles later on. The authority of the youngest Politburo member, Mikhail Gorbachev, was enhanced. He was charged with oversight of the economy and was probably Andropov's favoured successor. Other, lesser known figures, such as the future prime minister, Nikolai Ryzhkov, received important promotions at this time, while much of the dead wood left over from the Brezhnev period was swept aside. High-level appointments, moreover, seemed increasingly to reflect competence rather than personal connections to the leader, a marked contrast with the preceding decades.

THE CHERNENKO INTERLUDE

Andropov's successor, Konstantin Chernenko, proved to be the shortest-serving – and arguably the least likely – of all the Soviet Union's leaders. A career party official specialising in agitation and propaganda, Chernenko had formed a close relationship with Brezhnev when he served under the latter in Moldavia in the early 1950s. Chernenko thereafter became Brezhnev's political shadow, following him from post to post up the party hierarchy. In early 1965, shortly after his election as First Secretary, Brezhnev transferred Chernenko to the Central Committee apparatus to head the powerful General Department. As its head, Chernenko worked more closely with Brezhnev than any other department chief and was effectively the secretary to the Politburo. Moreover, the General Department's role expanded during Chernenko's tenure, as a result of his close ties to Brezhnev. Influential though he was, Chernenko's profile nevertheless remained relatively low. Only from the mid-1970s was Brezhnev politically strong enough to advance the career of his favourite openly. The Central Committee's Department for Organisational Party Work, which controlled personnel policy, was overseen by Chernenko from the late 1970s; Chernenko also appears to have supervised the Central Committee's Administrative Organs Department (military and police).

Nevertheless, Chernenko remained an unlikely contender for the succession. His political position depended entirely on Brezhnev's personal support: Chernenko had no natural constituency within the elite, no real experience of leadership or policy-making, and no independent political identity. He seemed to offer nothing more than continuity with the Brezhnev era. Although he failed to block Andropov's rise in 1982, Chernenko was strong enough to secure for himself the position of *de facto* second secretary, and as Andropov's health declined, Chernenko's political strength grew. From September 1983, he chaired meetings of the Politburo and Secretariat, and assumed an increasing array of the ailing Andropov's functions. Ironically, when Andropov died, Chernenko's age – he was 72 – was probably a political advantage. Elderly holdovers from the Brezhnev era, already worried by Andropov's politically motivated anti-corruption drive and his attempts to introduce new blood into the elite, saw Chernenko as the safest available option, while members of the younger generation were confident that he would not be in power for long. With none of the younger members of the elite ready to take power, Chernenko was the obvious interim choice. Few, however, probably realised just how transitory he would prove to be: Chernenko led the Soviet Union for only 13 months. When he died in March 1985, provoking the third change of leader in 28 months, Moscow wags claimed that the Central Committee had decided to simplify matters in future by voting 'to elect Comrade X as General Secretary and bury him beneath the Kremlin wall'.

Chernenko's time in office was one of drift, deadlock and the postponement of difficult choices. The discipline and anti-corruption campaigns of the Andropov era faded (they had lost much of their impetus even while Andropov was alive), the composition of the top leadership bodies virtually froze, and policy in every realm was characterised by continuity with the Brezhnev years. This probably suited Chernenko, who evinced little real interest in high policy. By contrast, he remained deeply interested in his original field: propaganda. Thus, while content to adopt a passive stance with respect to questions of economic policy, he energetically examined and corrected the lists of propaganda slogans drawn up in advance of major political holidays (Volkogonov, 1995). He also took a keen interest in a letter from Stalin's long-time lieutenant, Vyacheslav Molotov, requesting readmission to the Communist Party. A hard-line Stalinist, the 94-year-old Molotov had been expelled from the party in 1957 for attempting to oust Khrushchev. Chernenko, who looked back on Stalin's rule with a feeling of nostalgia, summoned various files on Molotov from the archives, which he examined before deciding to readmit him to the party. The General Secretary personally informed Molotov of his decision. The episode was indicative of both Chernenko's political leanings and his political style.

As Andropov's had done, Chernenko's health rapidly deteriorated, and this led to periodic disappearances from public view and his gradual disengagement from official business. The political vacuum thus created was filled by the Politburo's youngest member, Mikhail Gorbachev, who emerged as Chernenko's number two and who was fulfilling many of the General Secretary's functions by the time of Chernenko's death on 10 March 1985. Behind the scenes, therefore, Chernenko's thirteen-month interregnum was, like Andropov's rule, an important part of the pre-history of *perestroika*. Chernenko's broader historical significance lies not in what he did as leader of the USSR but simply in the fact that he became leader at all. His elevation to the leadership despite his advanced age, poor health and obviously limited abilities underscored the extent to which the Soviet leadership was unable or unwilling to address the hard choices before it. Chernenko was the most visible symptom of the crisis of the Soviet system.

STATE AND SOCIETY AT THE END OF THE BREZHNEV ERA

Throughout his eighteen years in power, Leonid Brezhnev sought always to ensure peace, order and tranquillity within both the leadership and society at large. This is arguably what the Soviet Union needed after a half-century of war and domestic upheaval, and it is certainly what Brezhnev promised to the October plenum of 1964. Over the years, however, the search for consensus, for incremental solutions and for stability at almost any price became a caricature of itself. From the beginning, the Brezhnev regime was essentially conservative. It was bound to be, given its commitment to certainty and stability. However, its conservatism was, in the early years at least, 'flexible and adaptive' (Colton, 1986: 24), open to at least a cautious reformism in areas like economic management or environmental protection. By the late 1970s, however, the leadership had lost its way, and its response was to cling ever more tightly to familiar ideas, institutions and policies. Brezhnev and his colleagues failed to grasp fully the extent of the country's problems and lacked both the imagination to consider new solutions to the problems facing their country, as well as the political will to impose them on a well entrenched and essentially conservative party–state bureaucracy.

Many of these problems were, ironically enough, as much a product of the Soviet system's success as of its failure. The traditional methods of planning and administrative allocation that had forced the USSR through its crash industrialisation in the 1930s were ill suited to managing a complex, highly industrialised economy in which innovation, quality and efficiency were all paramount concerns if growth was to continue. Similarly, methods of political socialisation that had been reasonably effective when directed at a largely illiterate or semi-literate populace lost much of their effectiveness when directed at the much more educated and sophisticated population that had grown up under Soviet power. Rising levels of urbanisation, industrialisation and educational attainment in non-Russian regions enhanced the self-confidence of the country's minority populations and made them less willing to accept Russian leadership. Their educated classes pursued diminishing opportunities for professional advancement, often in competition with Russians, and their political elites sought greater freedom from central interference. Finally, the regime fell victim to the expectations it had created. It had produced a generation of remarkably rapid growth and rising living standards after the Second World War, and its citizens expected this to continue.

Failure to meet these expectations, moreover, was dangerous, for the party's claim to legitimacy rested largely on successful economic performance. Whatever its formal claims, the CPSU's success as an economic manager formed the basis for its legitimation strategy. The party claimed that it was leading the Soviet people in the construction of communism; what this in fact had come to mean by the 1970s was that the party knew how to manage the process of economic development. As long as economic performance was reasonably good, this claim enjoyed some credibility. By the early 1980s, accumulating evidence of economic stagnation had left it looking decidedly shaky. Poor economic performance also undermined the Soviet Union's ability to sustain its ambitious foreign and defence policies at a time when the United States was growing more confident and assertive. Yet not competing with America was simply not an option, for the country's superpower status formed another important element of the party's claim to legitimacy. The gap between promise and performance, both at home and abroad, was rendered all the more striking by the self-congratulatory tone of the propaganda that continued to trumpet Soviet achievements, not to mention the cult surrounding Brezhnev himself. Neither could conceal the accumulating evidence of political and economic stagnation or the physical deterioration of the country's increasingly feeble leaders.

Nevertheless, few could have imagined at the end of Brezhnev's long reign that the Soviet Union had entered its final decade. Most observers, within the USSR and abroad, believed that more vigorous, perhaps more reformist, leadership could improve the performance of the system and sustain Soviet power at home and abroad. This was not to be. It is easy, in hindsight, to see in the stagnation of Brezhnev's last years the 'beginning of the end'. Easy but mistaken. While there is plenty of reason to doubt the long-term viability of the Soviet system as a competitor to western capitalism, there is little reason to believe that the USSR was, by the early 1980s, heading towards a speedy and inevitable collapse. A determined conservative in the Andropov mould could probably have preserved the system more or less intact and kept it going for a good deal longer. As it turned out, what Soviet communism could not survive was the determined and energetic attempt by a dynamic reformer to save it.

PART FOUR   DOCUMENTS

DOCUMENT 1   KHRUSHCHEV'S REMOVAL

Nikita Khrushchev's departure from the political scene was announced to the Soviet people and the world in a terse statement published on 16 October 1964, which gave virtually no explanation for the change of leader beyond a reference to Khrushchev's age and health.

A plenum of the Central Committee of the CPSU took place on 14 October of this year.

The plenum of the CC CPSU granted the request of Comrade N. S. Khrushchev to be released from his duties as First Secretary of the CC CPSU, member of the Presidium of the CC CPSU and Chairman of the USSR Council of Ministers, in connection with his advanced age and the deterioration of his health.

The plenum of the CC CPSU elected L. I. Brezhnev as First Secretary of the CC CPSU.

Pravda, 16 October 1964

The above statement was accompanied by an announcement that the Presidium of the USSR Supreme Soviet had convened on 15 October to elect Aleksei Kosygin as Chairman of the USSR Council of Ministers. A day later, a Pravda editorial on the 'Unshakeable Leninist General Line of the CPSU' cast some light on the real reasons for Khrushchev's fall, albeit without mentioning him by name. Pravda initially seemed to offer some reassurance to those fearing a neo-Stalinist reaction in the wake of Khrushchev's removal, as it confirmed the Party's opposition to the 'cult of personality' (i.e. Stalinism) and its continued commitment to the line adopted by the Twentieth, Twenty-first, and Twenty-second Party Congresses, which had taken place under Khrushchev.

The monolithic unity of the Party, its unshakeable faithfulness to Lenin's principles, was demonstrated with renewed force at the plenum of the Central Committee of the CPSU which took place on 14 October.

Uniting and directing the creative activity of the masses towards a single goal, the Party is guided by a precise compass – the life-giving Marxist-Leninist theory. The Party analyses deeply the complex processes of economic, political and cultural life and works out correct decisions on this basis. A Leninist party is the enemy of subjectivism and drift in communist construction. Hare-brained scheming, hasty conclusions and hurried decisions and actions that are cut off from reality are alien to such a party, as are boasting, idle talk, a passion for bureaucratic methods and a reluctance to take account of that which science and practical experience have already shown....

Carrying out its general line, the Party has consistently and un-compromisingly opposed – and continues to oppose – the ideology and practice of the cult of personality, which is alien to Marxism-Leninism, alien to the very nature of our socialist structure.

Pravda, 17 October 1964

DOCUMENT 2   PODGORNYI'S 'RETIREMENT'

On 24 May 1977, the Central Committee approved a resolution calling for Brezhnev to take over the largely ceremonial post of Chairman of the Presidium of the USSR Supreme Soviet (head of state) from Nikolai Podgornyi. In a hand-written letter to Brezhnev the following day, Podgornyi complained about the omission from the resolution of any face-saving explanation for his retirement.

Personal
Dear Leonid Il'ich!

You should understand my condition today, on account of which it is difficult and perhaps even impossible to say everything as I would wish to.

For me, yesterday's decision was simply staggering. I fully and completely agree that it is necessary to combine the post of General Secretary of the CC CPSU and the post of Chairman of the Presidium of the USSR Supreme Soviet....

As for the form and the essence of the formulation adopted and published in the press, radio and television, '*Released from the duties of a member of the Politburo of the CC CPSU*', without any explanation – I think, Leonid Il'ich, that *I do not deserve this.*

After all, if all this was predetermined in advance, you could have told me to submit my resignation on grounds of health or age or some other reasons, or you could have explained my departure in connection with my retirement.

Now, everyone can think whatever pops into his head, that I am a political criminal or a thief, or that I did not get on with others in the CC Politburo, etc.

Dear Leonid Il'ich!

I've been in the party over 52 years. I have always and in everything performed those tasks the party gave me, without asking anything in return. You and I are old friends, at least until recently. And 1964 brought us so close together that, it seemed, our friendship would never end – and so we vowed.... I always felt your friendship, your support, and this supported and encouraged me in our work together with you, *for which I sincerely thank you.*

Of course, anything can happen in working, and much happened with us. But believe me, L. I., I always wished you, and through you, the Politburo and the whole party, all good things and great successes. All the good things – and there were many – will remain to the end of my life. I wish you health and great success to the good of our party and Motherland.

N. Podgornyi

25/V-77

P.S. I will leave this for a bit, calm down and try to write more coherently. For now, if something is not quite right, forgive me.

Podgornyi's appeal was not without effect. He submitted to the Politburo a formal request to be released from his duties in view of his age and the state of his health. On 26 May, the Politburo, on Brezhnev's advice, approved Podgornyi's request and amended the earlier CC resolution accordingly.

Podgornyi (1995: 146), emphasis in original

DOCUMENT 3   BREZHNEV PRESENTS HIS VISION OF 'DEVELOPED SOCIALISM'

Introduction

A developed socialist society is a natural stage in the socio-economic maturing of the new system in the framework of the first phase of the communist formation. This, to use Lenin's words, is the fully established socialism from which the gradual transition to communism begins. This is precisely the stage in the development of socialism that has been achieved in our country....

The experience of the USSR, of other countries of the socialist community, testifies to the fact that laying the foundations of socialism, that is, abolishing the exploiting classes and establishing public ownership of the means of production in all sectors of the national economy, does not yet make it possible to launch the direct transition to communism. Before this certain stages in the development of socialism on its own basis must be traversed. Moreover, practice has shown that the development, the perfecting of socialism is a task no less complex, no less responsible than the laying of its foundations.

It is self-evident that a mature socialist society must rest on *highly developed productive forces, on a powerful, advanced industry, on a large-scale, highly mechanised agriculture built on collectivist principles.* Such today is the Soviet economy....

Thanks to the convergence of the diverse forms of socialist property, the gradual obliteration of any essential distinctions between town and country, between mental and physical labour, and adoption by all working people of the ideological and political positions of the working class, the interests and goals, the social ideals and psychology of all strata of the population have drawn closer together than ever before. On this basis, substantial changes have also occurred in the political system. Essentially they consist *in the growing of the state of the dictatorship of the proletariat into a socialist state of all the people.*

Such are the objective processes that led our party to the conclusion that *developed socialism has now been built in the USSR, that is to say, a degree, a stage in the maturing of the new society has been reached when the repatterning of the totality of social relations on the collectivist principles inherent in socialism is completed.*

Brezhnev (1977: 3–5, 7).

DOCUMENT 4   SHELEST RECEIVES THE 'INVITATION' TO INVADE CZECHOSLOVAKIA

In early August 1968, a small group of hardliners in the leadership of the Communist Party of Czechoslovakia transmitted a letter to Brezhnev via Ukrainian party chief Petr Shelest requesting urgent military assistance to thwart the imminent 'counter-revolution' that was about to take place in that country. Soviet leaders had been trying for some time to get the Czechoslovak conservatives to present them with such an appeal. Below is an extract from Shelest's diary describing the transfer of the letter.

... Aside from the meeting itself among the fraternal Parties, I'm particularly eager to link up with V. Bil'ak to receive the letter that is of such great interest to us. During one of my conversations with Bil'ak in Cierna, he told me that he'll have the letter and will transmit it to me. It's very difficult to believe there will be positive results from the Bratislava meeting.

...

Late in the evening I managed to link up and speak with V. Bil'ak. All of this was done after taking great precautions. I reminded Bil'ak that we were awaiting the letter promised by him and his group. During the conversation with me, Bil'ak was very ill at ease and disturbed by something, but he did not renege on his promise and requested only that he be given a bit more time, until the following day.

...

Toward evening [of 3 August] I met again with Bil'ak, and he and I arranged that at 8:00 p.m. he would go into the public lavatory, and that I also should show up there at that time. He would then transmit the letter to me via our KGB employee, Savchenko. This is precisely what happened. We met "by chance" in the lavatory, and Savchenko inconspicuously transferred from his hand to mine an envelope containing the long-awaited letter. It assessed the situation in the KSC and the country, the nefarious activities of rightist elements, and the political and psychological terror being waged against Communists, that is, people supporting correct positions. The gains of socialism are under threat. An anti-Soviet frenzy has overtaken the country, and the economy and politics of Czechoslovakia are fully oriented toward the West. A very alarming and complicated situation has emerged in the country. The letter expresses a request that if circumstances so warrant, we should intervene to block the path of counter-revolution and prevent the outbreak of civil war and bloodshed. The letter was signed by Indra, Bil'ak, Kolder, Barbirek, Kapek, Rigo, Piller, Svestka, Hoffmann, Lenart, and Strougal.

Kramer (1998b: 244)

DOCUMENT 5   **TREATY BETWEEN THE UNITED STATES OF AMERICA AND THE UNION OF SOVIET SOCIALIST REPUBLICS ON THE LIMITATION OF ANTI-BALLISTIC MISSILE SYSTEMS (THE ABM TREATY)**

The cornerstone of the arms control regime negotiated by the two super-powers during the 1970s was the ABM Treaty, signed in Moscow on 26 May 1972. By means of this agreement, the United States and the USSR sought to avoid an expensive and potentially destabilising race in the development of defensive systems. It remained in force until 2002, when the United States withdrew from it to pursue its own plans for national missile defence.

...

Article I

1. Each Party undertakes to limit anti-ballistic missile (ABM) systems and to adopt other measures in accordance with the provisions of this Treaty.
2. Each Party undertakes not to deploy ABM systems for a defense of the territory of its country and not to provide a base for such a defense, and not to deploy ABM systems for defense of an individual region except as provided for in Article III of this Treaty.

Article II

1. For the purpose of this Treaty an ABM system is a system to counter strategic ballistic missiles or their elements in flight trajectory, currently consisting of:

(a) ABM interceptor missiles, which are interceptor missiles constructed and deployed for an ABM role, or of a type tested in an ABM mode;

(b) ABM launchers, which are launchers constructed and deployed for launching ABM interceptor missiles; and

(c) ABM radars, which are radars constructed and deployed for an ABM role, or of a type tested in an ABM mode.

2. The ABM system components listed in paragraph 1 of this Article include those which are:

(a) operational;

(b) under construction;

(c) undergoing testing;

(d) undergoing overhaul, repair or conversion; or

(e) mothballed.

Article III

Each Party undertakes not to deploy ABM systems or their components except that:

(a) within one ABM system deployment area having a radius of one hundred and fifty kilometers and centered on the Party's national capital, a Party may deploy: (1) no more than one hundred ABM launchers and no more than one hundred ABM interceptor missiles at launch sites, and (2) ABM radars within no more than six ABM radar complexes, the area of each complex being circular and having a diameter of no more than three kilometers; and

(b) within one ABM system deployment area having a radius of one hundred and fifty kilometers and containing ICBM silo launchers, a Party may deploy: (1) no more than one hundred ABM launchers and no more than one hundred ABM interceptor missiles at launch sites, (2) two large phased-array ABM radars comparable in potential to corresponding ABM radars operational or under construction on the date of signature of the Treaty in an ABM system deployment area containing ICBM silo launchers, and (3) no more than eighteen ABM radars each having a potential less than the potential of the smaller of the above-mentioned two large phased-array ABM radars.

http://www.state.gov/www/global/arms/treaties/abmpage.html

DOCUMENT 6   INTERIM AGREEMENT BETWEEN THE UNITED STATES OF AMERICA AND THE UNION OF SOVIET SOCIALIST REPUBLICS ON CERTAIN MEASURES WITH RESPECT TO THE LIMITATION OF STRATEGIC OFFENSIVE ARMS (THE SALT I TREATY)

Signed along with the ABM Treaty, the first SALT treaty, which was to last for five years, confirmed the Soviet superiority that had emerged in the preceding years in terms of both numbers of launchers and total megatonnage. However, it failed to cover strategic bombers, in which the United States enjoyed a substantial advantage, or US aircraft based at sea or on the territory of US allies close to the USSR. The United States also enjoyed an edge in both accuracy and the deployment of missiles carrying multiple, independently targetable warheads (multiple independent re-entry vehicles, or MIRVs), which were not identifiable by satellite and were therefore excluded from the agreement.

...

Article I

The Parties undertake not to start construction of additional fixed land-based intercontinental ballistic missile (ICBM) launchers after July 1, 1972.

Article II

The Parties undertake not to convert land-based launchers for light ICBMs, or for ICBMs of older types deployed prior to 1964, into land-based launchers for heavy ICBMs of types deployed after that time.

Article III

The Parties undertake to limit submarine-launched ballistic missile (SLBM) launchers and modern ballistic missile submarines to the numbers operational and under construction on the date of signature of this Interim Agreement, and in addition to launchers and submarines constructed under procedures established by the Parties as replacements for an equal number of ICBM launchers of older types deployed prior to 1964 or for launchers on older submarines.

Article IV

Subject to the provisions of this Interim Agreement, modernization and replacement of strategic offensive ballistic missiles and launchers covered by this Interim Agreement may be undertaken.

Article V

1. For the purpose of providing assurance of compliance with the provisions of this Interim Agreement, each Party shall use national technical means of verification at its disposal in a manner consistent with generally recognized principles of international law.

2. Each Party undertakes not to interfere with the national technical means of verification of the other Party operating in accordance with paragraph 1 of this Article.

3. Each Party undertakes not to use deliberate concealment measures which impede verification by national technical means of compliance with the provisions of this Interim Agreement. This obligation shall not require changes in current construction, assembly, conversion, or overhaul practices.

...

Article VIII

2. This Interim Agreement shall remain in force for a period of five years unless replaced earlier by an agreement on more complete measures limiting strategic offensive arms. It is the objective of the Parties to conduct active follow-on negotiations with the aim of concluding such an agreement as soon as possible.

http://www.state.gov/www/global/arms/treaties/salt1-2.html

DOCUMENT 7 **TREATY BETWEEN THE UNITED STATES OF AMERICA AND THE UNION OF SOVIET SOCIALIST REPUBLICS ON THE LIMITATION OF STRATEGIC OFFENSIVE ARMS, TOGETHER WITH AGREED STATEMENTS AND COMMON UNDERSTANDINGS REGARDING THE TREATY (THE SALT II TREATY)**

Signed at Vienna on 18 June 1979, the SALT II treaty was never ratified, falling victim to the sharp deterioration in superpower relations that occurred at the end of the 1970s. Nevertheless, the two sides continued to adhere to the terms of SALT II, more or less, through the 1980s. The greater length and detail of this treaty and the difficulty in agreeing it both reflected the increasing complexity of the issues and technologies involved, as well as the fact that the 'easy' arms control bargains had been struck with the ABM Treaty and SALT I.

...

Article III

1. Upon entry into force of this Treaty, each Party undertakes to limit ICBM launchers, SLBM launchers, heavy bombers, and ASBMs to an aggregate number not to exceed 2,400.

2. Each Party undertakes to limit, from January 1, 1981, strategic offensive arms referred to in paragraph 1 of this Article to an aggregate number not to exceed 2,250, and to initiate reductions of those arms which as of that date would be in excess of this aggregate number.

3. Within the aggregate numbers provided for in paragraphs 1 and 2 of this Article and subject to the provisions of this Treaty, each Party has the right to determine the composition of these aggregates.

4. For each bomber of a type equipped for ASBMs, the aggregate numbers provided for in paragraphs 1 and 2 of this Article shall include the maximum number of such missiles for which a bomber of that type is equipped for one operational mission.

5. A heavy bomber equipped only for ASBMs shall not itself be included in the aggregate numbers provided for in paragraphs 1 and 2 of this Article.

6. Reductions of the numbers of strategic offensive arms required to comply with the provisions of paragraphs 1 and 2 of this Article shall be carried out as provided for in Article XI.

Article IV

1. Each Party undertakes not to start construction of additional fixed ICBM launchers.

2. Each Party undertakes not to relocate fixed ICBM launchers.

3. Each Party undertakes not to convert launchers of light ICBMs, or of ICBMs of older types deployed prior to 1964, into launchers of heavy ICBMs of types deployed after that time.

4. Each Party undertakes in the process of modernization and replacement of ICBM silo launchers not to increase the original internal volume of an ICBM silo launcher by more than thirty-two percent. Within this limit each Party has the right to determine whether such an increase will be made through an increase in the original diameter or in the original depth of an ICBM silo launcher, or in both of these dimensions.

Article V

1. Within the aggregate numbers provided for in paragraphs 1 and 2 of Article III, each Party undertakes to limit launchers of ICBMs and SLBMs equipped with MIRVs, ASBMs equipped with MIRVs, and heavy bombers equipped for cruise missiles capable of a range in excess of 600 kilometers to an aggregate number not to exceed 1,320.

2. Within the aggregate number provided for in paragraph 1 of this Article, each Party undertakes to limit launchers of ICBMs and SLBMs equipped with MIRVs, and ASBMs equipped with MIRVs to an aggregate number not to exceed 1,200.

3. Within the aggregate number provided for in paragraph 2 of this Article, each Party undertakes to limit launchers of ICBMs equipped with MIRVs to an aggregate number not to exceed 820.

4. For each bomber of a type equipped for ASBMs equipped with MIRVs, the aggregate numbers provided for in paragraphs 1 and 2 of this Article shall include the maximum number of ASBMs for which a bomber of that type is equipped for one operational mission.

http://www.state.gov/www/global/arms/treaties/salt2-2.html

DOCUMENT 8   THE JACKSON–VANIK AMENDMENT

The attachment of emigration conditions to US-Soviet trade relations in the Jackson–Vanik amendment was regarded by the Kremlin as a major affront. Though ready to ease restrictions on Jewish emigration substantially in pursuit of détente, it was not prepared to accept explicit US conditions on this issue. In response to passage of the amendment, Moscow abrogated its 1972 trade agreement with the United States.

SEC. 402. FREEDOM OF EMIGRATION IN EAST–WEST TRADE

(a) To assure the continued dedication of the United States to fundamental human rights, and notwithstanding any other provision of law, on or after the date of the enactment of this Act products from any nonmarket economy country shall not be eligible to receive non-discriminatory treatment (most-favored nation treatment), such country shall not participate in any program of the Government of the United States which extends credits or credit guarantees or investment guarantees, directly or indirectly, and the President of the United States shall not conclude any commercial agreement with any such country, during the period beginning with the date on which the president determines that such country –

(1) denies its citizens the right or opportunity to emigrate;

(2) imposes more than a normal tax on emigration or on the visas or other documents required for emigration, for any purpose or cause whatsoever; or

(3) imposes more than nominal tax, levy, fine, fee, or other charge on any citizen as a consequence of the desire of such citizens to emigrate to the country of his choice, and ending on the date on which the President determines that such country is no longer in violation of paragraph (1), (2), or (3).

Trade Act, P.L. 93–618 of 3 January 1975, USGPO, Washington DC.

The perceived threat from the People's Republic of China was much on the Soviet leader's mind during Brezhnev's 1973 visit to the United States, not least because US President Nixon's dramatic opening to China the year before had aroused Soviet fears of encirclement. In his memoirs, Nixon's Secretary of State, Henry Kissinger, later recorded the force with which the Soviet leaders sought to convey these concerns.

As it turned out, the two most significant conversations of the summit occurred on that last full day in San Clemente, June 23. They were unscheduled and descended upon us without warning. At a noon meeting between Nixon and Brezhnev, attended only by me and interpreter Sukhodrev, Brezhnev vented his hatred for the Chinese.... His ire was not free of racial overtones. The Chinese were perfidious and they were sly in concealing their real aims. He considered the Chinese Cultural Revolution an example of moral degeneracy, asking what kind of leader would oppress their people while making propaganda all around the world – as if the Gulag Archipelago concentration camps and extermination had never been heard of in his fatherland of socialism. He strongly implied that Soviet doctors believed that Mao suffered from a mental disorder. At any rate, sane or not, 'Mao had a treacherous character.'

But Brezhnev was not interested in simply making a theoretical point. His purpose was eminently practical. He proposed a secret exchange of views on China through the Presidential Channel. He warned that in ten years, China's nuclear weapons programme might be equal to the Soviet programme of 1973.... Brezhnev added that he had no objection to state-to-state relations between Washington and Peking. Military arrangements would be another matter. ... The Soviet Union had no intention of attacking China, but a Chinese military arrangement with the United States would only confuse the issue, asserted Brezhnev, with a subtlety that showed Gromyko's fine drafting hand.

Nixon replied coolly that he was prepared to be in touch through the Channel 'on any subject' but he gave no analysis of his own of Chinese motives or purposes. I added that we had never had any military discussions with China. Neither Nixon nor I offered any reassurance about the future. Brezhnev seemed to imply a quid pro quo when he remarked out of the blue that the Soviet Union had stopped military deliveries to North Vietnam after the signing of the Paris accords....

In the afternoon... Gromyko took me aside. He was obviously worried that Brezhnev had been insufficiently explicit – though not even his worst enemy is likely to list vagueness of expression among Brezhnev's faults. At any rate, the foreign minister wanted to reaffirm unambiguously, for the third time in six weeks, that any military agreement between China and the United States would lead to war. I said I understood what he was saying. But I gave him no clue as to our intentions. I saw no sense in giving blanket reassurance in the face of a threat....

Kissinger (1982: 294–5).

DOCUMENT 10   THE DANGERS OF DISPATCHING TROOPS TO AFGHANISTAN

On 17–18 March 1979, the Politburo discussed the deteriorating situation in Afghanistan and the possible Soviet response. Despite a strong sense that the USSR could not afford to allow the PDPA regime in Kabul to fall, the Soviet leaders reached a consensus in their strong opposition to military intervention in the Afghan civil war. Many of their concerns look all the more prescient in light of the consequences of their decision to intervene in December 1979.

ANDROPOV: We know Lenin's teaching about a revolutionary situation. Whatever type of situation we are talking about in Afghanistan, it is not that type of situation. Therefore, I believe that we can suppress a revolution in Afghanistan only with the aid of our bayonets, but that is for us entirely inadmissable. We cannot take such a risk ...

GROMYKO: I fully support Comrade Andropov's proposal to exclude a measure such as the introduction of our troops into Afghanistan. The [Afghan] army there is unreliable. Thus our army if it enters Afghanistan will be an aggressor. Against whom will it fight? Against the Afghan people first of all, and it will have to shoot at them. Comrade Andropov correctly noted that indeed the situation in Afghanistan is not ripe for a [socialist] revolution. And all that we have done in recent years with such effort in terms of a détente in international tensions, arms reductions, and much more – all that would be thrown back. Of course, this will be a nice gift for China. All the nonaligned countries will be against us....

One must ask, and what would we gain? Afghanistan with its present government, with a backward economy, with inconsequential weight in international affairs... we must keep in mind that from a legal point of view too we would not be justified in sending troops. According to the UN Charter a country can appeal for assistance, and we could send troops, in case it is subject to external aggression....

GROMYKO: ...We would be throwing away everything which we achieved with such difficulty, particularly détente, the SALT-II negotiations which would fly by the wayside, there would be no signing of an agreement (and however you look at it that is for us the greatest political act), there would be no meeting of Leonid Il'ich with Carter, and it is very doubtful that Giscard d'Estaing would come to visit us, and our relations with Western countries, particularly the FRG, would be spoiled....

Cold War International History Project Bulletin 4 (Fall 1994), pp. 70–1.

DOCUMENT 11 AN UNWELCOME COUP IN KABUL

On 14 September 1979, President Nur Mohammad Taraki, the leader of the PDPA's Parcham ('Banner') faction, launched an ambush against his rival, Prime Minister Hafizullah Amin, the hardline leader of the party's Khalq ('People's Party') faction. The ambush failed, leaving Amin and his Khalq faction in the ascendant. Taraki's defeat was a major problem for the Kremlin: Amin's policies were even more radical than Taraki's and intensified opposition to the regime. A report to the Politburo on 15 September by Foreign Minister Gromyko, Defence Minister Ustinov and First Deputy Chairman of the KGB Semyon Tsvigun conveys the Soviet leaders' frustration at their inability to control events in Afghanistan and their continuing fear of being dragged into a military intervention that they wish to avoid.

...In the conditions now prevailing, it seems to us expedient to adhere to the following line:

First. Taking account of the real situation as it is now developing, we cannot refuse to do business with Amin and the leadership that he heads. At the same time, we must restrain him as best we can from taking repressive measures against Taraki's supporters....

Second. Our military advisers attached to Afghan units and those working with the security organs and the Ministry of Internal Affairs should remain in place, fulfilling their duties connected with the preparation and conduct of operations against rebel formations, but not, of course, taking any part in repressive measures against Amin's enemies, in the event that military units are used for this purpose.

Third. Supplies of Soviet armaments and military equipment to Afghanistan should be slowed up somewhat.

Fourth. Approach Amin and express our opinion that, if Taraki surrenders all his offices, there should be no repressive measures against him nor any condemnation....

The limits of Moscow's ability to restrain Amin soon became apparent. On 16 September, Taraki's retirement for reasons of health was announced. In fact, Taraki's health took a turn for the worse in early October: he was executed on Amin's orders. The repression of Taraki supporters by Amin followed.

'Dokumenty', 1996.

DOCUMENT 12   ON POSSIBLE MILITARY INTERVENTION IN POLAND

Though anxious to avoid military intervention in Poland if at all possible, the Politburo and the military high command in the late summer of 1980 were concerned with preparing for just such a contingency. As the following note, signed by Suslov, Andropov, Gromyko, Ustinov and Chernenko makes clear, an invasion of Poland would have been a difficult and large-scale undertaking.

SPECIAL DOSSIER
Top Secret
Copy No.

CPSU CC

The situation in the PPR remains tense. The strike movement is operating on a countrywide scale.

Taking account of the emerging situation, the Ministry of Defense requests permission, in the first instance, to bring three tank divisions (1 in the Baltic MD, 2 in the Beloruss. MD) and one mechanized rifle division (Transcarp. MD) up to full combat readiness as of 6:00 p.m. on 29 August to form a group of forces in case military assistance is provided to the PPR.

To fill out these divisions, it will be necessary to requisition from the national economy up to 25 thous. military reservists and 6 thous. vehicles, including 3 thous. to replace the vehicles taken from these troops to help out with the harvest. Without the extra vehicles, the divisions cannot bring their mobile reserves up to full readiness. The necessity to fill out the divisions at the expense of resources from the national economy arises because they are maintained at a reduced level in peacetime. The successful fulfillment of tasks during the entry of these divisions into the territory of the PPR requires combat arrangements to be established some 5–7 days in advance.

If the situation in Poland deteriorates further, we will also have to fill out the constantly ready divisions of the Baltic, Belorussian, and Transcarpathian Military Districts up to wartime level. If the main forces of the Polish Army go over to the side of the counterrevolutionary forces, we must increase the group of our own forces by another five–seven divisions. To these ends, the Ministry of Defense should be permitted to plan the call-up of as many as 75 thous. additional military reservists and 9 thous. additional vehicles.

In this case, it would mean that a total of up to 100 thous. military reservists and 15 thous. vehicles would have to be requisitioned from the national economy.

Kramer (1998a: 108)

DOCUMENT 13 THE POLITBURO DISCUSSES PLANS FOR MARTIAL LAW IN POLAND

On 10 December 1981, the Politburo discussed Polish leader Wojciech Jaruzelski's plans to impose martial law in Poland and his request for Soviet economic and possibly also military assistance. As the extracts below make clear, the Soviet leaders were extremely unenthusiastic about the prospect of direct military intervention in Poland. Most interesting are the hints that Jaruzelski himself was angling for Soviet military assistance.

ANDROPOV: ...I'd now like to mention that Jaruzelski has been more than persistent in setting forth economic demands from us and has made the implementation of "Operation X" contingent on our willingness to offer economic assistance; and I would say even more than that, he is raising the question, albeit indirectly, of receiving military assistance as well....

As far as economic assistance is concerned, it will of course be difficult for us to undertake anything of the scale and nature of what has been proposed....

If Comrade Kulikov actually did speak about the introduction of troops, then I believe he did this incorrectly. We can't risk such a step. We don't intend to introduce troops into Poland. That is the proper position, and we must adhere to it until the end....

GROMYKO: ... we must somehow try to dispel the notions that Jaruzelski and other leaders in Poland have about the introduction of troops. There cannot be any introduction of troops into Poland....

USTINOV: ...With regard to what Comrade Kulikov allegedly said about the introduction of troops into Poland, I can say in full responsibility that Kulikov never said this. He simply repeated what was said by us and by Leonid Ilyich that we would not leave Poland in the lurch. And he perfectly well knows that the Poles themselves requested us not to introduce troops.

Kramer (1995: 136–7)

DOCUMENT 14 KOSYGIN PROMISES A BETTER DEAL TO CONSUMERS

In April 1971, Prime Minister Aleksei Kosygin presented the Ninth Five-Year Plan to the Twenty-fourth Congress of the CPSU. Reflecting the regime's increasing readiness to give priority to popular living standards, he promised a major improvement in household welfare, at least partly in response to sporadic worker protests.

... In the new five-year period, our people's material well-being will increase first of all as a result of increases in the wages and salaries of workers and office employees and in the incomes of collective farmers in step with growing productivity and the improved skills of personnel....

In accordance with this programme, the minimum wage will be raised to 70 roubles a month in 1971 and, at the same time, the basic wage and salary rates of workers and office employees in the middle pay categories of railroad transport will be increased. The basic rates for machine operators in agriculture will be increased in the same year.

As of July 1, 1971, it is planned to raise the minimum size of the pension for collective farmers and to extend to them the procedure for fixing pensions that has been established for workers and office employees.

At the same time ... the minimum size of the old-age pension for workers and office employees will be increased...

A high growth rate in the population's cash incomes is to be ensured by an increase in the production of consumer goods and by the growth of trade turnover. The draft Directives envisage a growth of 40% in the population's cash incomes, sales of goods to the population will increase by 42% and the volume of paid services will increase by 47%.

In the new five-year plan, market supplies of such products as meat, fish, vegetable oil, eggs and vegetables will increase by 40% to 60%. The sale of clothing will increase by 35%, that of knitwear by 56% and that of cultural and everyday goods by 80%. The rate at which the population is supplied with refrigerators will increase from 32 per 100 families in 1970 to 64 in 1975; for television sets the corresponding figures will be 51 and 72, and for washing machines they will be 52 and 72....

Kosygin (1973: 131–3).

DOCUMENT 15   THE KGB REPORTS ON DISSIDENT ACTIVITIES IN MOSCOW

In January 1967, KGB Chairman Vladimir Semichastnyi and USSR Prosecutor-General Roman Rudenko reported to the Central Committee on dissident activity in the capital. As is evident from their recommendations, even at this stage the security organs were moving towards the 'pastoral-prophylactic' approach to dissidence in an effort to limit the number of actual arrests and prosecutions undertaken.

The Committee for State Security and the USSR Prosecutor's Office are reporting on measures taken to curtail anti-social, politically harmful activities on the part of certain individual, antagonistically inclined persons.

As has been reported before, beginning in December 1965, in Moscow there have been a number of attempts to organise various assemblies and provocations, whether in defence of Sinyavskii and Daniel or 'in memory of the victims of Stalinism' or with demagogic calls for the revision of laws....

These assemblies are as a rule preceded by the circulation of various politically harmful materials, including leaflets with demagogic demands.

The activities of the participants in these assemblies are not casual or accidental. They are to a considerable extent inspired and heated up by those who, in an environment characterised by the increased political activism of the masses and the measures adopted by the Party to strengthen and broaden socialist democracy, hide behind slogans about the struggle with the 'consequences of the cult of personality' and for '"true" democracy', but have in fact started on the path of demagogy and have in essence set themselves the goal of discrediting the democratic achievements of the Soviet system.

The report goes on to name a number of the leading participants in this activity, including Aleksandr Nekrich, Aleksandr Ginzburg and Lidiya Chukovskaya, who were to become among the best known Soviet dissidents of the Brezhnev era.

... a group has formed in Moscow numbering 35–40 people, who carry on their politically harmful activities by means of the preparation and circulation of anti-Soviet literature and by the organisation of various demonstrations and assemblies....

Taking the view that bringing criminal charges against the persons indicated would trigger a definite reaction within the country and abroad, we would consider it expedient to instruct the CC's Department for Propaganda and the Moscow City Party Committee of the CPSU to conduct the necessary explanatory work, including speeches by party officials, authoritative propagandists, leading officials of the procuracy and state security at enterprises, in institutions and especially among student youth.

The organs of the Prosecutor's Office and of state security have taken measures of a warning-preventative character towards these people, conducting conversations with many of them and exerting a positive influence on them through their places of work or social organisations....

http://psi.ece.jhu.edu/~kaplan/IRUSS/BUK/GBARC/pdfs/dis60/pb67-2.pdf

DOCUMENT 16   A KGB ASSESSMENT OF *SAMIZDAT* PUBLICATIONS

The extracts below are taken from a December 1970 KGB report to the Central Committee of the CPSU on the spread of so-called samizdat literature. Signed by the then KGB Chairman, Yuri Andropov, the report highlights a change in the nature of samizdat literature being circulated

within the USSR: while much dissent was still expressed through belles-lettres *forms, the KGB reports here that most of it consisted of 'political programmatic' materials.*

Analysis of the so-called '*samizdat*' literature circulating in *intelligentsia* circles and among students shows that '*samizdat*' has undergone qualitative changes in recent years. If five years ago, the dissemination of ideologically vicious artistic works was chiefly observed, at the present time documents with a programmatic-political character are being given ever wider circulation. During the period since 1965, over 400 different studies and articles on economic, political and philosophical questions have appeared, criticising from various angles the historical experience of the building of socialism in the Soviet Union, evaluating the internal and external policies of the CPSU, and putting forward various programmes of opposition activity.

Many of these documents propagate ideas and views borrowed from the political platforms of the Yugoslav leaders, the Czechoslovak Dubčekites and certain western communist parties....

The report goes on to trace the influence in samizdat *writings of the historian Roy Medvedev and the physicist Andrei Sakharov.*

In a number of proposals for the 'democratisation' of the USSR is envisaged 'the limitation or liquidation of the monopoly of power of the CPSU, the creation in the country of an opposition that is loyal to socialism'. Their authors and disseminators consider that the current level of development of socialist democracy gives the opposition views a right to exist and to demand the creation of legal opportunities for the expression of disagreement with the official course....

From around the end of 1968 and the beginning of 1969, the political nucleus of a so-called 'democratic movement' has formed from oppositionally inclined elements. It has, in their view, three characteristics of an opposition: 'it has leaders and activists, and it relies on a significant number of sympathisers; without acquiring a clear organisational form it nevertheless defines certain aims for itself and chooses definite tactics; and it is striving for legality'....

The centres of circulation of uncensored materials remain, as before, Moscow, Leningrad, Kiev, Gorky, Novosibirsk and Khar'kov....

The Committee for State Security is taking the necessary steps to block attempts by certain persons to use '*samizdat*' for the circulation of slanders against the Soviet state and social structure....

http://psi.ece.jhu.edu/~kaplan/IRUSS/BUK/GBARC/pdfs/dis70/ct119-71.pdf

DOCUMENT 17   DISCIPLINING DISSIDENTS' DEFENCE ATTORNEYS

On 10 July 1970, KGB chief Yuri Andropov reported to the Central Committee on the case of N. E. Gorbanevskaya, who had been charged under article 190 of the criminal code for participating in anti-social activities, including the preparation and transmission to the West of 'hostile' samizdat materials. The court found her to be suffering from schizophrenia and sentenced her to forced treatment in a psychiatric hospital. However, Andropov's chief concern was not Gorbanevskaya's fate but that of her defence attorney.

...the Committee for State Security simultaneously reports on the incorrect behaviour during the judicial proceedings of defence attorney S. V. KALISTRATOVA, who tried to deny that GORBANEVSKAYA'S activities were criminal in character. Moreover, obviously slanderous materials prepared by the accused that discredited the Soviet state and social structure were presented by KALISTRATOVA in her address to the court as 'evaluative', expressing the convictions of GORBANEVSKAYA....

Such behaviour by a defence attorney during judicial proceedings is not a one-off. According to our data, analogous positions have been adopted by a group of Moscow defence attorneys... when representing defendants accused of anti-Soviet and anti-social activities in the form of slander against the Soviet state and social structure.

The Central Committee instructed the Moscow City Party Committee (Mosgorkom) to examine the questions raised by Andropov's report. Below is Mosgorkom's account of its fulfilment of those instructions.

To the CC CPSU on No ST-102/10s

The Moscow City Party Committee conducted a meeting of heads of the city's administrative organs, at which they discussed the problems of fulfilling the Resolution of the Secretariat of the CC CPSU of 17 July of this year 'On the note of the Committee for State Security attached to the USSR Council of Ministers' and worked out measures for implementing the same.

The Prosecutor's Office for the city of Moscow, the Moscow Administration of the Committee for State Security, the Moscow City Court and the Presidium of the City Collegium of Defence Attorneys were instructed to improve the coordination of their activities in organising and conducting judicial processes of great socio-political significance.

The chairman of the Presidium of the City Collegium of Defence Attorneys, Comrade K. N. Apraksin, and the heads of the juridical consulting bureaux were instructed to adopt measures for improving ideo-educational work in lawyers' collectives and increasing the personal responsibility of defence attorneys for their performances in court.

Comrade K. N. Apraksin's statement that the attorneys Kaminskaya, Kalistratova, Pozdeev and Rom would not in future be permitted to participate in processes concerning cases of crimes under article 190 of the Criminal Code of the RSFSR[2] was taken into account.

Attorney Monakhov was excluded from the Collegium of Defence Attorneys for amoral behaviour.

The measures adopted have been reported to the USSR Committee for State Security.

(Signed) *Illegible*

Secretary, Moscow City Party Committee

10.viii.70

'Napravlena' (1993: 94–5).

DOCUMENT 18   OPEN LETTER TO SOVIET LEADERS FROM SAKHAROV, MEDVEDEV AND TURCHIN

At the beginning of the 1970s, three leading dissident intellectuals, the physicists Andrei Sakharov and Valentin Turchin and the historian Roy Medvedev published an open letter to the leaders of the Soviet government, the Soviet state and the CPSU, in which they linked their concern with intellectual freedom and democratisation to problems of artistic creativity and technical and economic progress. Ultimately, they warned, failure to democratise the Soviet system would threaten Soviet power.

Deeply Esteemed Leonid Ilyich[3], Aleksei Nikolayevich[4], Nikolai Viktorovich[5]:

In the course of the past decade, menacing signs of breakdown and stagnation have been discovered in the economy of our country... Comparing our economy with that of the U.S., we see that ours lags not only in quantitative but also – saddest of all – in qualitative respects. We surpass America in the mining of coal, but we lag behind in oil drilling, lag very much behind in gas drilling and in the production of electric power, hopelessly lag behind in chemistry and infinitely lag behind in computer technology. As for the use of computers in the economy... a phenomenon that has deservedly been called the second industrial revolution... here the gap is so wide that it is impossible to measure it. We simply live in another epoch....

---

[2] Article 190 of the Criminal Code covered such acts as anti-Soviet propaganda and slander against the state.

[3] Brezhnev.

[4] Kosygin.

[5] Podgornyi.

The source of our difficulties is not the socialist structure. On the contrary, it lies in those peculiarities and conditions of our life that run contrary to socialism and are hostile to it. This source is the antidemocratic traditions and norms of public life that appeared during Stalin's period and have not been completely liquidated at the present time...

There is no doubt that, with the beginning of the second industrial revolution, these phenomena have become a decisive economic factor. Problems of organisation and management cannot be solved by one or several individuals who have power. They demand the creative participation of millions of people on all levels of the economic system. But in the process of exchanging information we are facing difficulties that cannot be overcome. Real information on our faults and negative phenomena is kept secret because it may be used by hostile propaganda. Exchange of information with foreign countries is restricted on the ground of penetration of hostile ideology. Theoretical conceptions and practical proposals which may seem to be too bold are suppressed immediately without any discussion under the influence of fear that they may break the foundations....

The top administrators receive incomplete, falsified information and thus cannot exercise their power completely....

Freedom of information and creative labour are necessary for the intelligentsia due to the nature of its activities, due to the nature of its social function. The desire of the intelligentsia to have greater freedom is legal and natural. The state, however, suppresses this desire by introducing various restrictions, administrative pressure, dismissals and even the holding of trials. This brings about a gap, mutual distrust and a complete mutual lack of understanding, which makes it difficult for the state and the most active strata of the intelligentsia to co-operate fruitfully. In the conditions of the present-day industrial society, where the role of the intelligentsia is growing, this gap cannot but be termed suicidal....

What awaits our country if a course toward democratisation is not taken? Falling behind the capitalist countries in the process of the second industrial revolution and gradual transformation into a second-rate provincial power...

Newsweek, 13 April 1970.

DOCUMENT 19   SOLZHENITSYN'S *LETTER TO THE SOVIET LEADERS*

Aleksandr Solzhenitsyn's own letter to the Soviet leaders, published several years after Sakharov, Turchin and Medvedev's, presents a very different dissident agenda. In the tradition of Russia's nineteenth-century Slavophiles, Solzhenitsyn argues that Russia's tragedy stems from its embrace of western materialism and, in particular, of Marxism, a doctrine that came to Russia from the West.

... The murky whirlwind of *Progressive Ideology* swept in on us from the West at the end of the last century, and has tormented and ravaged our soul quite enough....

... we had to be dragged along the whole of the Western bourgeois-industrial and Marxist path in order to discover, toward the close of the twentieth century, and again from progressive Western scholars, what any village greybeard in Russia or Ukraine had understood from time immemorial and could have explained to the progressive commentators ages ago... that a dozen worms can't go on gnawing at the same apple *forever*; that if the earth is a *finite* object, then its expanses and resources are finite also, and the *endless, infinite* progress dinned into our heads by the dreamers of the enlightenment cannot be accomplished on it....

As it is, we have followed Western technology too long and too faithfully. We are supposed to be the 'first socialist country in the world', one which sets an example to other peoples.... so why, then, have we been so dolefully unoriginal in technology, and why have we so unthinkingly, so blindly, copied Western civilisation?...

One might have thought that, with the central planning of which we are so proud, we of all people had the chance *not* to spoil Russia's natural beauty, *not* to create anti-human, multi-million concentrations of people. But we've done everything the other way round: we have dirtied and defiled the wide Russian spaces and disfigured the heart of Russia, our beloved Moscow....

We have squandered our resources foolishly without so much as a backward glance, sapped our soil, mutilated our vast expanses with idiotic 'inland seas' and contaminated belts of wasteland around our industrial centres.... So let us come to our senses in time, let us change our course!...

Solzhenitsyn (1974).

DOCUMENT 20   ROY MEDVEDEV, ON SOCIALIST DEMOCRACY

In stark contrast to Solzhenitsyn, Roy Medvedev remained committed to socialism, convinced that the country's salvation lay in socialist democracy and that the Soviet system could overcome the legacies of the Stalin era to return to its genuinely democratic and socialist roots.

There is no doubt about the fact that democratisation is an objective necessity for our society. Its inevitability is related to economic and technical progress, the scientific and technological revolution and changes that have taken place in the social structure. The country cannot be governed in the old way, and this is beginning to be felt not only by many young government officials but also by certain seemingly dyed-in-the-wool bureaucrats. Yet the fact remains that democratisation will not come about automatically, nor will it be handed down 'from above'. It will occur only as a response to objective demands and determined efforts....

I speak of struggle and pressure coming from the people and particularly the intelligentsia; however, this does not exclude the possibility of initiative appearing at the top. If moves toward democratisation were taken at the higher levels of party and state, it would be an important guarantee that subsequent controversy involving so many difficult political problems would take place in the least painful manner and would be kept within bounds. But for the time being we do not have such a leadership....Yet the experience of Hungary, where over a period of years there has been a process of real democratisation directed 'from above', does show that cooperation between those 'above' and those 'below' is perfectly viable. Something similar happened in Poland in 1971–72 but only after a very bitter and dangerous political crisis, which could have been avoided by more rational leadership. The Czechoslovak experience of 1968–69, its achievements and failures, must also be carefully studied....

The realisation of a serious programme of democratic change must be a comparatively slow and gradual process. The actual time period will be determined by many factors, but it should not take less than ten or fifteen years. First of all, the democratic movement in our country is still too weak and would be unable to achieve rapid political changes. Secondly, we are still very much in the process of formulating political programmes. Therefore, as the democratic movement evolves, there must also be a development of socialist political thought, the creation of new political doctrines on the basis of Marxism-Leninism which will analyse our changed political circumstances. Without this kind of theoretical preparation, without a serious programme – even if it is discussed only in a relatively narrow circle – any kind of rapid political change would inevitably create overwhelming contradictions and disarray. Overhasty reform can also cause problems within the socialist bloc (as the experience of Czechoslovakia has shown). Improvisation in politics can easily result in anarchy....

Medvedev (1975: 311–14).

DOCUMENT 21   ANDROPOV ARGUES FOR SOLZHENITSYN'S EXPULSION FROM THE USSR

On 7 February 1974, KGB chief Yuri Andropov wrote to Brezhnev urging that the dissident Solzhenitsyn be expelled from the USSR and deprived of his Soviet citizenship within a matter of days. The issue of what to do about Solzhenitsyn was then much on the Soviet leaders' minds, having been discussed in the Politburo the previous month, at which time Andropov pointed out that he had been pressing for action against the writer since 1965 ('Delo o pisatele', 1993). Andropov's advice was heeded: Solzhenitsyn was expelled on 13 February.

Leonid Il'ich!

I am sending you a short report prepared by comrades V. M. Chebrikov and F. D. Bobkov which deals directly with the Solzhenitsyn question. From the report it follows that this question has now gone beyond being a criminal matter and turned into a not unimportant problem having a definite political character. As is evident from the report, the great majority of Soviet people have correctly evaluated the criticism addressed towards Solzhenitsyn. But it is precisely from them that one hears ever more often and in ever sharper forms the question: 'Why do the authorities not take steps against Solzhenitsyn, who has not put down his weapons following the criticism of his views but has rather spoken out even more brazenly against Soviet power?'

I am especially worried that such questions are heard more and more frequently among military personnel and certain segments of the party apparatus.

On the other hand, one cannot overlook the fact that Solzhenitsyn's book, despite the steps we have taken to expose its anti-Soviet character, has received a certain sympathy from some representatives of the creative *intelligentsia*....

We have also confirmed cases in which specific workers or students have made statements to the effect that Solzhenitsyn has called on the Soviet leadership to cut prices for consumer goods and curtail assistance to Cuba and other developing countries in the interests of raising the living standards of the Soviet people. These thoughts are not contained in the *Gulag Archipelago* but they are, as you recall, in the aforementioned letter of Solzhenitsyn 'To the Soviet Leaders'....

On the basis of this, Leonid Il'ich, it seems to me that it is simply impossible to put off a resolution of the Solzhenitsyn question, despite all our desire not to harm our foreign relations, for further delay could bring about extremely undesirable consequences for us within the country.

Andropov then summarises for Brezhnev the state of discussions with the West German authorities concerning the willingness of the latter to allow Solzhenitsyn to live in that country.

If agreement is reached along these lines, then it seems to me that the Presidium of the Supreme Soviet of the USSR should adopt a decision no later than 9–10 February depriving Solzhenitsyn of his Soviet citizenship and expelling him from the country (a draft decree is enclosed). The actual operation expelling Solzhenitsyn could in this case be executed on 10–11 February.

It is important to do all this quickly, because, as is clear from operational documents, Solzhenitsyn is starting to guess our intentions and could issue a public document, which would put both us and [German Federal Chancellor Willy] Brandt in an embarrassing position.

If for some reason this operation to expel Solzhenitsyn fails, I think it would be advisable to launch criminal proceedings (with arrest) against him no later than 15 February. The prosecutors are ready for this.

http://psi.ece.jhu.edu/~kaplan/IRUSS/BUK/GBARC/pdfs/solgh/kgb74-7.pdf

DOCUMENT 22　A NOSTALGIC LOOK BACK AT THE 'TIME OF STAGNATION'

Important though dissident intellectual currents were, their impact within the USSR was limited. For most Soviet people, the Brezhnev era had much to recommend it and a nostalgia for the period became increasingly noticeable in the years of upheaval that followed 1985. In a humorous and evocative description of his own life in Brezhnev's Soviet Union, journalist Vladimir Konstantinov highlights the sense of stability and security that the old system gave to most people.

I spent my journalistic youth working on a provincial newspaper. It was the full flowering of stagnation. The better local publicists wrote on moral themes. Society was shaken, for example, by the story of a dog thrown overboard from a pleasure boat by drunken hooligans. Universal condemnation befell the *Komsomolka*[6] who went about wearing a T-shirt depicting the American flag. Nationality problems were not discussed because there were none. I once ascertained in conversation with an acquaintance that she thought that an Ingush was some sort of national dish. Like *lavash*[7].

---

[6] (Female) member of the Communist Youth League.
[7] The Ingush are a Caucasian people closely related to the Chechens. *Lavash* is a flat white bread popular in the Caucasus.

When not writing, local publicists drank. Not especially often – just every day. Each afternoon, as five o'clock approached, the corridors of the editorial departments would come to life, as the democratically elected (on a show of hands) representatives of the work collective raced to the *gastronom* across the street. Moreover, a vodka bottle, like a party card, was a great social equaliser. Thus, for example, it was not considered shameful late at night for a junior member of staff to help the editor-in-chief enter the lift. The problem was to synchronise the movement of the editor's body with the opening and closing of the lift's doors. This seemingly simple task was greatly complicated by the fact that both the editor and his voluntary helper were in one and the same state of deep creative contemplation.

As a new journalist, I was accepted warmly and treated with consideration by my senior colleagues, who day by day initiated me in the secrets of the trade. But they did not spare me in the event of blunders. Playing the miser on one occasion, I tried to save myself a few kopecks and returned from the shop across the street with a bottle of some sort of vermouth for a rouble eighty. My department head issued a stern rebuke which I shall never forget. 'Vova,' he said, 'the most important thing for a journalist is the liver. You've got to preserve it. Masters of the pen drink vodka.'

But it was not only 'publicists of the Leninist school' (as my colleague, the feuilletonist Yesipov, dubbed us) who drank vodka. Vodka glued together in one great monolith all the groups, classes and nations living on one-sixth of the earth's land mass. The elite drank. Publicists who spent their lives singing the praises of the most outstanding class in the world drank, too. So did the class itself....

In general, provincial Russia lived modestly and generously. The first time I ever saw a real live dissident in my life was in the Supreme Soviet of the Russian Soviet Federated Socialist Republic. True, a rumour once raced around our city to the effect that someone in one of the outlying districts had pasted up portraits of the members of the Politburo under the heading 'These men are wanted by the police'. To this day, I personally suspect that this was done by the members of the local KGB, simply in order to justify their own existence in our peacefully drinking province.

Reflecting on those glorious years, to which, judging from the polls, provincial Russia increasingly looks back with yearning, I think that their excellence lay not simply in the permanent presence in the shops of cheap macaroni and eggs for a rouble thirty. Rather, the very spirit of the time, its obvious defects notwithstanding, simply met certain deep needs of Soviet Man (*homo sovieticus*, who was, in my view, formed long before 1917): the need for tutelage, for paternal care, for certainty about tomorrow, or, more specifically, for the certainty that you didn't need to think about tomorrow, because someone else had already thought about it for you.

Konstantinov (1993: 8).

GLOSSARY

Anti-Ballistic Missile (ABM) Treaty   1972 agreement limiting deployment of anti-ballistic missile (ABM) systems. The treaty restricted each side to two ABM deployments of not more than 100 launchers, one around its capital city and a second at another location containing some part of its ICBM force. Launchers so deployed were to be static and land-based, limited to one missile with one warhead per launcher. Restrictions on associated radar systems were also agreed.

Baikal–Amur Mainline (BAM)   Mainline railway built across Siberia beginning in 1974. The BAM's completion, scheduled for 1983, was announced in 1984, but the line was unfit for freight traffic until 1989.

Big Five   Politburo Commission formed at the end of the 1960s to oversee the Strategic Arms Limitation Talks (SALT)*. The Big Five included the foreign and defence ministers, the KGB chief, the CC Secretary in charge of the defence industry and the deputy head of the Military-Industrial Commission.

Brezhnev doctrine   Also called the *doctrine of limited sovereignty*. In the wake of the 1968 Czechoslovak intervention, the Soviet leadership enunciated the principle that the interests of the socialist commonwealth transcended those of individual socialist states and that socialist states were duty-bound to come to the aid of socialism wherever it was threatened. It was an explicit declaration of the limits of Moscow's tolerance for doctrinal deviation and a rationale for intervention to check such deviation.

Cadres   In Soviet parlance, party and state officials were not referred to as 'bureaucrats' (*'chinovniki'*), as this had Tsarist, and therefore pejorative, connotations. They were instead referred to as 'cadres' (*kadry*). Cadres policy – the selection and preparation of personnel for important posts – was always an important concern of the top leadership.

Central Committee (CC) of the Communist Party of the Soviet Union   Elected by party Congresses (which were held every five years during the Brezhnev era), the Central Committee was, in theory, the most authoritative party body after the Congress itself. The Brezhnev-era CC, which grew to over 400 full and candidate members, brought together the country's top military, political and administrative elite but was far too large to meet frequently or to conduct the day-to-day business of running the party. Real power resided in its administrative organ, the Secretariat*, and its policy-making body, the Politburo*.

Communist Party of the Soviet Union (CPSU)   The most important political institution in the Soviet system and the only permitted political party until the very end of the Soviet period. As an administrative party (Gill, 1994), the CPSU did more than control the reins of power at the top of the state hierarchy: it was deeply involved in the actual running of all political, economic and social institutions of any significance. Its leader was, *de facto*, recognised as the leader of the country, even though the party leader was not always head of state or even head of government.

Council of Ministers   The Soviet cabinet. The Chairman of the Council of Ministers was the head of government and is often referred to in English as the Premier or Prime Minister.

derevenshchiki   The writers of the so-called 'village prose' school, who enjoyed some official favour under Brezhnev*, despite the fact that many of their views were at odds with the regime's ideology. The *derevenshchiki* focused on rural Russia, which they saw as the last repository of those truly Russian values of honesty, simplicity, harmony and close ties to both family and the land that might yet save society from the spiritual bankruptcy of western materialism.

détente   Literally 'relaxation'. The term used to refer to the reduction in tensions between the US and Soviet blocs during the 1970s, which was, for a time, the chief foreign policy goal of statesmen on both sides of the Cold War divide.

First Secretary   See *General Secretary*.

General Secretary   The leading official of the party's executive arm, the Central Committee Secretariat*. The General Secretary (known as the 'First Secretary' from 1953 to 1966) was for most of the Soviet period the country's *de facto* leader, although this was not immediately apparent: Stalin, Khrushchev* and Brezhnev* took some time to establish their clear pre-eminence within the leadership.

Gosplan   The State Planning Committee. Gosplan was charged with working out the state economic plans on the basis of directives from the country's political leadership. It coordinated and controlled the activities of branch ministries and other institutions in implementing those plans. It was, in many respects, the nerve centre of the Soviet economic system.

KGB   The Committee for State Security (*Komitet gosudarstvennyi bezopasnosti*). The Soviet security service during the period from 1953 to 1991. The KGB was responsible for all aspects of state security, from espionage and counter-espionage activities at home and abroad to the monitoring and suppression of dissent and the protection of members of the country's top leadership.

Kosygin reforms   The package of economic reforms adopted in 1965 and associated with the new prime minister of the day, Aleksei Kosygin*. The aim of the reforms was to introduce elements of market efficiency into the economic system while preserving the fundamentals of the centrally planned economy. By 1970, little remained of the reforms, which had fallen victim to a combination of bureaucratic resistance and contradictions within the reforms themselves.

nationalities policy   The Soviet regime's policies towards the country's hundreds of ethnic groups. The USSR was a multi-national state, with over 100 different nationalities appearing in the census data. Coping with such ethnic diversity was a major challenge for the authorities, especially as demographic trends shifted in directions the Kremlin found threatening during the Brezhnev era.

Non-Proliferation Treaty   International agreement aimed at limiting the spread of nuclear weapons. First adopted in 1968, it obliged states possessing nuclear weapons to refrain from transferring nuclear-weapons technology to states not possessing them. The latter undertook not to develop such weapons, in return for which promise the nuclear weapons states promised to work towards nuclear disarmament and to ease non-weapons states' access to nuclear technology for non-military purposes.

perestroika　Literally 'restructuring'; the name given to the programme of political and economic reform launched under Mikhail Gorbachev* after 1985.

Politburo　The Politburo (political bureau) of the Central Committee* (known as the Presidium from 1952 to 1966) was the party's highest policy-making body and to a great extent was 'the real cabinet of the Soviet system' (Hough & Fainsod, 1979: 466). During the Brezhnev era, power within the Politburo was concentrated in the hands of a sub-group of that body, consisting of those individuals who combined membership of the Politburo with membership of the CC Secretariat*, as well as the leaders of important all-union institutions like the KGB*, the foreign ministry and the defence ministry. Politburo members outside Moscow often had limited input into major policy decisions.

'Prague Spring'　The period of political liberalisation in Czechoslovakia that began with a re-shuffle of the Czechoslovak Communist Party leadership in January 1968 and ended with a Soviet-led military intervention in August of that year. The invasion of Czechoslovakia underscored the limits to Moscow's willingness to tolerate ideological and institutional deviation within the Communist bloc.

Presidium　See *Politburo*.

SALT　Strategic Arms Limitation Talks (or Treaty). The most important of the many strands of disarmament talks conducted by the United States and the USSR in the 1970s. The negotiations produced a five-year Interim Agreement on the Limitation of Strategic Arms (SALT I) in May 1972. This set the basis for a second round of SALT talks but the resulting treaty, the 1979 SALT II agreement, fell victim to the breakdown of *détente** at the end of the 1970s and was never ratified.

Samizdat　The reproduction and circulation of unpublished writings in manuscript form came to be known as *samizdat* (literally 'self-publishing'). Despite major efforts to curtail the practice – including the imposition of controls on the use of mimeo machines and photocopiers – *samizdat* writings were able to reach significant audiences, particularly when they were passed to the western media.

Secretariat　The Secretariat of the Central Committee* (CC) of the CPSU was the party's highest administrative body. Though formally subordinate to the Politburo and generally overshadowed by it, the Secretariat's role in implementing policy, managing 'cadres policy' and controlling the flow of information among the top elite made it extremely powerful. The CC Secretaries also oversaw a substantial central party bureaucracy with departments monitoring – and sometimes directly shaping – every major field of policy.

'social contract'　A tacit agreement between regime and society that western scholars like Hauslohner (1987) and Cook (1992, 1993) believed was essential to the Soviet regime's legitimation strategy. The state provided such benefits as job security, free housing, free medical care, and generous social welfare provision, as well as limiting income differentials, in return for political quiescence and compliance on the part of the population.

Solidarity　Independent trade union formed during the Polish labour unrest of July–August 1980. Solidarity rapidly emerged as a major force in Polish politics but was suppressed in late 1981, when martial law was imposed. It re-emerged in the late 1980s to negotiate Poland's transition from communist rule.

Andropov, Yuri (1914–84)   KGB Chairman, 1967–82; General Secretary of the CC CPSU and Chairman of the Presidium of the Supreme Soviet, 1982–84. While Andropov did not remain in power long enough to effect substantial changes in policy, he managed during his brief tenure as Soviet leader to replace many of Leonid Brezhnev's* elderly cronies and to promote individuals who were to play crucial roles in the Gorbachev era.

Brezhnev, Leonid (1906–82)   General Secretary of the CC CPSU, 1964–82. Brezhnev was the longest-serving Soviet leader after Stalin; he held the top party post for just over 18 years and the position of head of state (Chairman of the Presidium of the Supreme Soviet) for more than five. Though an effective back-room operator, he failed to comprehend, let alone to resolve, many of the emerging socio-economic problems that began to beset the Soviet regime during his time in power.

Chernenko, Konstantin (1911–85)   General Secretary of the CC CPSU and Chairman of the Presidium of the Supreme Soviet, 1984–5. A close personal associate of Leonid Brezhnev* for over 30 years, he was clearly Brezhnev's preferred successor. Thwarted by Yuri Andropov* at the time of Brezhnev's death, he assumed power when Andropov died 15 months later. His brief reign was characterised by political deadlock and policy drift.

Gorbachev, Mikhail (b. 1931)   General Secretary of the CC CPSU and Soviet head of state, 1985–91. The youngest man to lead the Soviet Union since Stalin's rise in the 1920s, Gorbachev embarked on a bold but ultimately unsuccessful attempt to reform both the Soviet political and economic systems and to transform the USSR's relations with the rest of the world. His tumultuous period in office ended with a pair of coups d'état against him. The first, in August 1991, failed, but the second, in December of that year, brought about Gorbachev's resignation and the dissolution of the Soviet Union.

Grechko, Andrei (1903–76)   Minister of Defence, 1967–76, and member of the Politburo of the CC CPSU, 1973–6. Grechko seems to have been a rather un-imaginative martinet whose hardline views on defence and foreign policy and lack of political acumen often left him isolated on key issues during the period of high détente.

Gromyko, Andrei (1909–89)   USSR Foreign Minister, 1957–85 and member of the Politburo of the CC CPSU, 1973–6. Among the best known of Soviet politicians, Gromyko was one of the most authoritative members of the Brezhnev leadership and largely controlled Soviet foreign policy during the Andropov–Chernenko interregnum. A tough-minded realist, Gromyko came virtually to personify Soviet foreign policy by the late 1970s. He later played a key role in the accession to power of Mikhail Gorbachev* but was nevertheless speedily replaced by Gorbachev.

Khrushchev, Nikita (1894–1971)   First Secretary of the CC CPSU, 1953–64, and Chairman of the USSR Council of Ministers, 1958–64. Having prevailed in the struggle to succeed Stalin, Khrushchev sought to renovate and rejuvenate the Soviet system while leaving its fundamentals intact. His impulsiveness in both policy-making and personnel policy, together with his 'de-Stalinisation' campaign, ultimately alienated much of the elite and led to his removal in October 1964.

Kosygin, Aleksei (1904–80)   Chairman of the USSR Council of Ministers (i.e. Prime Minister), 1964–80. A member of the top leadership from the early 1940s, Kosygin succeeded Nikita Khrushchev* as head of government. Kosygin rapidly came to be overshadowed by Khrushchev's successor as party leader, Leonid Brezhnev*. Though relations between Kosygin and Brezhnev were cool, the former's administrative competence and authority among the managerial elite enabled him to remain in office until shortly before his death in 1980.

Podgornyi, Nikolai (1903–83)   Chairman of the Presidium of the Supreme Soviet (head of state), 1965–77. A former party leader of the Ukraine, Podgornyi played a key role in the plot to overthrow Khrushchev* in 1964. His large political following made him a potential rival to Brezhnev*, who rapidly moved to demote many of Podgornyi's close associates and to marginalise Podgornyi himself, giving him a largely ceremonial post, where he remained until Brezhnev forced him out in 1977.

Sakharov, Andrei (1921–89)   Nuclear physicist, dissident and Nobel laureate. Widely known as the 'father' of the Soviet hydrogen bomb, Sakharov was one of the USSR's leading physicists in the early post-war era. During the 1960s, he became one of the USSR's leading dissidents. In January 1980, he was sent into internal exile in the closed city of Gorky, returning to Moscow in 1987 on the initiative of Gorbachev*. He was soon recognised as one of the fathers of the emerging democratic movement in the USSR and was elected to the new Soviet legislature, the Congress of People's Deputies, in 1989.

Shelepin, Aleksandr (1918–95)   KGB Chairman, 1958–61; Central Committee Secretary, 1961–7; Chairman of the All-Union Council of Trade Unions, 1967–75. Shelepin, like Podgornyi*, seems to have been viewed by Brezhnev* as a potential rival. After Khrushchev's removal, the new General Secretary moved rapidly to marginalise Shelepin politically. Shelepin was long seen by many observers as the leading 'neo-Stalinist' within the leadership, a perception which, while somewhat oversimplified, did have some basis in Shelepin's own views.

Solzhenitsyn, Aleksandr (b. 1918)   Writer, dissident and Nobel·laureate for literature. A veteran of Stalin's prison camps, Solzhenitsyn had a difficult relationship with the Soviet regime under Nikita Khrushchev* but was able to publish much of his work. During the Brezhnev years, however, he became an increasingly open critic of the regime and enraged the authorities by publishing his history of the Soviet labour camp system, *The Gulag Archipelago*, in the West. He was charged with treason, stripped of his citizenship and expelled from the USSR. The Gorbachev-era thaw and subsequent collapse of the USSR made it possible for Solzhenitsyn once again to be published in his native land, and to return there to live, but his attempts to shape post-Soviet Russian politics have had little impact.

Suslov, Mikhail (1902–82)   Secretary of the CC CPSU, 1947–82, and member of the Presidium/Politburo of the CC CPSU, 1955–82. One of the longest-serving and most conservative members of the Soviet leadership, Suslov was *de facto* ideologist-in-chief during the Brezhnev years and one of the four or five members of the Politburo inner circle that resolved most key policy issues.

Ustinov, Dmitrii (1908–84)   Minister of Defence, 1976–84, and candidate member (1965–76) and then full member (1976–84) of the Politburo of the CC CPSU. Grechko's* successor as defence minister, Ustinov had spent his career not in the armed forces but in the defence industrial complex, which he effectively headed for most of the post-war period. By the late 1970s, he was one of the four or five men who really dominated the Politburo, and his influence grew during the long post-Brezhnev interregnum. Had he not died three months before Chernenko*, it is possible that he would have thwarted the accession of Gorbachev*.

Vysotskii, Vladimir (1938–80)   'Guitar poet' and actor. As a film actor, Vysotskii became wildly popular with his portrayal of tough-guy anti-heroes, his songs of liquor, sex and delinquency, and his lampooning of much official culture. His verses challenged the cultural values propagated by the regime and dealt with the marginal and dispossessed elements of Soviet society. Vysotskii's funeral in 1980 was one of the largest outpourings of mass emotion of the post-war period, despite the fact that the official media largely ignored his death.

GUIDE TO FURTHER READING

The Brezhnev era probably remains the least-studied period in the twentieth-century history of Russia/the USSR. Interest in the Brezhnev period fell rapidly in the late 1980s, as Soviet politics grew more turbulent under Mikhail Gorbachev. The increasing availability of archival and other primary sources, as well as the flood of memoirs that began to appear in the late 1980s, created fantastic opportunities for historians to re-examine virtually the entire Soviet period, but historians' energies have been overwhelmingly directed at the period before 1964, whereas political scientists have focused their attention on the Gorbachev era and the collapse of the USSR. As Bacon (2002: 1) observes, 'scarcely anything has been written in English on the subject of Brezhnev or the Brezhnev years – and not much more in Russian – since the days when the topic was current affairs'. Strikingly, Brezhnev remains the only Soviet leader without a 'post-Soviet' biography in English: the two English biographies that exist (Dornberg, 1974; Murphy, 1981) both appeared during Brezhnev's lifetime. The closest to a recent biography in English is the section devoted to Brezhnev in Dmitri Volkogonov's *The Rise and Fall of the Soviet Empire: Political Leaders from Lenin to Gorbachev* (London, 1998).

Some twenty years after Brezhnev's death, this is beginning to change, not least thanks to the efforts of Bacon and his colleagues. Readers looking for the best recent scholarly overview of the period would do well, therefore, to turn to Edwin Bacon and Mark Sandle (eds), *Brezhnev Reconsidered* (Basingstoke, 2002). Otherwise, the best overviews of the period are still to be found in recent general histories of the Soviet Union, most notably Robert Service's *A History of Twentieth-Century Russia* (Cambridge, MA, 1997) and Ronald G. Suny's *The Soviet Experiment: Russia, the USSR and the Successor States* (Oxford, 1998). Stephen Kotkin's excellent *Armageddon Averted: The Soviet Collapse, 1970–2000* (Oxford, 2001) also provides a brief but very sharp analysis of the period, taking the middle of the Brezhnev years as the starting point for his account of the Soviet collapse.

PRIMARY SOURCES IN ENGLISH

While there has been remarkably little in the way of scholarly monographs on Brezhnev and the Brezhnev era, a large number of memoirs of the period have been published, mostly in Russian but some also in English. Among the latter are former Foreign Minister Andrei Gromyko's *Memories* (London, 1989), as well as Mikhail Gorbachev's *Memoirs* (London, 1995). Revealing views from those just outside the top leadership but working closely with the country's leaders are provided by academician Georgy Arbatov's *The System: An Insider's Life in Soviet Politics* (New York, 1993) and by Fedor Burlatsky's *Khrushchev and the First Russian Spring* (New York, 1991), which, despite its title, covers the Brezhnev years as well. Short but valuable reminiscences by a number of former senior Soviet officials may be found in Michael Ellman and Vladimir Kontorovich (eds), *The Destruction of the Soviet Economic System: An Insiders' History* (Armonk, 1998). Aleksandr Savel'ev and Nikolai Detinov's *The Big Five: Arms Control Decision-making in the Soviet Union* (Westport, CT, 1995) provides a fascinating inside account of arms-control policy-making during the Brezhnev era.

Those seeking key documents in English will find the *Cold War International History Project Bulletin*, which has appeared at intervals since 1992, an invaluable source, containing, as it does, both translations of key archival documents on the Cold War and commentaries on the same. Also useful in this connection is Robert V. Daniels' two-volume *A Documentary History of Communism* (London, 1985), which contains English translations of official documents as well as extracts from dissident writings.

CHAPTER 1: BACKGROUND TO THE BREZHNEV ERA

Readers interested in the historical background to Brezhnev's accession are likely to find any number of good general histories of the USSR valuable, including those by Service and Suny already mentioned. In addition, there has been a good deal of recent work on the Khrushchev period in particular, including William J. Tompson's *Khrushchev: A Political Life* (Basingstoke, 1995), William Taubman *et alii* (eds), *Nikita Khrushchev* (New Haven, CT, 2000), and Sergei Khrushchev's *Nikita Khrushchev and the Creation of a Superpower* (University Park, PA, 2000). There has also been a great deal written on Soviet foreign policy under Khrushchev, with a particular 'boom' in writing on the missile crisis. The best general overview is to be found in Michael Beschloss's massive two-volume treatment, *MAYDAY: Eisenhower, Khrushchev and the U-2 Affair* (London, 1986) and *Kennedy and Khrushchev: The Crisis Years* (London and Boston, 1991). On the interaction between domestic and international politics, which largely defined the political agenda for Khrushchev's successors, see James Richter, *Khrushchev's Double Bind: International Pressures and Domestic Coalition Politics* (Baltimore and London, 1994). Finally, readers interested in the missile crisis itself are referred to Aleksandr Fursenko and Timothy Naftali, *'One Hell of a Gamble': The Secret History of the Cuban Missile Crisis* (London, 1997).

CHAPTERS 2–3: POLITICS AND POLICY UNDER BREZHNEV AND KOSYGIN

Fifteen years of scholarly neglect of the Brezhnev era mean that many of the key works on high politics and policy-making remain those written by western 'Sovietologists' prior to 1985. In this respect, Jerry F. Hough and Merle R. Fainsod, *How the Soviet Union is Governed* (Cambridge, MA, 1979) remains well worth reading. Many of its conclusions were extremely controversial at the time and many more look highly problematic (to say the least) in view of subsequent events, but it remains an excellent introduction to the Soviet political system and to the men who dominated it during the period to the early 1980s. In much the same way, George Breslauer's *Khrushchev and Brezhnev as Leaders: Building Authority in Soviet Politics* (London, 1982) remains an important contribution to the literature. Among more recent works, the opening chapters of Archie Brown's *The Gorbachev Factor* (Oxford, 1996) provide a valuable picture of Soviet elite politics in the Brezhnev era, while an excellent recent assessment of Brezhnev's own role as politician and policy- maker can be found in Ian Thatcher's (2002) contribution to the Bacon and Sandle volume. Both of these latter two works draw on a great deal of material published in Russian in recent years but still unavailable in English. Finally, excellent case studies of specific issues include Thane Gustafson's *Reform in Soviet Politics* (Cambridge, 1981) and *Crisis amid Plenty: The Politics of Soviet Energy under Brezhnev and Gorbachev* (Princeton, 1989).

CHAPTERS 4–5: THE SOVIET UNION AND THE WORLD, 1964–1985

For an excellent, readable and brief introduction to Soviet foreign policy, see Caroline Kennedy-Pipe, *Russia and the World, 1917–1991* (London, 1998), which handles the Brezhnev period better than most such works. Although many of its conclusions remain highly contestable, the up-dated version of Raymond Garthoff's *Détente and Confrontation: Soviet-American Relations from Nixon to Reagan* (Washington DC, 1994) remains perhaps the best single-volume treatment of East–West relations in the Brezhnev years. Though rather older, Harry Gelman's *The Brezhnev Politburo and the Decline of Détente* (Ithaca, 1984) also remains valuable. Richard D. Anderson's *Public Politics in an Authoritarian State: Making Foreign Policy during the Brezhnev Years* (Ithaca, 1993) explores the internal politics of Soviet foreign policy and the role Brezhnev played in brokering agreement within the leadership on major issues. A good deal of recent work has been done on specific episodes in Soviet foreign policy during the Brezhnev era, including Kieran Williams's prize-winning *The Prague Spring and Its Aftermath: Czechoslovak Politics, 1968–1970* (Cambridge, 1997) and Fred Wehling's *Irresolute Princes: Kremlin Decision-making in Middle East Crises, 1967–1973* (Basingstoke, 1997). Finally, as noted above, the successive issues of the *International Cold War History Project Bulletin* offer extensive primary documents in translation, along with commentary and scholarly articles.

CHAPTERS 6–7: THE SOVIET ECONOMY IN THE BREZHNEV ERA

For a non-specialist, the best introduction to the Soviet economic system, its rise and its fall, probably remains the last edition of the late Alec Nove's classic *An Economic History of the USSR, 1917–1991*, 4th edition (Harmondsworth, 1992). Brief and more specialised is Mark Harrison's (2002) outstanding contribution to Bacon and Sandle's *Brezhnev Reconsidered*. The first five chapters or so of Ellman and Kontorovich's *The Destruction of the Soviet Economic System* are also both readable and valuable, although they will probably make sense only to readers who are already reasonably familiar with the Soviet system. On living standards and the 'social contract', Linda Cook's *The Soviet Social Contract and Why It Failed: Welfare Policy and Workers' Politics from Brezhnev to Yeltsin* (Cambridge, MA, 1993) is indispensable. See also Vladimir Shlapentokh's contribution to the Ellman and Kontorovich volume and Gertrude Schroeder's 'Soviet Living Standards in Comparative Perspective', in Horst Herlemann (ed.), *Quality of Life in the Soviet*

Union (Boulder, 1987). Finally, for the classic treatment of one of the key weaknesses of the Soviet system, see Joseph Berliner's *The Innovation Decision in Soviet Industry* (Cambridge, MA, 1976).

Readers looking for something less dry than straight economic analysis that nevertheless casts light on the way the Soviet economic system worked should not miss Loren R. Graham's slender but masterful *The Ghost of the Executed Engineer: Technology and the Fall of the Soviet Union* (Cambridge, MA, 1993). Graham's short study of the life of Petr Palchinsky, a little-known Soviet engineer executed in 1929 for his views on engineering and its place in society, makes an important contribution to our understanding of the Soviet economic system and why it failed.

CHAPTERS 8–9: SOCIETY AND CULTURE IN THE USSR, 1964–1985

Readers seeking introductions to the social and cultural histories of the Brezhnev era might well begin with Vladimir Andrle's *A Social History of Twentieth-Century Russia* (London, 1998) on the former and Richard Stites's brief but very readable *Russian Popular Culture: Entertainment and Society since 1900* (Cambridge, 1992). On demographic issues, see Nicholas Eberstadt, *The Poverty of Communism*, (New Brunswick and Oxford, 1988), as well as Murray Feshbach and Alfred Friendly, Jr, *Ecocide in the USSR: Health and Nature Under Siege* (New York, 1995), and Stephen G. Wheatcroft's path-breaking article, 'The Great Leap Upwards: Anthropometric Data and Indicators of Crises and Secular Change in Soviet Welfare Levels, 1880–1960', *Slavic Review* 58:1 (Spring, 1999). Wheatcroft's views remain very controversial, and readers will find in the same issue of *Slavic Review* a number of articles engaging the same issues from different perspectives, as well as a reply by Wheatcroft to his critics.

For a discussion of the dissident movement and its place in Soviet society, Ludmilla Alexeyeva's *Soviet Dissent: Contemporary Movements for National, Religious and Human Rights* (Middletown, CT, 1983) is a good place to start. See also Peter Reddaway's 'Dissent in the Soviet Union', *Problems of Communism* 32:6 (November–December 1983) and Vladimir Shlapentokh's *Soviet Intellectuals and Political Power* (London, 1990). A good deal of the dissident literature of the period has also appeared in English, such as Roy Medvedev's *On Soviet Dissent* (New York, 1980) and Aleksandr Zinoviev's *The Reality of Communism* (London, 1984) and *The Yawning Heights* (Harmondsworth, 1981). However, the impact of heterodox thinking within the system should not be overlooked; here, John Gooding's chapter in the Bacon and Sandle volume is extremely valuable, as is one of the most famous examples of such 'within-system dissent' – Tat'yana Zaslavskaya's 'Novosibirsk Report', an English translation of which may be found in *Survey* 28:1 (1984).

On nationality issues, Bohdan Nahaylo and Victor Swoboda's *Soviet Disunion: A History of the Nationalities Problem in the USSR* (London, 1990) provides a thorough but highly polemical account of the issue. For a view sharply at odds with theirs, see the contribution by Mike Bowker (2002) to the Bacon and Sandle volume. See also Mark Beissinger and Lubomyr Hajda (eds), *The Nationalities Factor in Soviet Politics and Society* (Boulder, 1990).

CHAPTER 10: FROM BREZHNEV TO GORBACHEV

In addition to Gorbachev's own *Memoirs* and Brown's *The Gorbachev Factor*, the key works on the transition from Brezhnev to Gorbachev include Donald R. Kelley's *Soviet Politics from Brezhnev to Gorbachev* (Boulder, 1987) and John W. Parker's two-volume *Kremlin in Transition* (London, 1991), which covers the period from 1978 to 1989. The relevant chapters of Volkogonov's *Rise and Fall* are also well worth reading, particularly for the portrait of Chernenko. For a view of Chernenko sharply at odds with the conventional one, see Ilya Zemtsov's *Chernenko: The Last Bolshevik* (New York, 1989). Relatively little has been written about the intriguing figure of Andropov since his death; the sole English-language biography remains Zhores Medvedev's *Andropov* (Oxford, 1983). For a good analysis of the Soviet economy and its difficulties during these years, see Philip Hanson's *From Stagnation to Catastroika: Commentaries on the Soviet Economy, 1983–1991* (New York and London, 1992) and the relevant chapters in Ellman and Kontorovich's *Destruction of the Soviet Economic System*.

BIBLIOGRAPHY

PRIMARY SOURCES

1 Afanas'ev, Viktor G. (1994), *4-aya vlast' i 4 genseka: ot Brezhneva do Gorbacheva v "Pravde"*, Moscow.

2 Andropov, Yu V., A. A. Gromyko, D. F. Ustinov and B. N. Ponomarev (1995), 'Dlya spaseniya Rodiny i revolyutsii', *Istochnik* 3(10), May–June.

3 Arbatov, Georgy A. (1993), *The System: An Insider's Life in Soviet Politics*, New York.

4 Baibakov, Nikolai (1991), 'Bez glubokogo analiza i vsveshennogo podkhoda', in Yu. V. Aksyutin (ed.), *L. I. Brezhnev: Materialy k biografii*, Moscow.

5 Belanovsky, Sergei (1998), 'The Arms Race and the Burden of Military Expenditures', in Michael Ellman and Vladimir Kontorovich (eds), *The Destruction of the Soviet Economic System: An Insiders' History*, Armonk, NY.

6 Brezhnev, Leonid Il'ich (1970–1983), *Leninskim kursom: rechi i stat'i* (nine volumes), Moscow.

7 Brezhnev, Leonid Il'ich (1977), 'A Historic Stage on the Road to Communism', *World Marxist Review* 20:12 (December).

8 Brezhnev, Leonid Il'ich (1978a), *Little Land*, Moscow.

9 Brezhnev, Leonid Il'ich (1978b), *Rebirth*, Moscow.

10 Brezhnev, Leonid Il'ich (1978c), *The Virgin Lands*, Moscow.

11 Brezhnev, Leonid Il'ich (1979), *Peace, Détente and Soviet-American Relations*, New York and London.

12 Chazov, Yevgenii Ivanovich (1992), *Zdorov'e i vlast'*, Moscow.

13 Chernyaev, Anatolii (1993), *Shest' let s Gorbachevym: po dnevnikovym zapisyam*, Moscow.

14 Churbanov, Yu. M. (1993), *Ya rasskazhu vse, kak bylo*, Moscow.

15 'Delo o pisatele A. I. Solzhenitsyne' (1993), *Istochnik* 3, May–June.

16 'Dogovarivayutsya go togo, chto ne bylo zalpa "Avrory"' (1996), *Istochnik* 2(21), March–April.

17 Dokuchaev, M. S. (1995), *Moskva, Kreml', Okhrana*, Moscow.

18 'Dokumenty' (1996), 'Dokumenty sovetskogo rukovodstva o polozehnii v Afganistane, 1979–1980', *Novaya i noveishaya istoriya* 3, May–June.

19 Egorychev, Nikolai (1989), 'Napravlen poslom', *Ogonek* 6:6–7, 28–30.

20 Eydelman, Moisei (1998), 'Monopolized Statistics under a Totalitarian Regime', in Michael Ellman and Vladimir Kontorovich (eds), *The Destruction of the Soviet Economic System: An Insiders' History*, Armonk, NY.

21 Gorbachev, Mikhail S. (1995), *Memoirs*, London.

22 Grishin, V. V. (1996), *Ot Khrushcheva do Gorbacheva: politicheskie portrety pyati gensekov i A. N. Kosygina*, Moscow.

23 Gromov, B. V. (1994), *Ogranichennyi kontingent*, Moscow.

24 Gromyko, Andrei A. (1990), *Pamyatnoe*, 2 vols, Moscow.

25 Gromyko, Andrei A. (1991), 'Koe-chto o periode zastoya', in Yu. V. Aksyutin (ed.), *L. I. Brezhnev: Materialy k biografii*, Moscow.

26 Israelyan, Viktor (1995), *Inside the Kremlin During the Yom Kippur War*, Pittsburgh.

27 Kaminskaya, Dina (1982), *Final Judgement: My Life as a Soviet Defense Attorney*, New York.

28 Karpinski, L. (1989), 'The Autobiography of a Half-Dissident', in Stephen Cohen and K. van den Heuvel (eds), *Voices of Glasnost*, New York.

29 Kissinger, Henry (1980), *The White House Years*, Washington.

30 Kissinger, Henry (1982), *Years of Upheaval*, Washington.

31 Konstantinov, Vladimir (1993), 'Sovetskii kharakter: zametki provintsial'nogo pessimista', *Moskovskie novosti* No 10 (7 March).

32 Kornienko, G. M. (1993), 'Kak prinimalis' resheniya o vvode sovetskhikh voisk v Afganistan i ikh vyvode', *Novya i noveishaya istoriya* 3 (May–June).

33 Kosygin, Aleksei N. (1973), 'Report on the Directives of the 24th CPSU Congress for the Five-Year Plan for the Development of the USSR National Economy in 1971–1975', 6 April 1971, in *Current Soviet Policies VI*, Columbus, OH.

34 Leonov, N. (1995), *Likholet'e*, Moscow.

35 Mazurov, Kirill T. (1989), 'Ya govoryu ne tol'ko o sebe', *Sovetskaya Rossiya*, 19 February.

36 Medvedev, Roy A. (1975), *On Socialist Democracy*, New York.

37 Medvedev, Vladimir (1994), *Chelovek za spinoi*, Moscow.

38 'Napravlena' (1993), 'Napravlena v spetial'nuyu psikhiatricheskuyu bol'nitsu', *Istochnik* 2 (May–June).

39 Pechenev, Vadim (1991), *Gorbachev: k vershinam vlasti*, Moscow.

40 Podgornyi, Nikolai V. (1995), 'Ya ne zasluzhil, chtoby bez vsyakoi motivirovki', *Istochnik* 1, January–February.

41 Rodionov, P. A. (1989), 'Kak nachinalsya zastoi', *Znamya* 8 (August).

42 Sakharov, Andrei (1968), *Progress, Coexistence and Intellectual Freedom*, tr by *The New York Times*, London.

43 Savel'ev, Aleksandr G. and Nikolai Detinov (1995), *The Big Five: Arms Control Decision-making in the Soviet Union*, Westport, CT.

44 Semichastnyi, V. E. (1995), 'Net paradnoi shumikhi i kriklivykh fraz', *Istochnik* 1, January–February.

45 Shelepin, Aleksandr N. (1991), 'Istoriya: uchitel' surovyi', *Trud*, 19 March.

46 Shelest, Petr E. (1989), 'O Khrushcheve, Brezhneve i drugikh', *Argumenty i fakty* 2 (January).

47 Shelest, Petr E. (1991), 'On umel vesti apparatnye igry, a stranu zabrosil...', in Yu. V. Aksyutin (ed.), *L. I. Brezhnev: Materialy k biografii*, Moscow.

48 Shelest, Petr E. (1995), *Da ne sudimy budete...*, Moscow.

49 Shevardnadze, Eduard (1991), *The Future Belongs to Freedom*, London.

50 Shevchenko, Arkady (1985), *Breaking with Moscow*, New York.

51 Solzhenitsyn, Aleksandr I. (1974), *Letter to the Soviet Leaders*, tr Hilary Sternberg, New York.

52 Strelyanyi, Anatolii (1988), 'Poslednii romantik', *Druzhba narodov* 11 (November).

53   Tsentral'noe statisticheskoe upravlenie SSSR (TsSU) (1966), *Narodnoe khozyaistvo SSSR v 1965g: statisticheskii ezhegodnik*, Moscow.
54   Tsentral'noe statisticheskoe upravlenie SSSR (TsSU) (1976), *Narodnoe khozyaistvo SSSR v 1975g: statisticheskii ezhegodnik*, Moscow.
55   Tsentral'noe statisticheskoe upravlenie SSSR (TsSU) (1985), *Narodnoe khozyaistvo SSSR v 1984g: statisticheskii ezhegodnik*, Moscow.
56   Tsentral'noe statisticheskoe upravlenie SSSR (TsSU) (1991), *Narodnoe khozyaistvo SSSR v 1990g: statisticheskii ezhegodnik*, Moscow.
57   Voronov, Gennadii (1991), 'Oshibki s Brezhnevym my sebe ne proshchaem', in Yu. V. Aksyutin (ed.), *L. I. Brezhnev: Materialy k biografii*, Moscow.
58   Yun', Oleg (1998), 'A Promising Departure', in Michael Ellman and Vladimir Kontorovich (eds), *The Destruction of the Soviet Economic System: An Insiders' History*, Armonk, NY.
59   Zoteev, Gennadii (1998a), 'Economic Policy in the Interregnum between Andropov and Gorbachev-Ryzhkov', in Michael Ellman and Vladimir Kontorovich (eds), *The Destruction of the Soviet Economic System: An Insiders' History*, Armonk, NY.
60   Zoteev, Gennadii (1998b), 'The View from Gosplan: Growth to the Year 2000', in Michael Ellman and Vladimir Kontorovich (eds), *The Destruction of the Soviet Economic System: An Insiders' History*, Armonk, NY.
61   *XXII S"ezd Kommunisticheskoi Partii Sovetskogo Soyuza: stenograficheskii otchet* (1962), Moscow.

SECONDARY SOURCES: BOOKS

1   Adomeit, Hannes (1973), *Soviet Risk-taking and Crisis Behaviour: from Confrontation to Coexistence*, London.
2   Aganbegyan, Abel (1988), *The Challenge of Perestroika*, London.
3   Aksyutin, Yu. V., ed. (1991), *L. I. Brezhnev: Materialy k biografii*, Moscow.
4   Alexeyeva, Ludmilla (1985), *Soviet Dissent: Contemporary Movements for National, Religious and Human Rights*, Middletown, CT.
5   Anderson, Richard D. (1993), *Public Politics in an Authoritarian State: Making Foreign Policy During the Brezhnev Years*, Ithaca, NY.
6   Andrle, Vladimir (1998), *A Social History of Twentieth-Century Russia*, London.
7   Beissinger, Mark and Lubomyr Hajda, eds (1990), *The Nationalities Factor in Soviet Politics and Society*, Boulder, CO.
8   Bennigsen, Alexandre and Marie Broxup (1983), *The Islamic Threat to the Soviet State*, London and Canberra.
9   Berliner, Joseph (1976), *The Innovation Decision in Soviet Industry*, Cambridge, MA.
10   Birman, Igor (1989), *Personal Consumption in the USSR and the USA*, London.
11   Bloch, Sidney and Peter Reddaway (1977), *Russia's Political Hospitals: The Abuse of Psychiatry in the Soviet Union*, London.
12   Breslauer, George (1982), *Khrushchev and Brezhnev as Leaders: Building Authority in Soviet Politics*, London.
13   Brown, Archie (1974), *Soviet Politics and Political Science*, Basingstoke.
14   Brown, Archie (1996), *The Gorbachev Factor*, Oxford.

15 Brubaker, Rogers (1996), *Nationalism Reframed: Nationhood and Nationalism in the New Europe*, Cambridge.

16 Burlatsky, Fedor (1990), *Vozhdi i sovetniki: O Khrushcheve, Andropove i ne tol'ko o nikh...*, Moscow.

17 Collins, Randall (1986), *Weberian Sociological Theory*, Cambridge.

18 Colton, Timothy (1986), *The Dilemma of Reform in the Soviet Union*, New York.

19 Cook, Linda (1993), *The Soviet Social Contract and Why It Failed: Welfare Policy and Workers' Politics from Brezhnev to Yeltsin*, Cambridge, MA.

20 Daniels, Robert V. (1993), *The End of the Communist Revolution*, London and New York.

21 Dawisha, Karen (1984), *The Kremlin and the Prague Spring*, Berkeley.

22 Donaldson, Robert H. and Joseph L. Nogee (1998), *The Foreign Policy of Russia: Changing Systems, Enduring Interests*, London.

23 Dornberg, John (1974), *Brezhnev: The Masks of Power*, London.

24 Dunlop, John B. (1983), *The Faces of Contemporary Russian Nationalism*, Princeton.

25 Dunlop, John B. (1985), *The New Russian Nationalism*, Washington.

26 Eberstadt, Nicholas (1988), *The Poverty of Communism*, New Brunswick and Oxford.

27 Edmonds, Robin (1983), *Soviet Foreign Policy: The Brezhnev Era*, Oxford.

28 Ellman, Michael, and Vladimir Kontorovich, eds (1998), *The Destruction of the Soviet Economic System: An Insider's History*, Armonk, NY.

29 Feshbach, Murray and Alfred Friendly, Jr (1995), *Ecocide in the USSR: Health and Nature Under Siege*, New York.

30 Fortescue, Stephen (1990), *Science Policy in the Soviet Union*, London.

31 Gelman, Harry (1984), *The Brezhnev Politburo and the Decline of Détente*, London.

32 Gill, Graeme (1994), *The Collapse of a Single-Party System*, Cambridge.

33 Gleason, Gregory (1990), *Federalism and Nationalism: the Struggle for Republican Rights in the USSR*, Boulder.

34 Graham, Loren R. (1993), *The Ghost of the Executed Engineer: Technology and the Fall of the Soviet Union*, Cambridge, MA.

35 Griko, T. I. (1997), *Sovetskoe gosudarstvo i obschestvo 50-kh–serediny 80-kh godov*, Moscow.

36 Gros, Daniel and Alfred Steinherr (1995), *Winds of Change: Economic Transition in Central and Eastern Europe*, London.

37 Gustafson, Thane (1981), *Reform in Soviet Politics*, Cambridge.

38 Gustafson, Thane (1989), *Crisis amid Plenty: The Politics of Soviet Energy under Brezhnev and Gorbachev*, Princeton, NJ.

39 Halliday, Fred (1986), *The Making of the Second Cold War*, 2nd edition, London.

40 Henze, Paul B. (1996/97), 'Moscow, Mengistu and the Horn: Difficult Choices for the Kremlin', *Cold War International History Project Bulletin* 8–9 (Winter).

41 Hoffman, Erik P. and Robin F. Laird (1982), *The Politics of Economic Modernization in the Soviet Union*, Ithaca.

42 Hough, Jerry F. and Merle Fainsod (1979), *How the Soviet Union is Governed*, Cambridge, MA.

43 Jain, Rajendra K. (1993), *Germany, the Soviet Union and Eastern Europe, 1949–1991*, London.
44 Janossy, Ferenc (1971), *The End of the Economic Miracle: Appearance and Reality in Economic Development*, White Plains, NY.
45 Joll, James (1992), *The Origins of the First World War*, 2nd edition, London.
46 Joravsky, David (1970), *The Lysenko Affair*, Cambridge, MA.
47 Josephson, Paul R. (1997), *New Atlantis Revisited: Akademgorodok, the Soviet City of Science*, Princeton.
48 Kanet, Roger E., ed. (1982), *Soviet Foreign Policy in the 1980s*, New York.
49 Kelley, Donald R. (1986), *The Politics of Developed Socialism: The Soviet Union as a Post-Industrial State*, New York and London.
50 Kelley, Donald R. (1987), *Soviet Politics from Brezhnev to Gorbachev*, New York.
51 Kennedy-Pipe, Caroline (1998), *Russia and the World, 1917–1991*, London.
52 Kohler, Foy D. *et alii* (1977), *Soviet Strategy for the Seventies*, Washington.
53 Kotkin, Stephen (2001), *Armageddon Averted: The Soviet Collapse, 1970–2000*, Oxford.
54 Lane, David S. (1990), *Soviet Society under Perestroika*, London.
55 Lee, William T. (1997), *The ABM Treaty Charade: A Study in Elite Illusion and Delusion*, Washington.
56 Linden, Carl A. (1966), *Khrushchev and the Soviet Leadership*, Baltimore.
57 Löwenhardt, John, James R. Ozinga and Erik van Ree (1992), *The Rise and Fall of the Soviet Politburo*, London.
58 Malik, Hafez (1994), *Soviet-Pakistan Relations and Post-Soviet Dynamics*, Basingstoke.
59 Marrese, Michael and Jan Vanous (1983), *Soviet Subsidization of Trade with Eastern Europe: A Soviet Perspective*, Berkeley, CA.
60 Martel, Gordon (1986), *The Origins of the First World War*, 2nd edition, London.
61 Mau, Vladimir (1996), *The Political History of Economic Reform in Russia, 1985–1994*, London.
62 Medvedev, Roy (1979), *On Stalin and Stalinism*, Oxford.
63 Medvedev, Roy (1982), *Khrushchev*, Oxford.
64 Medvedev, Roy (1991), *Lichnost' i epokha: politicheskii portret L. I. Brezhneva*, 2 vols, Moscow.
65 Medvedev, Zhores (1969), *The Rise and Fall of T. D. Lysenko* (tr I. Michael Lerner), New York and London.
66 Millar, James R., ed. (1987), *Politics, Work and Daily Life in the USSR: A Survey of Former Soviet Citizens*, Cambridge.
67 Millar, James R. (1991), *The Soviet Economic Experiment*, Urbana, Ill.
68 Murphy, Paul J. (1981), *Brezhnev: Soviet Politician*, Jefferson, NC.
69 Nahaylo, Bohdan and Victor Swoboda (1990), *Soviet Disunion: A History of the Nationalities Problem in the USSR*, London.
70 Naishul', Vitalii (1991), *The Supreme and Last Stage of Socialism*, London.
71 Nelson, Keith (1995), *The Making of Détente: Soviet-American Relations in the Shadow of Vietnam*, Baltimore.
72 Nove, Alec (1989), *An Economic History of the USSR*, 2nd edition, London.
73 Parrish, Michael (1996), *The Lesser Terror: Soviet State Security, 1939–1953*, Westport, CT.

74 Pavlov, Yuri (1994), *The Soviet-Cuban Alliance, 1959–1991*, London.

75 Reisinger, William M. (1992), *Energy and the Soviet Bloc: Alliance Politics after Stalin*, Ithaca.

76 Rigby, T. H., Archie Brown and Peter Reddaway, eds (1980), *Authority, Power and Policy in the USSR: Essays Dedicated to Leonard Schapiro*, London.

77 Roberts, Geoffrey (1999), *The Soviet Union in World Politics: Coexistence, Revolution and Cold War, 1945–1991*, London.

78 Rowen, Henry S. and Charles Wolf, Jr. (1989), *The Impoverished Superpower: Perestroika and the Soviet Military Burden*, San Francisco.

79 Rywkin, Michael (1982), *Moscow's Muslim Challenge: Soviet Central Asia*, London.

80 Samuelson, Robert J., ed. (1990), *The Economist Book of Vital World Statistics*, New York.

81 Shmelev, Nikolai, and Vladimir Popov (1989), *The Turning Point: Revitalizing the Soviet Economy*, New York.

82 Shtromas, Alexander (1981), *Political Change and Social Development: The Case of the Soviet Union*, Frankfurt am Main.

83 Shubin, Aleksandr (1997), *Istoki perestroiki*, Moscow.

84 Simis, Konstantin (1982), *USSR: The Corrupt Society: The Secret World of Soviet Capitalism*, New York.

85 Simm, Gerhard (1991), *Nationalism and Policy toward the Nationalities*, Boulder.

86 Skidelsky, Robert (1996), *The Road from Serfdom*, New York and London.

87 Smith, Hedrick (1990), *The New Russians*, New York.

88 Snyder, Jack (1991), *Myths of Empire*, Ithaca.

89 Steinberg, Dmitri (1990), *The Soviet Economy, 1970–1990: A Statistical Analysis*, San Francisco.

90 Stites, Richard (1992), *Russian Popular Culture: Entertainment and Society since 1900*, Cambridge.

91 Suny, Ronald Grigor (1998), *The Soviet Experiment: Russia, the USSR and the Successor States*, Oxford.

92 Tatu, Michel (1969), *Power in the Kremlin: From Khrushchev's Decline to Collective Leadership*, tr Helen Katel, London.

93 Terras, Victor (1991), *A History of Russian Literature*, New Haven and London.

94 Thompson, Terry (1989), *Ideology and Policy: The Political Uses of Doctrine in the Soviet Union*, Boulder.

95 Tompson, William J. (1995), *Khrushchev: A Political Life*, Basingstoke.

96 Valenta, Jiri, *Soviet Intervention in Czechoslovakia, 1968: Anatomy of a Decision*, Baltimore.

97 Volkogonov, Dmitri (1995), *Sem' vozhdei*, 2 vols, Moscow.

98 Walker, Martin (1986), *The Waking Giant: Gorbachev's Russia*, London.

99 Wehling, Fred (1997), *Irresolute Princes: Kremlin Decision-making in Middle East Crises, 1967–1973*, Basingstoke.

100 White, Stephen and Evan Mawdsley (2000), *The Soviet Elite from Lenin to Gorbachev: The Central Committee and Its Members*, Oxford.

101 Williams, Kieran (1997), *The Prague Spring and Its Aftermath: Czechoslovak Politics, 1968–1970*, Cambridge.

102 Yanov, Alexander (1978), *The Russian New Right*, Berkeley.
103 Yanowitch, Murray (1977), *Social and Economic Inequality in the Soviet Union*, White Plains, NY.

SECONDARY SOURCES: ARTICLES AND CHAPTERS

 1 Adam, Jan S. (1989), 'Incremental Activism in Soviet Third World Policy: The Role of the International Department of the CPSU Central Committee', *Slavic Review* 48:4.
 2 Bacon, Edwin (2002), 'Reconsidering Brezhnev', in Edwin Bacon and Mark Sandle (eds), *Brezhnev Reconsidered*, Basingstoke.
 3 Balakin, V. S. and L. P. Balakina (1995), 'Sotsiokul'turnyi raskol nauchnoi intelligentsii 60-kh godov XX veka', in L. Zemlyanskaya (ed.), *Chelovek. Istoriya. Obshchestvo: uchenye zapiski*, Chelyabinsk.
 4 Barghoorn, Frederick C. (1983), 'Regime–Dissenter Relations after Khrushchev: Some Observations', in Susan Gross Solomon (ed.), *Pluralism in the Soviet Union: Essays in Honor of Gordon Skilling*, Basingstoke.
 5 Barry, Donald D. and Harold J. Berman (1971), 'The Jurists', in H. Gordon Skilling and Franklyn Griffiths (eds), *Interest Groups in Soviet Politics*, Princeton, NJ.
 6 Beissinger, Mark (1992), 'Ethnicity, the Personnel Weapon and Neo-Imperial Integration: Ukrainian and RSFSR Provincial Party Officials Compared', in Rachel Denber (ed.), *The Soviet Nationality Reader: The Disintegration in Context*, Boulder.
 7 Beliaev, Edward and Pavel Butorin (1982), 'The Institutionalization of Soviet Sociology: Its Social and Political Context', *Social Forces* 61:2.
 8 Birman, Aleksandr (1966), 'Prodolzhenie razgovora', *Novyi mir* (May).
 9 Birman, Aleksandr (1969), 'Samaya blagodarnaya zadacha', *Novyi mir* (December).
10 Bond, A. R., M. V. Belkindas and A. I. Treyvish (1990), 'Economic Development Trends in the USSR, 1970–1988: Part 1', *Soviet Geography* 31:3.
11 Boretskii, Rudol'f (1993), 'Sekretnaya "papka Suslova" – bol'she voprosov chem otvetov', *Novoe vremya* 47 (November).
12 Bornstein, Morris (1985), 'Improving the Soviet Economic Mechanism', *Soviet Studies* 37:1.
13 Bovin, Aleksandr (1991), 'Kurs na stabil'nost' porodil zastoi', in Yu. V. Aksyutin (ed.), *L. I. Brezhnev: Materialy k biografii*, Moscow.
14 Bowker, Mike (2002), 'Brezhnev and Superpower Relations', in Edwin Bacon and Mark Sandle (eds), *Brezhnev Reconsidered*, Basingstoke.
15 Breslauer, George W. (1978), 'On the Adaptability of Soviet Welfare-State Authoritarianism', in Karl W. Ryavec (ed.), *Soviet Society and the Communist Party*, Amherst, MA.
16 Brown, Archie, (1980), 'The Power of the General Secretary of the CPSU', in T. H. Rigby, Archie Brown and Peter Reddaway (eds), *Authority, Power and Policy in The USSR: Essays Dedicated To Leonard Schapiro*, London.
17 Brown, Archie (1983), 'Pluralism, Power and the Soviet Political System: A Comparative Perspective', in Susan Gross Solomon (ed.), *Pluralism in the Soviet Union: Essays in Honour of H. Gordon Skilling*, London and Basingstoke.

18 Burlatsky, Fedor (1988), '"Mirnyi zagovor" protiv N. S. Khrushcheva', in Yu. V. Aksyutin (ed.), *N. S. Khrushchev: materialy k biografii*, Moscow.

19 Collins, Randall (1981), 'Long-term Social Change and the Territorial Power of States', in Randall Collins, *Sociology since Mid-Century: Essays in Theory Cumulation*, New York.

20 Cook, Linda (1992), 'The Soviet "Social Contract" and Gorbachev's Reforms', *Soviet Studies* 44:1.

21 Davis, Christopher (1984), 'The Economics of the Soviet Health Care System', in *Political Economy of the Soviet Union*, Washington.

22 Easterly, William and Stanley Fischer (1995), 'The Soviet Economic Decline', *World Bank Economic Review* 9:3.

23 Ellman, Michael (1980), 'A Note on the Distribution of Earnings in the USSR under Brezhnev', *Slavic Review* 39:4 (December).

24 Evangelista, Matthew (1996), 'Stalin's Revenge: Institutional Barriers to Internationalization in the Soviet Union', in Helen Milner and Robert O. Keohane (eds), *Internationalization and Domestic Politics*, Cambridge.

25 Feshbach, Murray (1982), 'The Soviet Union: Population Trends and Dilemmas', *Population Bulletin* 37 (August).

26 Fitzpatrick, Sheila (1976), 'Culture and Politics under Stalin: A Reappraisal', *Slavic Review* 35:2 (Summer).

27 Fitzpatrick, Sheila (1979), 'Stalin and the Making of the New Elite, 1928–1935', *Slavic Review* 38:3 (Fall).

28 Fowkes, Ben (2002), 'The National Question in the Soviet Union under Brezhnev', in Edwin Bacon and Mark Sandle (eds), *Brezhnev Reconsidered*, Basingstoke.

29 Freeze, Gregory L. (1998), 'From Stalinism to Stagnation, 1953–1985', in Gregory L. Freeze (ed.), *Russia: A History*, Oxford.

30 Gaiduk, Ilya (1995/96), 'The Vietnam War and Soviet-American Relations, 1964–1973: New Russian Evidence', *Cold War International History Project Bulletin* 6–7 (Winter).

31 Garthoff, Raymond (1998), 'The Conference on Poland, 1980–1982: Internal Crisis, International Dimensions', *Cold War International History Project Bulletin* 11 (Winter).

32 George, Victor (1991), 'Social Security in the USSR', *International Social Security Review* 44:4.

33 Gleijeses, Piero (1996/97), 'Havana's Policy in Africa, 1959–76: New Evidence from the Cuban Archives', *Cold War International History Project Bulletin* 8–9 (Winter).

34 Gooding, John (2002), 'The Roots of Perestroika', in Edwin Bacon and Mark Sandle (eds), *Brezhnev Reconsidered*, Basingstoke.

35 Gorlin, Alice (1976), 'Industrial Reorganization: the Associations', in *Soviet Economy in a New Perspective: A Compendium of Papers Submitted to the Joint Economic Committee, Congress of the United States*, Washington.

36 Gribkov, A. I. (1992), 'Doktrina Brezhneva i pol'skii krizis nachala 80-kh godov', *Voenno-istoricheskii zhurnal* 9 (September).

37 Harmstone, Richard C. and John F. Patackas (1997), 'Unearthing a Root Cause of Soviet Economic Disintegration', *Europe-Asia Studies* 49:4.

38 Harrison, Mark (1993), 'Soviet Economic Growth Since 1928: the Alternative Statistics of G. I. Khanin', *Europe-Asia Studies* 45:1.

39   Harrison, Mark (2002), 'Economic Growth and Slowdown', in Edwin Bacon and Mark Sandle (eds), *Brezhnev Reconsidered*, Basingstoke.

40   Hauslohner, Peter (1987), 'Gorbachev's Social Contract', *Soviet Economy* 3:1.

41   Hodnett, Grey (1967), 'The Debate over Soviet Federalism', *Soviet Studies* 18:4.

42   Hodnett, Grey (1981), 'The Pattern of Leadership Politics', in Seweryn Bialer (ed.), *The Domestic Context of Soviet Foreign Policy*, New York.

43   Hosking, Geoffrey (1994), 'Predposylki obrazovaniya grazhdanskogo obshchestva v period "zastoya"', in I. D. Koval'chenko *et alii* (eds), *Rossiya v XX veke: Istoriki mira sporyat*, Moscow.

44   Jaruzelski, Wojciech (1998), 'Commentary', *Cold War International History Project Bulletin* 11 (Winter).

45   Jian, Chen and David Wilson (1998), 'All under the Heaven is Great Chaos: Beijing, the Sino-Soviet Border Clashes and the Turn towards Sino-American Rapprochement', *Cold War International History Project Bulletin* 11 (Winter).

46   Jones, Ellen and Fred W. Grupp (1983), 'Infant Mortality Trends in the Soviet Union', *Population and Development Review* 9:2 (June).

47   Jones, Ellen and Fred W. Grupp (1984), 'Modernisation and Ethnic Equalisation in the USSR', *Soviet Studies* 36:2 (April).

48   Joravsky, David (1965), 'The Debacle of Lysenkoism', *Problems of Communism* 14:6 (November–December).

49   Josephson, Paul R. (1992), 'Soviet Scientists and the State: Politics, Ideology and Fundamental Research from Stalin to Gorbachev', *Social Research* 59:3 (Fall).

50   Juviler, Peter H. (1967), 'Family Reforms on the Road to Communism', in Peter H. Juviler and Henry W. Morton (eds), *Soviet Policy-Making: Studies of Communism in Transition*, London.

51   Khanin, G. I. (1991), *Dinamika ekonomicheskogo razvitiya SSSR*, Moscow.

52   Khanin, G. I. (1996), 'Otsenka dinamiki valovogo vnutrennego produkta Rossii za period 70-kh–90-kh godov', Novosibirsk, mimeo.

53   Khanin, G. and V. Selyunin (1987), 'Lukavye tsifry', *Novyi mir* 2 (February).

54   Kirsanov, Nikolai (1991), 'Ne osobenno tseremonyas' s faktami: voennaya biografiya L. I. Brezhneva v istoricheskoi literature', in Yu. V. Aksyutin (ed.), *L. I. Brezhnev: Materialy k biografii*, Moscow.

55   Kontorovich, Vladimir (1988), 'Lessons of the 1965 Soviet Economic Reform', *Soviet Studies* 40:2 (April).

56   Kornienko, G. M. (1995), 'A "Missed Opportunity": Carter, Brezhnev, SALT II, and the Vance Mission to Moscow, November 1976–March 1977', *Cold War International History Project Bulletin* 5 (Spring).

57   Kramer, Mark (1992), 'New Sources on the 1968 Soviet Invasion of Czechoslovakia', *Cold War International History Project Bulletin* 2 (Fall).

58   Kramer, Mark (1993), 'The Prague Spring and the Soviet Invasion of Czechoslovakia: New Interpretations', *Cold War International History Project Bulletin* 3 (Fall).

59   Kramer, Mark (1995), 'New Evidence on the Polish Crisis, 1980–81', *Cold War International History Project Bulletin* 5 (Spring).

60   Kramer, Mark (1998a), 'Jaruzelski, the Soviet Union and the Imposition of Martial Law in Poland: New Light on the Mystery of December 1981', *Cold War International History Project Bulletin* 11 (Winter).

61   Kramer, Mark (1998b), 'Ukraine and the Soviet–Czechoslovak Crisis of 1968 (Part 1): New Evidence from the Diary of Petro Shelest', *Cold War International History Project Bulletin* 11 (March)

62   Kudrov, V. (1997), 'The Comparison of the USSR and USA Economies by IMEMO in the 1970s', *Europe-Asia Studies* 49:5.

63   Machiewicz, Pawel (1998), 'The Assistance of Warsaw Pact Forces is not Ruled Out', *Cold War International History Project Bulletin* 11 (Winter).

64   Mastny, Vojtech (1999), 'The Soviet Non-Invasion of Poland in 1980–81 and the End of the Cold War', *Europe-Asia Studies* 51:2.

65   Matthews, Mervyn (1987), 'Aspects of Poverty in the Soviet Union', in Horst Herlemann (ed.), *Quality of Life in the Soviet Union*, Boulder, CO.

66   McCauley, Martin (1998), 'From Perestroika Towards a New Order, 1985–1995', in Gregory L. Freeze (ed.), *Russia: A History*, Oxford.

67   Menon, Rajan (1982), 'Military Power, Intervention and Soviet Policy in the Third World', in Roger E. Kanet (ed.), *Soviet Foreign Policy in the 1980s*, New York.

68   Millar, James R. (1985), 'The Little Deal: Brezhnev's Contribution to Acquisitive Socialism', *Slavic Review* 44:4 (Winter).

69   Moody, Stephen S. (1991), 'Fallen Star', *The New Republic* (September).

70   Nekrasova, I. M. and S. I. Degtev (1994), 'Ekonomicheskaya reforma 60-kh godov: Istoriya, problemy, resheniya', in I. D. Koval'chenko *et alii* (eds), *Rossiya v XX veke: Istoriki mira sporyat*, Moscow.

71   Nemtsov, Aleksandr V. (2001), 'Alkogol' i smertnost' v Rossii: 1980-e–1990-e gody', *Demoskop Weekly* 19/20 (15 May).

72   Noren, James H. (1995), 'The Controversy over Western Measures of Soviet Defense Expenditures', *Post-Soviet Affairs* 11:3.

73   Nove, Alec (1982), 'Income Distribution in the USSR: A Possible Explanation of Some Recent Data', *Soviet Studies* 34:2 (April).

74   Pravda, Alex (1982), 'The Soviet Union: "From Getting There to Being Here"', *Political Studies* 30:1.

75   Rathjens, George, Abram Chayes and J. P. Ruina (1974), *Nuclear Arms Control Agreements: Process and Impact*, Washington.

76   Reddaway, Peter (1980), 'Policy towards Dissent since Khrushchev', in T. H. Rigby, Archie Brown and Peter Reddaway (eds), *Authority, Power and Policy in the USSR: Essays in Honour of Leonard Schapiro*, Basingstoke.

77   Reddaway, Peter (1983), 'Dissent in the Soviet Union', *Problems of Communism* 32:6 (November–December).

78   Rigby, T. H. (1970), 'The Soviet Leadership: Towards a Self-Stabilising Oligarchy?', *Soviet Studies* 22:4 (October).

79   Rigby, T. H. (1979), 'Forward from "Who Gets What, When, How"', *Slavic Review* 39:2 (Summer).

80   Rutkevich, M. (1984), 'Reforma obrazovaniya, potrebnosti obshchestva, molodezh", *Sotsiologicheskie issledovaniya* 4 (October–December).

81   Sandle, Mark (2002), 'A Triumph of Ideological Hairdressing? Intellectual Life in the Brezhnev Era Reconsidered', in Edwin Bacon and Mark Sandle (eds), *Brezhnev Reconsidered*, Basingstoke.

82   Schroeder, Gertrude (1979), 'The Soviet Economy on a Treadmill of "Reforms"', in *Soviet Economy in a Time of Change: A Compendium of Papers Submitted to the Joint Economic Committee, Congress of the United States*, Washington.

83   Schroeder, Gertrude and M. Elizabeth Denton (1982) 'An Index of Consumption in the USSR', in *USSR: Measures of Economic Growth and Development, 1950–1980*, Washington.

84   Schroeder, Gertrude (1985), 'The Slowdown in Soviet Industry', *Soviet Economy* 1:1 (January–March).

85   Schroeder, Gertrude (1987), 'Soviet Living Standards in Comparative Perspective', in Horst Herlemann (ed.), *Quality of Life in the Soviet Union*, Boulder, CO.

86   Schroeder, Gertrude (1995), 'Reflections on Economic Sovietology', *Post-Soviet Affairs* 11:3.

87   Sherlock, Thomas (1990), 'Khrushchev Reconsidered', *Report on the USSR*, 8 June.

88   Shlapentokh, Vladimir (1998), 'Standard of Living and Popular Discontent', in Michael Ellman and Vladimir Kontorovich (eds), *The Destruction of the Soviet Economic System: An Insiders' History*, Armonk, NY.

89   Shtromas, Alexander (1979), 'Dissent and Political Change in the Soviet Union', *Studies in Comparative Communism* 12:2–3 (Summer/Autumn).

90   Sidorenko, G. I. and V. N. Krut'ko (1990), 'Sokhranit' zdorov'e natsii', *Ekologicheskaya al'ternativa*, Moscow.

91   Tabachnik, Dmitrii (1991), 'Zapyataya v biografii genseka', in Yu. V. Aksyutin (ed.), *L. I. Brezhnev: Materialy k biografii*, Moscow.

92   Thatcher, Ian D. (2002), 'Brezhnev as Leader', in Edwin Bacon and Mark Sandle (eds), *Brezhnev Reconsidered*, Basingstoke.

93   Tompson, William J. (1991), 'The Fall of Nikita Khrushchev', *Soviet Studies* 43:6.

94   Tompson, William (2000), 'An Opportunity Missed – Or Wisely Passed Up? Khrushchev, Industrial Management and Economic Reform', in William Taubman, Sergei Khrushchev and Abbott Gleason (eds), *Nikita Khrushchev*, New Haven, CT.

95   von Beyme, Klaus (1975), 'A Comparative View of Democratic Centralism', *Government and Opposition* 10:3.

96   Webber, Mark (2002), '"Out of Area Operations": The Third World', in Edwin Bacon and Mark Sandle (eds), *Brezhnev Reconsidered*, Basingstoke.

97   Westad, Arne (1996/97a), 'Moscow and the Angolan Crisis, 1974–1976: A New Pattern of Intervention', *Cold War International History Project Bulletin* 8–9 (Winter).

98   Westad, Odd Arne (1996/97b), 'Concerning the Situation in "A": New Russian Evidence on the Soviet Intervention in Afghanistan', *Cold War International History Project Bulletin* 8–9 (Winter).

99   Wheatcroft, Stephen G. (1999), 'The Great Leap Upwards: Anthropometric Data and Indicators of Crises and Secular Change in Soviet Welfare Levels, 1880–1960', *Slavic Review* 58:1 (Spring).

100   White, Stephen (1986), 'Economic Performance and Communist Legitimacy', *World Politics* 38:3.

101   Williams, Kieran (1996), 'New Sources on Soviet Decision-Making during the 1968 Czechoslovak Crisis', *Europe-Asia Studies* 48:3.

102   Wohlforth, William (1994/95), 'Realism and the End of the Cold War', *International Security* 19:3.

103 Woodruff, David (2000), 'Rules for Followers: Institutional Theory and the New Politics of Economic Backwardness in Russia', *Politics and Society* 28:4 (December).

104 Zakulin, Gleb (1971), 'The Contemporary Countryside in Soviet Literature: A Search for New Values', in James R. Millar (ed.), *The Soviet Rural Community*, Urbana, Ill.

105 Zaslavskaya, Tat'yana (1984), 'The Novosibirsk Report', *Survey* 28:1.

INDEX

STUART BRITAIN

Social Change and Continuity: England 1550–1750 (Second edition)
Barry Coward
0 582 29442 8

James I (Second edition)
S J Houston
0 582 20911 0

The English Civil War 1640–1649
Martyn Bennett
0 582 35392 0

Charles I, 1625–1640
Brian Quintrell
0 582 00354 7

The English Republic 1649–1660 (Second edition)
Toby Barnard
0 582 08003 7

Radical Puritans in England 1550–1660
R J Acheson
0 582 35515 X

The Restoration and the England of Charles II (Second edition)
John Miller
0 582 29223 9

The Glorious Revolution (Second edition)
John Miller
0 582 29222 0

EARLY MODERN EUROPE

The Renaissance (Second edition)
Alison Brown
0 582 30781 3

The Emperor Charles V
Martyn Rady
0 582 35475 7

French Renaissance Monarchy: Francis I and Henry II (Second edition)
Robert Knecht
0 582 28707 3

The Protestant Reformation in Europe
Andrew Johnston
0 582 07020 1

The French Wars of Religion 1559–1598 (Second edition)
Robert Knecht
0 582 28533 X

Phillip II
Geoffrey Woodward
0 582 07232 8

The Thirty Years' War
Peter Limm
0 582 35373 4

Louis XIV
Peter Campbell
0 582 01770 X

Spain in the Seventeenth Century
Graham Darby
0 582 07234 4

Peter the Great
William Marshall
0 582 00355 5

EUROPE 1789–1918

Britain and the French Revolution
Clive Emsley   0 582 36961 4

Revolution and Terror in France 1789–1795 (Second edition)
D G Wright   0 582 00379 2

Napoleon and Europe
D G Wright   0 582 35457 9

The Abolition of Serfdom in Russia, 1762–1907
David Moon   0 582 29486 X

Nineteenth-Century Russia: Opposition to Autocracy
Derek Offord   0 582 35767 5

The Constitutional Monarchy in France 1814–48
Pamela Pilbeam   0 582 31210 8

The 1848 Revolutions (Second edition)
Peter Jones   0 582 06106 7

The Italian Risorgimento
M Clark   0 582 00353 9

Bismarck & Germany 1862–1890 (Second edition)
D G Williamson   0 582 29321 9

Imperial Germany 1890–1918
Ian Porter, Ian Armour and Roger Lockyer   0 582 03496 5

The Dissolution of the Austro-Hungarian Empire 1867–1918 (Second edition)
John W Mason   0 582 29466 5

Second Empire and Commune: France 1848–1871 (Second edition)
William H C Smith   0 582 28705 7

France 1870–1914 (Second edition)
Robert Gildea   0 582 29221 2

The Scramble for Africa (Second edition)
M E Chamberlain   0 582 36881 2

Late Imperial Russia 1890–1917
John F Hutchinson   0 582 32721 0

The First World War
Stuart Robson   0 582 31556 5

Austria, Prussia and Germany, 1806–1871
John Breuilly   0 582 43739 3

EUROPE SINCE 1918

The Russian Revolution (Second edition)
Anthony Wood   0 582 35559 1

Lenin's Revolution: Russia, 1917–1921
David Marples   0 582 31917 X

Stalin and Stalinism (Second edition)
Martin McCauley   0 582 27658 6

The Weimar Republic (Second edition)
John Hiden   0 582 28706 5

The Inter-War Crisis 1919–1939
Richard Overy   0 582 35379 3

Fascism and the Right in Europe, 1919–1945
Martin Blinkhorn   0 582 07021 X

Spain's Civil War (Second edition)
Harry Browne   0 582 28988 2

The Third Reich (Third edition)
D G Williamson   0 582 20914 5

The Origins of the Second World War (Second edition)
R J Overy   0 582 29085 6

The Second World War in Europe
Paul MacKenzie   0 582 32692 3

The French at War, 1934–1944
Nicholas Atkin   0 582 36899 5

Anti-Semitism before the Holocaust
Albert S Lindemann   0 582 36964 9

The Holocaust: The Third Reich and the Jews
David Engel   0 582 32720 2

Germany from Defeat to Partition, 1945–1963
D G Williamson   0 582 29218 2

Britain and Europe since 1945
Alex May   0 582 30778 3

Eastern Europe 1945–1969: From Stalinism to Stagnation
Ben Fowkes   0 582 32693 1

Eastern Europe since 1970
Bülent Gökay   0 582 32858 6

The Khrushchev Era, 1953–1964
Martin McCauley   0 582 27776 0

NINETEENTH-CENTURY BRITAIN

Britain before the Reform Acts: Politics and Society 1815–1832
Eric J Evans   0 582 00265 6

Parliamentary Reform in Britain c. 1770–1918
Eric J Evans   0 582 29467 3

Democracy and Reform 1815–1885
D G Wright   0 582 31400 3

Poverty and Poor Law Reform in Nineteenth-Century Britain, 1834–1914:
From Chadwick to Booth
David Englander   0 582 31554 9

The Birth of Industrial Britain: Economic Change, 1750–1850
Kenneth Morgan   0 582 29833 4

Chartism (Third edition)
Edward Royle   0 582 29080 5

Peel and the Conservative Party 1830–1850
Paul Adelman   0 582 35557 5

Gladstone, Disraeli and later Victorian Politics (Third edition)
Paul Adelman   0 582 29322 7

Britain and Ireland: From Home Rule to Independence
Jeremy Smith   0 582 30193 9

TWENTIETH-CENTURY BRITAIN

The Rise of the Labour Party 1880–1945 (Third edition)
Paul Adelman   0 582 29210 7

The Conservative Party and British Politics 1902–1951
Stuart Ball   0 582 08002 9

The Decline of the Liberal Party 1910–1931 (Second edition)
Paul Adelman   0 582 27733 7

The British Women's Suffrage Campaign 1866–1928
Harold L Smith   0 582 29811 3

War & Society in Britain 1899–1948
Rex Pope   0 582 03531 7

The British Economy since 1914: A Study in Decline?
Rex Pope   0 582 30194 7

Unemployment in Britain between the Wars
Stephen Constantine   0 582 35232 0

The Attlee Governments 1945–1951
Kevin Jefferys   0 582 06105 9

The Conservative Governments 1951–1964
Andrew Boxer   0 582 20913 7

Britain under Thatcher
Anthony Seldon and Daniel Collings   0 582 31714 2

Britain and Empire, 1880–1945
Dane Kennedy   0 582 41493 8

INTERNATIONAL HISTORY

The Eastern Question 1774–1923 (Second edition)
A L Macfie   0 582 29195 X

India 1885–1947: The Unmaking of an Empire
Ian Copland   0 582 38173 8

The Origins of the First World War (Second edition)
Gordon Martel   0 582 28697 2

The United States and the First World War
Jennifer D Keene   0 582 35620 2

Anti-Semitism before the Holocaust
Albert S Lindemann   0 582 36964 9

The Origins of the Cold War, 1941–1949 (Second edition)
Martin McCauley   0 582 27659 4

Russia, America and the Cold War, 1949–1991
Martin McCauley   0 582 27936 4

The Arab–Israeli Conflict
Kirsten E Schulze   0 582 31646 4

The United Nations since 1945: Peacekeeping and the Cold War
Norrie MacQueen   0 582 35673 3

Decolonisation: The British Experience since 1945
Nicholas J White   0 582 29087 2

The Origins of the Vietnam War
Fredrik Logevall   0 582 31918 8

The Vietnam War
Mitchell Hall   0 582 32859 4

WORLD HISTORY

China in Transformation 1900–1949
Colin Mackerras   0 582 31209 4

Japan Faces the World, 1925–1952
Mary L Hanneman   0 582 36898 7

Japan in Transformation, 1952–2000
Jeff Kingston   0 582 41875 5

China since 1949
Linda Benson   0 582 35722 5

US HISTORY

American Abolitionists
Stanley Harrold   0 582 35738 1

The American Civil War, 1861–1865
Reid Mitchell   0 582 31973 0

America in the Progressive Era, 1890–1914
Lewis L Gould   0 582 35671 7

The United States and the First World War
Jennifer D Keene   0 582 35620 2

The Truman Years, 1945–1953
Mark S Byrnes   0 582 32904 3

The Korean War
Steven Hugh Lee   0 582 31988 9

The Origins of the Vietnam War
Fredrik Logevall   0 582 31918 8

The Vietnam War
Mitchell Hall   0 582 32859 4